The Ultimate Ninja Foodi Cookbook Guide

365
Easy and Quick, Pressure Cook, Slow Cook, Dehydrate, and More Recipes for Beginners and Advanced Users

Robert Lanier

All Rights Reserved:

The content contained within this book may not be reproduced, duplicated, or transmitted without direct written permission from the author or the publisher. Under no circumstances will any blame or legal responsibility be held against the publisher, or author, for any damages, reparation, or monetary loss due to the information contained within this book, either directly or indirectly.

Legal Notice: This book is copyright protected. It is only for personal use. You cannot amend, distribute, sell, use, quote or paraphrase any part, or the content within this book, without the consent of the author or publisher.

Disclaimer Notice:

Please note the information contained within this document is for educational and entertainment purposes only. All effort has been executed to present accurate, up to date, reliable, complete information. No warranties of any kind are declared or implied. Readers acknowledge that the author is not engaged in the rendering of legal, financial, medical, or professional advice. The content within this book has been derived from various sources. Please consult a licensed professional before attempting any techniques outlined in this book. By reading this document, the reader agrees that under no circumstances is the author responsible for any losses, direct or indirect, that are incurred as a result of the use of the information contained within this document, including, but not limited to, errors, omissions, or inaccuracies.

Table of Contents

Table of Contents 3
Introduction 7
How to Use the Ninja Foodi Pressure Cooker 7
Tips and Tricks for the Perfect TenderCrisp 8
Accessories to Help with
Your Ninja Foodi Pressure Cooker 8
Frequently Asked Questions 9

Snacks, Appetizers & Sides 10

Garlicky Tomato 10
Honey-garlic Chicken Wings 10
Salmon Croquettes 10
Spinach Hummus 10
Asian Chicken Nuggets 11
Caponata 11
Parmesan Stuffed Mushrooms 11
Cheesy Bacon Brussel Sprouts 11
Cheesy Jalapeno Boats 12
White Bean Hummus 12
Mini Crab Cakes 12
Zucchini Egg Tots 12
Swiss Onion Dip 13
Crispy Spiced Cauliflower Bites 13
Caramelized Cauliflower With Hazelnuts 13
Chicken Meatballs With Dill Dipping Sauce 13
Japanese Eggs 14
Sweet Potato Skins 14
Tiny Tostadas 14
Jalapeno Salsa 14
Rosemary Potato Fries 14
Apple Pecan Cookie Bars 15
Crispy Sesame Shrimp 15
Crispy Cheesy Straws 15
Herby Fish Skewers 15
Glazed Walnuts 15
Spicy Black Bean Dip 16
Dill Butter 16
Steak And Minty Cheese 16
Cheesy Onion Dip 16
Rosemary And Garlic Mushrooms 16
Cauliflower Gratin 17
Mini Steak Kebabs 17
Spicy Turkey Meatballs 17
Teriyaki Chicken Wings 17
Butter-flower Medley 18
Shallots With Mushrooms 18
Loaded Potato Skins 18
Cheesy Chicken Dip 19
Scalloped Potatoes 19
Chili Chicken Dip 19
Three-layer Taco Dip 19
Mushrooms Stuffed With Veggies 20
Mexican Street Corn Queso Dip 20
Nutmeg Peanuts 20
Cashew Cream 20
Cheesy Stuffed Onions 21
Pork Shank 21
Cheesy Fried Risotto Balls 21
Sweet Potato Gratin 22

Breakfast 23

Carrot Cake Oats 23
Ham & Spinach Breakfast Bake 23
Zucchini Pancakes 23
Chocolate Hazelnut Toaster Pastries 23
Blueberry Muffins 24
Prosciutto, Mozzarella Egg In A Cup 24
Spanish Potato And Chorizo Frittata 24
Pumpkin Coconut Breakfast Bake 24
Nutmeg Pumpkin Porridge 25
Pumpkin Breakfast Bread 25
Baked Eggs In Mushrooms 25
Pancetta Hash With Baked Eggs 25
Curried Chickpea And Roasted Tomato Shakshuka 25
Double Chocolate Quinoa Bowl 26
Breakfast Burritos 26
Southwest Tofu Scramble 26
Spinach & Sausage Casserole 27
Plum Breakfast Clafoutis 27
Banana Coconut Loaf 27
Prosciutto Egg Bake 28
Bacon And Gruyère Egg Bites 28
Butternut Squash Cake Oatmeal 28
Crustless Quiche 28
Waffle Bread Pudding With Maple-jam Glaze 29
Broccoli, Ham, And Cheddar Frittata 29
Egg Spinach Bites 29
Baked Eggs In Spinach 30
Carrot Cake Muffins 30
Glazed Lemon Muffins 30
Stuffed Baked Potatoes 30
Cheesy Meat Omelet 31
Broccoli Egg Scramble 31
Cinnamon Crumb Donuts 31
Poached Egg Heirloom Tomato 31
Bacon And Sausage Cheesccake 32
Sausage & Egg Stuffed Peppers 32
Walnut Orange Coffee Cake 32
Double Berry Dutch Baby 32
Flaxseeds Granola 33
Breakfast Souffles 33
Ricotta Raspberry Breakfast Cake 33
Banana Custard Oatmeal 33
Raspberry And Vanilla Pancake 34
Bell Pepper Frittata 34
Savory Oatmeal 34

Ninja Foodi Cookbook Guide

Fish & Seafood ... 35

- Fish Broccoli Stew ... 35
- Blackened Tilapia With Cilantro-lime Rice And Avocado Salsa ... 35
- Tuna Zoodle Bake ... 35
- Coconut Curried Mussels ... 36
- Shrimp & Asparagus Risotto ... 36
- Penne All Arrabbiata With Seafood And Chorizo ... 36
- New England Lobster Rolls ... 36
- Herb Salmon With Barley Haricot Verts ... 37
- Steamed Sea Bass With Turnips ... 37
- Salmon Kale Meal ... 37
- Pepper Smothered Cod ... 37
- Mussel Chowder With Oyster Crackers ... 38
- Caramelized Salmon ... 38
- Panko Crusted Cod ... 39
- Swordfish With Caper Sauce ... 39
- Air Fried Scallops ... 39
- Italian Flounder ... 39
- Lemon Cod Goujons And Rosemary Chips ... 39
- Paella Señorito ... 40
- Potato Chowder With Peppery Prawns ... 40
- Haddock With Sanfaina ... 40
- Salmon With Dill Chutney ... 41
- Shrimp Etouffee ... 41
- Shrimp Fried Rice ... 41
- Sweet & Spicy Shrimp ... 41
- Easy Clam Chowder ... 42
- Glazed Salmon ... 42
- Buttered Fish ... 42
- Awesome Shrimp Roast ... 42
- Flounder Veggie Soup ... 43
- Baked Cod Casserole ... 43
- Coconut Shrimp ... 43
- Oyster Stew ... 43
- Crab Cakes With Spicy Dipping Sauce ... 43
- Smoked Salmon Pilaf With Walnuts ... 44
- Pistachio Crusted Salmon ... 44
- Shrimp And Chorizo Potpie ... 44
- Coconut Cilantro Shrimp ... 45
- Farfalle Tuna Casserole With Cheese ... 45
- Cheesy Crab Pie ... 45
- Salmon & Quinoa Patties ... 45
- Mediterranean Cod ... 46
- Clam Fritters ... 46
- Spicy "grilled" Catfish ... 46
- Sweet Sour Fish ... 46

Vegan & Vegetable ... 47

- Okra Stew ... 47
- Pineapple Appetizer Ribs ... 47
- Balsamic Cabbage With Endives ... 47
- Veggie Potpie ... 47
- Southern Pineapple Casserole ... 48
- Palak Paneer ... 48
- Italian Spinach & Tomato Soup ... 48
- Cheesy Green Beans With Nuts ... 48
- Cauliflower Cakes ... 48
- Hearty Veggie Soup ... 49
- Creamy Carrot Soup ... 49
- Cheese And Mushroom Tarts ... 49
- Colorful Vegetable Medley ... 49
- Pomegranate Radish Mix ... 50
- Cheese Crusted Carrot Casserole ... 50
- Burrito Bowls ... 50
- Sesame Radish ... 50
- Radish Apples Salad ... 51
- Stuffed Summer Squash ... 51
- Cabbage With Carrots ... 51
- Hot & Sour Soup ... 51
- Cheesy Baked Spinach ... 51
- Zucchinis Spinach Fry ... 52
- Paneer Cutlet ... 52
- Asparagus With Feta ... 52
- Quinoa Stuffed Butternut Squash ... 52
- Cauliflower Enchiladas ... 53
- Cauliflower Chunks With Lemon Sauce ... 53
- Potato Filled Bread Rolls ... 53
- Minestrone With Pancetta ... 53
- Eggplant Lasagna ... 54
- Creamy Polenta & Mushrooms ... 54
- Eggplant With Kale ... 54
- Broccoli Cauliflower ... 54
- Beets And Carrots ... 54
- Quick Indian-style Curry ... 55
- Artichoke With Mayo ... 55
- Pepper And Sweet Potato Skewers ... 55
- Garlic Potatoes ... 55
- Zucchini Quinoa Stuffed Red Peppers ... 56
- Hawaiian Tofu ... 56
- Carrot Gazpacho ... 56
- Italian Sausage With Garlic Mash ... 56
- Stuffed Manicotti ... 57
- Garlic Bread Pizza ... 57
- Roasted Cauliflower Salad ... 57
- Creamy Golden Casserole ... 57
- Roasted Squash And Rice With Crispy Tofu ... 58
- Creamy Spinach Soup ... 58
- Italian Baked Zucchini ... 58

Poultry ... 59

- Chicken Cacciatore ... 59
- Korean Barbecued Satay ... 59
- Sticky Drumsticks ... 59
- Lemon Turkey Risotto ... 59
- Sweet Garlicky Chicken Wings ... 59
- Refried Black Beans And Chicken Fajitas ... 60
- Mexican Style Green Chili Chicken ... 60
- Sesame Crusted Chicken ... 60
- Chicken Meatballs Primavera ... 61
- Country Chicken Casserole ... 61
- Cheesy Chicken And Broccoli Casserole ... 61
- Tuscan Chicken & Pasta ... 62
- Shredded Chicken With Lentils And Rice ... 62
- Sour Cream & Cheese Chicken ... 62
- Mexican Chicken Soup ... 62
- Chipotle Raspberry Chicken ... 62
- Turkey And Brown Rice Salad With Peanuts ... 63
- Buttermilk Fried Chicken ... 63

Healthy Chicken Stew 63	Creamy Turkey And Mushroom Ragu 68
Turkey Enchilada Casserole 64	Buffalo Chicken And Navy Bean Chili 68
Roasted Chicken With Potato Mash 64	Chicken Chickpea Chili 68
Shredded Chicken And Wild Rice 64	Hainanese Chicken 68
Chicken With Black Beans 65	Butternut Turkey Stew 69
Coq Au Vin 65	Butter Chicken 69
Buttermilk Chicken Thighs 65	Chicken Thighs With Cabbage 69
Chicken With Prunes 65	Thyme Chicken With Veggies 69
Whole Chicken With Lemon And Onion Stuffing 66	Lemon, Barley & Turkey Soup 70
Simple Chicken Parmesan 66	Chicken And Sweet Potato Corn Chowder 70
Taco Stuffed Avocados 66	Moo Shu Chicken 70
Crunchy Chicken Schnitzels 66	Greek Chicken 70
Creamy Tuscan Chicken Pasta 67	Honey Chicken & Veggies 71
Chicken With Mushroom Sauce 67	Chicken With Roasted Red Pepper Sauce 71
Pulled Chicken And Peach Salsa 67	Skinny Chicken & Dumplings 71
Red Chili Chicken 67	Spicy Onion Crusted Chicken Tenders 71

Beef, Pork & Lamb 72

Pork Tenderloin With Warm Balsamic And Apple Chutney 72	Hamburger & Macaroni Skillet 80
Caribbean Ropa Vieja 72	Cheesy Ham & Potato Casserole 81
Asian Beef 72	Beef Broccoli 81
Braised Lamb Shanks 73	Sticky Baby Back Ribs 81
Beef Stir Fry 73	Jamaican Pork 82
Short Ribs With Egg Noodles 73	Italian Sausage And Cannellini Stew 82
Beef And Garbanzo Bean Chili 73	Flank Steak With Bell Pepper Salsa 82
Beef Lasagna 74	Simple Beef & Shallot Curry 82
Carne Guisada 74	Italian Pasta Potpie 83
Crusted Pork Chops 74	Braised Short Ribs With Mushrooms 83
Chinese Bbq Ribs 75	Sausage & Roasted Red Pepper Linguine 83
Smoky Horseradish Spare Ribs 75	Cheddar Cheeseburgers 84
Peppercorn Meatloaf 75	Crispy Korean-style Ribs 84
Caribbean Pork Pot 75	Pork Pie 84
Lone Star Chili 75	Pork Tenderloin With Ginger And Garlic 84
Picadillo Dish 76	Taco Meatballs 85
Garlicky Pork Chops 76	Sticky Barbeque Baby Back Ribs 85
Beef And Bacon Chili 76	Corned Beef 85
Mexican Pork Stir Fry 76	Spiced Lamb Meatballs 85
Honey Short Ribs With Rosemary Potatoes 77	Steak And Chips 86
Lamb Chops And Potato Mash 77	Pesto Pork Chops & Asparagus 86
Braised Short Ribs With Creamy Sauce 77	Stuffed Cabbage Rolls 86
Meatballs With Spaghetti Sauce 78	Beef Bourguignon(1) 86
Healthier Meatloaf 78	Crunchy Cashew Lamb Rack 87
Crispy Pork Chops 78	Thai Roasted Beef 87
Adobo Steak 78	Ropa Vieja 87
Chunky Pork Meatloaf With Mashed Potatoes 79	Beef Brisket & Carrots 88
Italian Pot Roast 79	Beef And Cherry Tagine 88
Ground Beef Stuffed Empanadas 79	Herbed Lamb Chops 88
Pot Roast With Biscuits 80	Tex Mex Beef Stew 88
Bolognese Pizza 80	Korean Cabbage Cups 89
Cuban Pork 80	Beef In Basil Sauce 89
	Pork Chops With Gravy 89

Soups & Stews 90

Chicken Tomatillo Stew 90	Chicken Noodle Soup 92
Chickpea, Spinach, And Sweet Potato Stew 90	Pho Tom 93
Roasted Tomato And Seafood Stew 90	Loaded Potato Soup 93
Lasagna Soup 91	Chicken Potpie Soup 93
Chicken Enchilada Soup 91	Jamaican Jerk Chicken Stew 94
Mushroom And Wild Rice Soup 91	Braised Pork And Black Bean Stew 94
Butternut Squash, Apple, Bacon And Orzo Soup 92	Italian Sausage, Potato, And Kale Soup 94
Chicken Chili 92	

Ninja Foodi Cookbook Guide

Desserts 95

Peanut Butter Pie	95	Milk Dumplings In Sweet Sauce	101
Apricots With Honey Sauce	95	Coconut Rice Pudding	101
Date Orange Cheesecake	95	Brownie Pie	101
Fried Snickerdoodle Poppers	95	Lime Muffins	102
Steamed Lemon Pudding	96	Carrot Raisin Cookie Bars	102
Blueberry Peach Crisp	96	Baked Apples With Pecan Stuffing	102
Chocolate Soufflé	96	Raspberry Crumble	102
Chocolate Cake	96	Chocolate Fondue	102
Mini Chocolate Cheesecakes	96	Berry Vanilla Pudding	103
Blueberry Lemon Pound Cake	97	Maply Soufflés	103
Hot Fudge Brownies	97	Raspberry Cobbler	103
Cherry Cheesecake	97	Poached Peaches	103
Double Chocolate Cake	98	Tres Leches Cake	104
Churro Bites	98	Strawberry Crumble	104
Coconut Cream "custard" Bars	98	Cinnamon Mulled Red Wine	104
Chocolate Cheesecake	99	Raspberry Cream Tart	104
Tiramisu Cheesecake	99	Pumpkin Latte Cake	105
Cranberry Pie	100	Red Velvet Cheesecake	105
Flourless Chocolate Cake	100	Mocha Cake	105
Pecan Stuffed Apples	100	Dark Chocolate Brownies	106
Filling Coconut And Oat Cookies	100	Créme Brulee	106
Coconut Milk Crème Caramel	101	Apple Strudels	106
Delicious Almond And Apple	101		

RECIPE INDEX 107

Introduction

For so many people, there are a few unspoken rules when it comes to cooking. It needs to be quick, it needs to be tasty, and it needs to be good for you. However, in the constant hustle and bustle of life, too often we sacrifice at least one of these areas to get the job done and move on to the next thing. Imagine being able to sauté vegetables, steam rice, and cook the perfect steak in just one pot. That's right. You can prepare a meal that has all your daily nutritional requirements using only one appliance. Even better? You can make desserts like a cobbler and flan in the very same unit.

Multi-cookers claim to do it all, and slow cookers have long been touted for their versatility and convenience. After all, they do the work for you: just toss ingredients into the pot and come back to a perfectly cooked meal. Pressure cookers take it a step further, making your food incredibly tender, exceptionally fast.

But what about texture? Tender food is great, but no one wants to eat stews and soups every night. We all crave the crispy and crunchy. What are chicken wings without a crispy exterior? Who wants to eat potpie without a flaky crust?

Enter the Ninja Foodi Pressure Cooker, the pressure cooker that crisps—a revolutionary appliance changing the multi-cooker game. That means, with the Foodi Pressure Cooker, you can make roast chicken that is juicy and tender within and beautiful bronzed and crisp outside.

This Ninja Foodi cookbook will introduce you to the functions and benefits of this revolutionary appliance. Whether you are new to the Foodi or you are a Foodi fanatic, I will break down cooking with the Ninja Foodi Pressure Cooker, giving you tips and tricks, and helping you unleash its full potential—flavor, texture, and speed. And, of course, I'll introduce you to a wide variety of recipes so you can use it every day. The 365 recipes in the Ninja Foodi cookbook offer air-frying, pressure-cooking, and sauté recipes from breakfast through dinner.

Now it's time to dive right into Ninja Foodi cooking journey!

How to Use the Ninja Foodi Pressure Cooker

Before using the device, it is essential to check all its components, if the power cord is intact, all the valves are in their position, and the sealing ring is properly fixed, etc. If any of the components are not properly set, the device will not function well. Now that everything is in place, you can plug in your device. Once plugged in, the LED screen of the control panel lights up.

1. Add Ingredients to the Ninja Foodi Cooking Pot:
To start with the cooking, you can either remove the cooking pot from the vessel and add ingredients to it or leave it in the vessel to cook a meal in which we need to start by sautéing the ingredients; the inner pot is left inside of the vessels and ingredients are added gradually to the pot. The inner markings of the pot provide a good measurement for the food, and it also marks the limit, do not add anything above its 2/3 full limit. There must be enough space above the food so that it could easily boil or expand.

2. Seal and Secure the Lid:
For pressure cooking, the pressure lid with the valve attached needs to be installed, sealed, and locked on top of the vessel. For that, simply place the lid over the vessel and rotate it until it sounds clicks. When the arrow on the vessel aligns with the close marking of the lid, it means your lid is sealed. Whenever the lid is not properly closed, the timer does not initiate. This is one of the security features of the Ninja Foodi, which does not initiate cooking without proper locking of the lid. For Air Crisping, use the crisping lid.

3. Select the Appropriate Cooking Mode:
As a multipurpose Ninja Foodi cooker offers you several different cooking modes, each of these modes has its own preset or integrated settings to adjust both the time and pressure according to the requirement. To start the cooking process, select any of the desired programs by pressing their respective buttons or keys. Remember that each mode has its own settings; to make changes in time and pressure, use the adjustment keys. Every standard control panel of a Ninja Foodi pressure cooker gives you these many options:

- Steam
- Air Crisp

- Sear/Sauté
- Pressure
- Slow Cook
- Bake/Roast
- Broil
- Dehydrate
- Keep Warm

Once the mode is selected, the Ninja Foodi will immediately switch to a Preheating State, which continues for 10 seconds. During this stage, the cooker sets its internal temperature and the internal pressure; then, it finally switches to the cooking state. Once the food is all cooked, the Ninja Foodi automatically switches to a standby mode where it is kept warm at low temperatures. The Keep Warm key allows you to either stop or cancel the operation or switch the appliance to the Warm mode. Once set, the warm mode will continue until the button is pressed again.

Once the mode is selected, use the time and temperature keys to increase or decrease the values. Then pressure the START/STOP button to initiate the cooking or stop it.

Tips and Tricks for the Perfect TenderCrisp

It's the TenderCrisp Technology that sets the Ninja Foodi apart from every other product out there. Here are seven basic, simple steps to get that tender and crispy finish every time you use your Ninja Foodi.

1. Heat it up. When using the Sear/Sauté, Air Crisp, or Broil functions, always preheat the Ninja Foodi for 5 minutes before adding food. This will ensure that you have reached the correct temperature before you begin to cook.
2. Shake it up. It is recommended to always shake (or toss with tongs) food that is layered on top of itself in the Cook & Crisp Basket at least once or twice during crisping. But the more you shake or toss, the more even and crispy the result will be.
3. Spritz with oil. Use a bottle with a nozzle or a cooking spray can to evenly coat large proteins and veggies with oil. You can also use a brush if you're applying thick sauces and marinades.
4. Keep it consistent. Foods that are the same size cook more evenly. Be sure to cut foods into similar-size pieces when prepping a recipe.
5. Rinse the rice. When using Pressure to cook rice and grains, for best results be sure to rinse them thoroughly, until the water runs clear.
6. Keep it separate. When following recipes for a 360 Meal, you will layer meats over veggies and rice using the Reversible Rack. This builds flavor and keeps the meal in one pot, all while maintaining texture. If you prefer to keep the meat drippings separate, place aluminum foil over the Revesible Rack before adding the meat.
7. Utensils matter. Keep your Ninja Foodi looking and performing its best by only using wooden, silicone, or silicone-tipped utensils.

Accessories to Help with Your Ninja Foodi Pressure Cooker

In addition to the accessories that came with your Ninja Foodi Pressure Cooker, there are a few additional accessories you can purchase so that you can truly get the most out of your Ninja Foodi.

1. Dehydrate Rack – This rack is specifically designed to expand the amount of food you can dehydrate at once. Arrange ingredients in a single layer and carefully place the rack in the cooking pot. Follow the Dehydrate Chart to create your own custom jerky, vegetable chips, dried fruit snacks, and more.
2. Glass Lid – With this new accessory, there is no second guessing with how your food is cooking. The glass allows you to check on your food as it steams and slow cooks without removing the lid. I also love using the glass lid with the Keep Warm setting as a buffet. Great for holidays or keeping dinner warm until the whole family is home to enjoy together!
3. Loaf Pan – This specially designed loaf pan fits perfectly on the Reversible Rack. The ideal baking accessory for quick breads, it works equally as well for your favorite meatloaf recipe. Plus, the loaf pan has ceramic coating and is nonstick for easy cleaning.
4. Multi-Purpose Pan – Perfect for baking everything from desserts to casseroles, the Multi-Purpose Pan is the must-have accessory for any Ninja Foodi fanatic and can be used across most Ninja Foodi products.
5. Multi-Purpose Sling – Aluminum foil is a hack used in many recipes for removing accessories and roasts from pressure cookers. The multi-purpose sling is a more durable,

Ninja Foodi Cookbook Guide

reusable option, and is great for that whole roasted chicken or the Multi-Purpose Pan.

6. Tube Pan – A tube pan is very similar to a Bundt pan but it has detachable sides like a springform pan, making it easy to remove foods. Use this pan for everything from cheesecakes and delicate desserts to cornbread and casseroles.

Frequently Asked Questions

1. Why does the Ninja Foodi come with two lids?
The Ninja Foodi is the only pressure cooker that crisps. For this reason, it comes with a Pressure Lid for the Pressure, Steam, Slow Cook, and Sear/Sauté functions, as well as a Crisping Lid for the Air Crisp, Bake/Roast, Broil, and Dehydrate functions. Use the lids individually or one right after the other to unlock a world of recipes you never knew you could make at home.

2. How do I convert my favorite recipes to the Ninja Foodi?
You can easily convert a number of your favorite recipes to the Ninja Foodi. When converting recipes from a conventional oven, use the Bake/Roast setting and reduce the temperature of the recipe by 25°F. So if a recipe is baked in the oven at 375°F/190 °C, you would set the Ninja Foodi for 350°F/175 °C. You will also likely be able to cut down the cook time. Check the food frequently to avoid overcooking.

You can also cook your favorite slow cooker recipes using Pressure so that they cook much quicker. A good rule of thumb is that recipes that slow cook for 8 hours on Low or 4 hours on High should take 25 to 30 minutes in the pressure cooker. It is also important to check your liquid level and ensure that your recipe includes ½ to 1 cup of liquid for the cooker to get to pressure. And as always, make sure the pressure release valve is in the Seal position.

A number of the recipes throughout this book are staples that my husband, Julien, and I have been cooking for years, but with the Ninja Foodi we no longer need to turn on a bunch of appliances and use numerous pots and pans. Instead, recipes like Crispy Chicken Thighs with Roasted Carrots are all made in one pot while maintaining their own unique textures. However, every recipe is different, and there is no one rule for doubling or halving all recipes in the book. I recommend trying the recipes as they are and then experimenting with ingredient swaps, cutting recipes in half, or doubling recipes. Note that cook times may change, too.

3. What is the difference between quick release and natural release?
Quick release is when you manually switch the pressure release valve to the Vent position. Quick release is used in the majority of this book's recipes. Natural release occurs when you let the Ninja Foodi decrease in pressure naturally after cooking is complete. This technique is most commonly used when cooking beans.

4. When doing a TenderCrisp recipe, should I remove the liquid after using the Pressure Lid, before switching to the Crisping Lid?
If you are following one of the TenderCrisp recipes in this book, there is no need to remove the liquid before switching to the Crisping Lid. These recipes are specifically designed to work with the amount of liquid in the bottom of the pot.

If you are creating your own recipe and would like to make sure the bottom of your food is browned in the Cook & Crisp™ Basket, make sure not to exceed the 3-cup mark (located on the inside of the pot) with liquid.

5. Can I cook frozen food in the Ninja Foodi?
Yes! One of the best things about the Ninja Foodi is that you can cook frozen food straight from the freezer without the need to defrost. Use Pressure to turn frozen chicken breasts into shredded chicken or ground beef into chili, or use the combination of Pressure and the Crisping Lid to roast a whole chicken from frozen or cook the perfect medium-rare steak.

Ninja Foodi Cookbook Guide

Snacks, Appetizers & Sides

Garlicky Tomato

Servings: 5
Cooking Time: 5 Minutes
Ingredients:
- 5 tomatoes
- ¼ cup chives, chopped
- ⅓ cup garlic clove, minced
- ½ teaspoon salt
- ½ teaspoon black pepper
- 1 tablespoon olive oil
- 7 ounces Parmesan cheese

Directions:
1. Wash the tomatoes and slice them into thick slices.
2. Place the sliced tomatoes in the Ninja Foodi's insert.
3. Combine the grated cheese and minced garlic and stir the mixture.
4. Sprinkle the tomato slices with chives, black pepper, and salt.
5. Then sprinkle the sliced tomatoes with the cheese mixture.
6. Close the Ninja Foodi's lid and cook the dish in the "Pressure" mode for 5 minutes.
7. Once done, remove the tomatoes carefully and serve.

Nutrition:
- InfoCalories: 224; Fat: 14g; Carbohydrates: 12.55g; Protein: 13g

Honey-garlic Chicken Wings

Servings: 4
Cooking Time: 43 Minutes
Ingredients:
- 2 pounds fresh chicken wings
- ¾ cup potato starch
- Cooking spray
- ¼ cup unsalted butter
- 4 tablespoons minced garlic
- ¼ cup honey
- ¼ teaspoon sea salt

Directions:
1. Insert Cook & Crisp Basket into pot and close crisping lid. Select AIR CRISP, set temperature to 390°F (200°C), and set time to 5 minutes. Select START/STOP to begin preheating.
2. Pat the chicken wings dry. In a large bowl, toss the chicken wings with potato starch until evenly coated.
3. Once unit has preheated, place the wings in the basket. Close lid.
4. Select AIR CRISP, set temperature to 390°F (200°C), and set time to 30 minutes. Select START/STOP to begin.
5. After 15 minutes, open lid, then lift the basket and shake the wings. Coat with cooking spray. Lower basket back into the pot. Close lid and continue cooking until the wings reach your desired crispiness.
6. Cooking is complete when the internal temperature of the meat reads at least 165°F (75°C) on a food thermometer.
7. Remove basket from pot. Cover with aluminum foil to keep warm.
8. Select SEAR/SAUTÉ and set to MD:LO. Select START/STOP to begin.
9. Add the butter and garlic and sauté until fragrant, about 3 minutes. Add the honey and salt and simmer for about 10 minutes, adding water as needed to thin out the sauce.
10. Place the wings in a large bowl. Drizzle with the sauce and toss the chicken wings to coat. Serve.

Nutrition:
- InfoCalories: 654, Total Fat: 33g, Sodium: 302mg, Carbohydrates: 53g, Protein: 39g.

Salmon Croquettes

Servings: 6
Cooking Time: 20 Minutes
Ingredients:
- Nonstick cooking spray
- 14 ¾ oz. pink salmon, drained, bones removed & flaked
- 1 egg
- 2 tbsp. yellow mustard
- 2 tsp fresh parsley, chopped
- ½ tsp onion powder
- ¼ tsp pepper
- ¾ cup herb-seasoned stuffing mix
- ½ cup flour

Directions:
1. Lightly spray fryer basket with cooking spray.
2. In a large bowl, combine salmon, egg, mustard, parsley, onion powder, and pepper and mix well. Form into 12 patties.
3. Place the flour in a shallow dish.
4. Dredge both sides of the patties in the flour and place in the basket in a single layer.
5. Add the tender-crisp lid and set to air fry on 375°F (190°C). Cook patties 8-10 minutes per side until gold brown. Serve immediately.

Nutrition:
- InfoCalories 245, Total Fat 7g, Total Carbs 24g, Protein 19g, Sodium 670mg.

Spinach Hummus

Servings: 12
Cooking Time: 1 Hr 10 Min
Ingredients:
- 2 cups spinach; chopped /260g
- ½ cup tahini /65g
- 2 cups dried chickpeas /260g
- 8 cups water /2000ml
- 5 garlic cloves, crushed
- 5 tbsp grapeseed oil /75ml
- 2 tsp salt; divided /10g
- 5 tbsp lemon juice /75ml

Directions:
1. In the pressure cooker, mix 2 tbsp oil, water, 1 tsp or 5g salt, and chickpeas. Seal the pressure lid, choose Pressure, set to High, and set the timer to 35 minutes. Press Start. When ready, release the pressure quickly. In a small bowl, reserve ½ cup of the cooking liquid and drain chickpeas.
2. Mix half the reserved cooking liquid and chickpeas in a food processor and puree until no large chickpeas remain; add remaining cooking liquid, spinach, lemon juice, remaining tsp salt, garlic, and tahini.
3. Process hummus for 8 minutes until smooth. Stir in the remaining 3 tbsp or 45ml of olive oil before serving.

Ninja Foodi Cookbook Guide

Asian Chicken Nuggets

Servings: X
Cooking Time: 20 Minutes
Ingredients:
- 1 lb. chicken breasts, boneless, skinless & cut in 1-inch pieces
- 1 tsp salt
- ½ tsp pepper
- 2 eggs
- 1 cup Panko bread crumbs
- ¼ cup lite soy sauce
- ¼ cup honey
- 4 cloves garlic, diced fine
- 2 tbsp. hoisin sauce
- 1 tablespoon freshly grated ginger
- 1 tablespoon Sriracha
- 2 green onions, sliced thin
- 2 tsp sesame seeds

Directions:
1. Place the rack in the cooking pot and top with a sheet of parchment paper.
2. Sprinkle the chicken with salt and pepper.
3. In a shallow dish, beat the eggs.
4. Place the bread crumbs in a separate shallow dish. Working in batches, dip the chicken first in the eggs then bread crumbs, pressing to coat the chicken well.
5. Place the chicken on the parchment paper in a single layer. Add the tender-crisp lid and select air fry on 400 °F (205°C). Bake the chicken 10-15 minutes until golden brown and cooked through, turning over halfway through cooking time. Transfer to serving plate and keep warm.
6. Set the cooker to sauté on med-high heat. Add the soy sauce, honey, garlic, hoisin, ginger, and Sriracha, stir to combine. Cook, stirring frequently, until sauce thickens, about 2 minutes.
7. Add chicken and toss to coat. Serve immediately garnished with green onions and sesame seeds.

Nutrition:
- InfoCalories 304,Total Fat 7g,Total Carbs 27g,Protein 32g,Sodium 1149mg.

Caponata

Servings: 10
Cooking Time: 30 Minutes
Ingredients:
- 2 tbsp. olive oil
- 1 eggplant, unpeeled & chopped
- 1 onion, chopped
- 2 tbsp. garlic powder
- ½ cup pimiento-stuffed green olives, chopped
- 3 stalks celery, chopped
- 8 oz. tomato sauce
- ¼ cup white vinegar
- 1/3 cup brown sugar, packed
- ¼ tsp hot pepper sauce

Directions:
1. Set cooker to sauté on med-high heat. Add oil and let it get hot.
2. Once oil is hot, add eggplant, onion, and garlic powder and cook 5 minutes, stirring occasionally, until eggplant starts to get soft.
3. Stir in remaining ingredients and reduce heat to low. Cook 25 minutes, or until all the vegetables are tender. Serve warm or cold.

Nutrition:
- InfoCalories 87,Total Fat 3g,Total Carbs 15g,Protein 1g,Sodium 16mg.

Parmesan Stuffed Mushrooms

Servings: 5
Cooking Time: 15 Minutes
Ingredients:
- 1 lb. button mushrooms, wash & remove stems
- 2 tbsp. olive oil, divided
- ¼ cup parmesan cheese, fat free
- 2 cloves garlic, diced fine
- ¼ cup cream cheese, fat free, soft
- ¼ cup whole wheat panko bread crumbs

Directions:
1. Place the rack in the cooking pot and top with a piece of parchment paper.
2. Brush the mushrooms with 1 tablespoon oil.
3. In a small bowl, combine parmesan, garlic, and cream cheese until smooth. Spoon 1 teaspoon of the mixture into each mushroom. Place mushrooms on parchment paper.
4. In a separate small bowl, stir together bread crumbs and remaining oil. Sprinkle over tops of mushrooms.
5. Add the tender-crisp lid and select bake on 375°F (190°C). Cook mushrooms 15 minutes, or until tops are nicely browned and mushrooms are tender. Serve immediately.

Nutrition:
- InfoCalories 121,Total Fat 6g,Total Carbs 10g,Protein 7g,Sodium 191mg.

Cheesy Bacon Brussel Sprouts

Servings: 6
Cooking Time: 15 Minutes
Ingredients:
- Nonstick cooking spray
- 3 slices turkey bacon, chopped
- 2 tsp olive oil
- 1 lb. Brussels sprouts, trimmed & cut in half
- 2 cloves garlic, diced fine
- ¼ cup water
- 3 oz. goat cheese, soft
- 2 tbsp. skim milk
- 1 tbsp. parmesan cheese
- ¼ tsp salt
- ¼ tsp pepper
- 1 tsp paprika

Directions:
1. Spray the cooking pot with cooking spray. Set to sauté on med-high heat.
2. Add bacon and cook until crisp, transfer to paper-towel line plate.
3. Add oil and let it get hot. Add Brussel sprouts and cook, stirring frequently, 5 minutes or until they start to brown.
4. Add water, cover and cook another 5 minutes or until fork-tender. Drain any water from the pot.
5. Add goat cheese, milk, parmesan, salt, and pepper. Cook, stirring frequently, until cheese has melted.
6. Stir in bacon and cook until heated through. Sprinkle with paprika and serve.

Nutrition:
- InfoCalories 106,Total Fat 6g,Total Carbs 8g,Protein 7g,Sodium 274mg.

Cheesy Jalapeno Boats

Servings: 12
Cooking Time: 25 Minutes
Ingredients:
- 8 oz. cream cheese, reduced fat, soft
- 1 cup cheddar cheese, reduced fat, grated
- 1 tsp garlic powder
- 2 eggs
- 2 tbsp. skim milk
- 1 cup panko bread crumbs
- ½ tsp paprika
- ½ tsp chili powder
- ½ tsp salt
- ¼ tsp pepper
- 12 jalapeno peppers, halved lengthwise, stems & seeds removed

Directions:
1. Place the rack in the cooking pot and line with parchment paper.
2. In a medium bowl, beat together cream cheese, cheddar, and garlic powder.
3. In a small bowl, whisk together eggs and milk.
4. In a shallow dish, stir together bread crumbs, paprika, chili powder, salt, and pepper.
5. Spread a tablespoon of cheese mixture in each jalapeno. Dip in egg mixture then coat with bread crumbs. Place on the parchment paper.
6. Add the tender-crisp lid and set to bake on 350°F (175°C). Cook 20-25 minutes or until golden brown. Serve immediately.
7. Bake 30 to 35 minutes, or until golden.

Nutrition:
- InfoCalories 107,Total Fat 5g,Total Carbs 9g,Protein 6g,Sodium 326mg.

White Bean Hummus

Servings: 8
Cooking Time: 8 Hours
Ingredients:
- 2 cups small white beans, soaked overnight
- 2 tbsp. pine nuts
- 1 tsp lemon zest, grated
- 1 tbsp. fresh lemon juice
- ¼ tsp garlic powder
- ¼ tsp salt

Directions:
1. Place beans with just enough water to cover them in the cooking pot. Add the lid and set to slow cooker function on low heat. Cook 8 hours, or until beans are tender.
2. Drain the beans, reserving some of the cooking liquid. Place beans in a food processor.
3. Wipe the cooking pot and set to sauté on low heat. Add the pine nuts and cook, stirring frequently, until lightly browned.
4. Add the lemon zest and juice, garlic powder, and salt to the beans. Pulse until almost smooth. If hummus is too thick, add reserved cooking liquid, a tablespoon at a time, until desired consistency.
5. Transfer hummus to a serving bowl and sprinkle with pine nuts. Serve.

Nutrition:
- InfoCalories 169,Total Fat 1g,Total Carbs 31g,Protein 12g,Sodium 81mg.

Mini Crab Cakes

Servings: 9
Cooking Time: 10 Minutes
Ingredients:
- Nonstick cooking spray
- 2/3 cup Italian seasoned bread crumbs
- ½ cup egg substitute
- ½ red bell pepper, chopped fine
- ½ red onion, chopped fine
- 1 stalk celery, chopped fine
- 3 tbsp. lite mayonnaise
- 2 tsp fresh lemon juice
- ½ tsp salt
- ¾ tsp pepper
- 1 tsp dried tarragon
- 2 cans lump crabmeat, drained

Directions:
1. Lightly spray fryer basket with cooking spray.
2. In a large bowl, combine all ingredients, except crab, until combined. Gently fold in crab. Form into 36 patties. Place them in a single layer in the fryer basket without overcrowding them.
3. Add the tender-crisp lid and set to air fry on 350°F (175°C). Cook patties 3-5 minutes per side until golden brown. Repeat with remaining patties. Serve warm.

Nutrition:
- InfoCalories 96,Total Fat 2g,Total Carbs 8g,Protein 10g,Sodium 543mg.

Zucchini Egg Tots

Servings: 8
Cooking Time: 9 Minutes
Ingredients:
- 2 medium zucchinis
- 1 egg
- 1 teaspoon salt
- ½ teaspoon baking soda
- 1 teaspoon lemon juice
- 1 teaspoon basil
- 1 tablespoon oregano
- ⅓ cup oatmeal flour
- 1 tablespoon olive oil
- 1 teaspoon minced garlic
- 1 tablespoon butter

Directions:
1. Wash the zucchini and grate it. Beat the egg in a suitable mixing bowl and blend it using a whisk.
2. Add the baking soda, lemon juice, basil, oregano, and flour to the egg mixture.
3. Stir it carefully until smooth. Combine the grated zucchini and egg mixture together.
4. Knead the dough until smooth. Mix olive oil with minced garlic together.
5. Set the Ninja Foodi's insert to" Sauté" mode.
6. Add butter and transfer the mixture to the Ninja Foodi's insert. Melt the mixture.
7. Make the small tots from the zucchini dough and place them in the melted butter mixture.
8. Sauté the dish for 3 minutes on each side.
9. Once the zucchini tots are cooked, remove them from the Ninja Foodi's insert and serve.

Nutrition:
- InfoCalories: 64; Fat: 4.4g; Carbohydrates: 4.35g; Protein: 2g

Swiss Onion Dip

Servings: 10
Cooking Time: 20 Minutes
Ingredients:
- ½ cup lite mayonnaise
- 2 cups Swiss cheese, grated
- 1 tsp garlic powder
- 1 green onion, sliced thin
- Paprika for sprinkling

Directions:
1. In a medium bowl, combine all ingredients except paprika and mix well.
2. Transfer to a 1-quart baking dish and sprinkle with paprika.
3. Place the rack in the cooking pot and place the dish on it. Add the tender-crisp lid and set to air fry on 350°F (175°C). Bake 15-20 minutes until cheese is melted and top is golden brown. Serve immediately.

Nutrition:
- InfoCalories 121,Total Fat 10g,Total Carbs 2g,Protein 6g,Sodium 100mg.

Crispy Spiced Cauliflower Bites

Servings: 12
Cooking Time: 15 Minutes
Ingredients:
- Nonstick cooking spray
- 1 egg
- 1 tbsp. water
- 1 cup whole wheat panko bread crumbs
- 1 tbsp. garlic powder
- ½ tsp onion powder
- 1 tbsp. fresh parsley, chopped
- 6 cups cauliflower florets
- ¼ cup light mayonnaise
- 2 tbsp. sweet chili sauce
- 2 tbsp. hot sauce

Directions:
1. Lightly spray the fryer basket with cooking spray and place in the cooking pot.
2. In a small bowl, whisk together egg and water.
3. In a separate small bowl, stir together bread crumbs, garlic powder, onion powder, and parsley.
4. Dip each floret first in egg then in bread crumbs. Place in fryer basket, in batches.
5. Add the tender-crisp lid and set to air fry on 400°F (205°C). Bake cauliflower 15 minutes or until golden brown and crispy.
6. In a small bowl, whisk together mayonnaise, chili sauce, and hot sauce. When all the cauliflower is done, drizzle sauce over the top and serve.

Nutrition:
- InfoCalories 77,Total Fat 3g,Total Carbs 11g,Protein 3g,Sodium 177mg.

Caramelized Cauliflower With Hazelnuts

Servings: 4
Cooking Time: 15 Minutes
Ingredients:
- 1 head cauliflower, cut in ½-inch thick slices
- 2 cups cold water
- 2 tbsp. olive oil
- 1 tbsp. honey
- ½ tsp fresh lemon juice
- ½ tsp salt
- ¼ tsp pepper
- 1 tbsp. fresh sage, chopped
- 1 tbsp. hazelnuts, toasted & chopped
- ¼ cup parmesan cheese, reduced fat

Directions:
1. Remove any core from the cauliflower slices. Lay them in a single layer in the cooking pot.
2. Add enough water to come halfway up the sides of the cauliflower. Add oil, honey, lemon, salt, and pepper.
3. Set cooker to sauté on high. Cover and cook cauliflower until the water has evaporated, about 6-8 minutes. When it begins to brown reduce heat to low.
4. Once water has evaporated, flip cauliflower over and cook another 5 minutes, or until bottom is golden brown.
5. Transfer to serving plates and top with sage, hazelnuts, and parmesan cheese. Serve.

Nutrition:
- InfoCalories 112,Total Fat 8g,Total Carbs 9g,Protein 3g,Sodium 407mg.

Chicken Meatballs With Dill Dipping Sauce

Servings: 8
Cooking Time: 15 Minutes
Ingredients:
- Nonstick cooking spray
- 1 lb. lean ground chicken
- 1 tsp oregano
- 1 cup whole wheat panko bread crumbs
- 1 egg, beaten
- 1/3 cup milk
- 2 cloves garlic, diced fine
- 1/3 cup red onions, diced fine
- 1/3 cup fresh parsley, chopped fine
- ¾ tsp salt, divided
- ¼ tsp black pepper
- 1 cup plain Greek yogurt, low fat
- 1/3 cup fresh dill, chopped fine
- 1 lemon, zest and juice
- ½ tsp cumin
- 1/8 tsp cayenne pepper

Directions:
1. Lightly spray the fryer basket with cooking spray.
2. In a large bowl, combine chicken, oregano, bread crumbs, egg, milk, garlic, onions, parsley, ½ teaspoon salt, and black pepper until thoroughly combined. Form into 1-inch meatballs.
3. Place meatballs in the basket in a single layer, do not over crowd. Add the tender crisp lid and set to air fry on 400°F (205°C). Cook meatballs 10-15 minutes until cooked through, turning over halfway through cooking time.
4. In a small bowl, stir together yogurt, dill, lemon zest and juice, remaining salt, cumin, and cayenne pepper until combined.
5. Serve meatballs with sauce for dipping.

Nutrition:
- InfoCalories 174,Total Fat 7g,Total Carbs 13g,Protein 14g,Sodium 386mg.

Japanese Eggs

Servings: 4
Cooking Time: 20 Minutes
Ingredients:
- 1 cup Chinese master stock
- 4 eggs
- 1 teaspoon salt

Directions:
1. Pour the Chinese master stock in the Ninja Foodi's insert and Close the Ninja Foodi's lid.
2. Cook the liquid on the "Pressure" mode for 10 minutes.
3. Remove the Chinese master stock from the Ninja Foodi's insert and chill it.
4. Meanwhile, place the eggs in the Ninja Foodi's insert.
5. Add water and boil the eggs on the "Pressure" mode for 10 minutes.
6. Once eggs are done, remove from the Ninja Foodi's insert and chill well.
7. Peel the eggs and place them in the Chinese master stock.
8. Leave the eggs in the liquid for 20 minutes.
9. Remove the eggs from the liquid. Cut the eggs into halves.

Nutrition:
- InfoCalories: 134; Fat: 9.7g; Carbohydrates: 2.01g; Protein: 9g

Sweet Potato Skins

Servings: 4
Cooking Time: 20 Minutes
Ingredients:
- 2 sweet potatoes, baked & halved lengthwise
- 1 tsp olive oil
- 2 cloves garlic, diced fine
- 1 tbsp. fresh lime juice
- 2 cups baby spinach
- ½ cup chicken, cooked & shredded
- 1 tsp oregano
- 1 tsp cumin
- 2 tsp chili powder
- ½ cup mozzarella cheese, grated
- ¼ cup cilantro, chopped

Directions:
1. Scoop out the center of the potatoes, leaving some on the side to help keep the shape.
2. Set the cooker to sauté on med-high heat and add the oil.
3. Once the oil is hot, add garlic, lime juice, and spinach. Cook 2-3 minutes until spinach is wilted.
4. In a large bowl, mash the sweet potato centers until almost smooth.
5. Stir in chicken, oregano, cumin, and chili powder. Stir in spinach until combined.
6. Place the rack in the cooking pot and top with parchment paper.
7. Spoon the potato mixture into the skins and top with cheese. Place on the rack.
8. Add the tender-crisp lid and set to bake on 400°F (205°C). Bake 15-20 minutes until cheese is melted and lightly browned. Let cool slightly then cut each skin in 4 pieces and serve garnished with cilantro.

Nutrition:
- InfoCalories 132, Total Fat 2g, Total Carbs 20g, Protein 9g, Sodium 155mg.

Tiny Tostadas

Servings: 8
Cooking Time: 10 Minutes
Ingredients:
- 8 corn tortillas
- 1 cup pork, cooked & shredded
- 1 ½ tbsp. taco seasoning
- 6 tbsp. salsa
- 1 lettuce leaf, shredded
- 1 tbsp. cheddar cheese, fine grated

Directions:
1. Set to air fryer function on 400°F (205°C). Place the rack in the cooker and top with a sheet of parchment paper.
2. Cut 3 mini tortillas from each large tortilla, so you have 24. Use a jar or other round object to do this.
3. In a small bowl, combine pork and taco seasoning.
4. Place a layer of mini tortillas on the rack, you will need to make these in batches, top with 1 teaspoon of the meat mixture.
5. Add the tender-crisp lid and bake 10-12 minutes or until tortillas are golden brown. Transfer to serving plate and top with salsa, lettuce, and cheese. Repeat with remaining ingredients.

Nutrition:
- InfoCalories 34, Total Fat 1g, Total Carbs 4g, Protein 2g, Sodium 84mg.

Jalapeno Salsa

Servings: 10
Cooking Time: 7 Minutes
Ingredients:
- 8 ounces jalapeno pepper
- ¼ cup Erythritol
- 5 tablespoon water
- 2 tablespoons butter
- 1 teaspoon paprika

Directions:
1. Wash the jalapeno pepper and remove the seeds.
2. Slice it into thin circles. Sprinkle the sliced jalapeno pepper with paprika and Erythritol.
3. Put the butter and jalaeno mixture into the Ninja Foodi's insert and add water.
4. Set the Ninja Foodi's insert to "Sauté" mode.
5. Once the butter melts, add the sliced jalapeno in the Ninja Foodi's insert.
6. Close the Ninja Foodi's lid and sauté the dish for 7 minutes.
7. Once done, remove the dish from the Ninja Foodi's insert.
8. Cool it and serve.

Nutrition:
- InfoCalories: 28; Fat: 2.5g; Carbohydrates: 7.5g; Protein: 0.4g

Rosemary Potato Fries

Servings: 4
Cooking Time: 30 Min
Ingredients:
- 4 russet potatoes, cut into sticks
- 2 garlic cloves, crushed
- 2 tbsp butter, melted /30ml
- 1 tsp fresh rosemary; chopped /5g
- Salt and pepper, to taste

Directions:
1. Add butter, garlic, salt, and pepper to a bowl; toss until the sticks are well-coated. Lay the potato sticks into the Ninja Foodi's basket. Close the crisping lid and cook for 15

Ninja Foodi Cookbook Guide

minutes at 370 °F or 185°C. Shake the potatoes every 5 minutes.
2. Once ready, check to ensure the fries are golden and crispy all over if not, return them to cook for a few minutes.
3. Divide standing up between metal cups lined with nonstick baking paper, and serve sprinkled with rosemary.

Apple Pecan Cookie Bars

Servings: 12
Cooking Time: 20 Minutes
Ingredients:
- Nonstick cooking spray
- 2/3 cup sugar
- 2 egg whites
- ½ tsp vanilla
- ½ cup flour
- 1 tsp baking powder
- 2 cups Granny Smith apples, chopped
- ¼ cup pecans, chopped

Directions:
1. Lightly spray an 8-inch baking pan with cooking spray.
2. In a large bowl, whisk together egg whites, sugar, and vanilla until frothy.
3. Whisk in flour and baking powder until combined.
4. Fold in apples and nuts and pour into pan.
5. Place the rack in the cooking pot and place the pan on it. Add the tender-crisp lid and set to air fry on 350°F (175°C). Bake 18-20 minutes or until the cookies pass the toothpick test.
6. Let cool before cutting and serving.

Nutrition:
- InfoCalories 90,Total Fat 2g,Total Carbs 18g,Protein 1g,Sodium 10mg.

Crispy Sesame Shrimp

Servings: 10
Cooking Time: 10 Minutes
Ingredients:
- 1 cup flour
- ¼ tsp salt
- ¼ tsp cayenne pepper
- ¾ cup club soda
- Nonstick cooking spray
- 1 lb. medium shrimp, peel & devein
- 2 tsp sesame seeds

Directions:
1. In a medium bowl, combine flour, salt, and pepper.
2. Whisk in club soda until combined.
3. Spray fryer basket with cooking spray.
4. Dip shrimp, one at a time, in the batter and place in basket in a single layer. Sprinkle with sesame seeds.
5. Add tender-crisp lid and set cooker to air fryer function on 400°F (205°C). Cook shrimp 8-10 minutes or until golden brown. Serve immediately.

Nutrition:
- InfoCalories 81,Total Fat 1g,Total Carbs 10g,Protein 7g,Sodium 319mg.

Crispy Cheesy Straws

Servings: 8
Cooking Time: 45 Min
Ingredients:
- 2 cups cauliflower florets, steamed /260g
- 5 oz. cheddar cheese /150g
- 3 ½ oz. oats /105g
- 1 egg
- 1 red onion; diced
- 1 tsp mustard /5g
- Salt and pepper, to taste

Directions:
1. Add the oats in a food processor and process until they resemble breadcrumbs. Place the steamed florets in a cheesecloth and squeeze out the excess liquid.
2. Put the florets in a large bowl, and add the rest of the ingredients to the bowl.
3. Mix well with your hands, to combine the ingredients thoroughly.
4. Take a little bit of the mixture and twist it into a straw. Place in the lined Ninja Foodi basket; repeat with the rest of the mixture.
5. Close the crisping lid and cook for 10 minutes on Air Crisp mode at 350 °F or 175°C. After 5 minutes, turn them over and cook for an additional 10 minutes.

Herby Fish Skewers

Servings: 4
Cooking Time: 75 Min
Ingredients:
- 1 pound cod loin, boneless, skinless; cubed /450g
- 2 garlic cloves, grated
- 1 lemon, juiced and zested
- 1 lemon, cut in wedges to serve
- 3 tbsp olive oil /45ml
- 1 tsp dill; chopped /5g
- 1 tsp parsley; chopped /5g
- Salt to taste

Directions:
1. In a bowl, combine the olive oil, garlic, dill, parsley, salt, and lemon juice. Stir in the cod and place in the fridge to marinate for 1 hour. Thread the cod pieces onto halved skewers.
2. Arrange into the oiled Ninja Foodi basket; close the crisping lid and cook for 10 minutes at 390 °F or 200°C. Flip them over halfway through cooking. When ready, remove to a serving platter, scatter lemon zest and serve with wedges.

Glazed Walnuts

Servings: 4
Cooking Time: 4 Minutes
Ingredients:
- ⅓ cup of water
- 6 ounces walnuts
- 5 tablespoon Erythritol
- ½ teaspoon ground ginger
- 3 tablespoons psyllium husk powder

Directions:
1. Combine Erythritol and water together in a mixing bowl.
2. Add ground ginger and stir the mixture until the erythritol is dissolved.
3. Transfer the walnuts to the Ninja Foodi's insert and add sweet liquid.
4. Close the Ninja Foodi's lid and cook the dish in the "Pressure" mode for 4 minutes.
5. Remove the walnuts from the Ninja Foodi's insert.
6. Dip the walnuts in the Psyllium husk powder and serve.

Nutrition:
- InfoCalories: 286; Fat: 25.1g; Carbohydrates: 10.4g; Protein: 10.3g

Spicy Black Bean Dip

Servings: 12
Cooking Time: 20 Minutes
Ingredients:
- 2 16 oz. cans black beans, rinsed & drained, divided
- 1 cup salsa, divided
- 1 tsp olive oil
- ¾ onion, diced fine
- 1 red bell pepper, diced fine
- 3 cloves garlic, diced fine
- 1 tbsp. cilantro
- 2 tsp cumin
- ¼ tsp salt
- ¼ cup cheddar cheese, reduced fat, grated
- 1 tomato, chopped

Directions:
1. Add 1 can beans and ¼ cup salsa to a food processor or blender. Pulse until smooth.
2. Set cooker to sauté on medium heat. Add oil and let it get hot.
3. Add the onion, pepper, and garlic and cook, stirring occasionally, 5-7 minutes, or until vegetables are tender.
4. Add the pureed bean mixture along with remaining ingredients except cheese and tomatoes, mix well. Reduce heat to low and bring to a simmer. Let cook 5 minutes, stirring frequently.
5. Transfer dip to serving bowl and top with cheese and tomato. Serve immediately.

Nutrition:
- InfoCalories 100,Total Fat 2g,Total Carbs 16g,Protein 6g,Sodium 511mg.

Dill Butter

Servings: 7
Cooking Time: 5 Minutes
Ingredients:
- 1 cup butter
- 1 teaspoon minced garlic
- 1 teaspoon dried oregano
- 1 teaspoon dried cilantro
- 1 tablespoon dried dill
- 1 teaspoon salt
- ½ teaspoon black pepper

Directions:
1. Set "Sauté" mode and place butter inside the Ninja Foodi's insert.
2. Add minced garlic, dried oregano, dried cilantro, butter, dried dill, salt, and black pepper.
3. Stir the mixture well and sauté it for 4-5 minutes or until the butter is melted.
4. Then switch off the cooker and stir the butter well.
5. Transfer the butter mixture into the butter mould and freeze it.

Nutrition:
- InfoCalories: 235; Fat: 26.3g; Carbohydrates: 0.6g; Protein: 0.4g

Steak And Minty Cheese

Servings: 4
Cooking Time: 15 Min
Ingredients:
- 2 New York strip steaks
- 8 oz. halloumi cheese /240g
- 12 kalamata olives
- Juice and zest of 1 lemon
- Olive oil
- 2 tbsp chopped parsley /30g
- 2 tbsp chopped mint /30g
- Salt and pepper, to taste

Directions:
1. Season the steaks with salt and pepper, and gently brush with olive oil. Place into the Ninja Foodi, close the crisping lid and cook for 6 minutes (for medium rare) on Air Crisp mode at 350 °F or 175°C. When ready, remove to a plate and set aside.
2. Drizzle the cheese with olive oil and place it in the Ninja Foodi; cook for 4 minutes.
3. Remove to a serving platter and serve with sliced steaks and olives, sprinkled with herbs, and lemon zest and juice.

Cheesy Onion Dip

Servings: 8
Cooking Time: 15 Minutes
Ingredients:
- 8 oz. cream cheese, soft
- 1 cup Swiss cheese, grated
- 1 cup mayonnaise
- 1 cup onion, grated

Directions:
1. In a medium bowl, combine all ingredients and mix thoroughly. Transfer to a small baking dish and cover tightly with foil.
2. Place the trivet in the cooking pot along with 1 cup of water. Place the dish on trivet.
3. Secure the lid and select pressure cooking on high. Set timer for 15 minutes.
4. When timer goes off, use quick release to remove the lid.
5. Remove the foil and add the tender-crisp lid. Set to air fryer on 400°F (205°C) cook 1-2 minutes until the top is golden brown. Serve warm.

Nutrition:
- InfoCalories 352,Total Fat 35g,Total Carbs 3g,Protein 6g,Sodium 290mg.

Rosemary And Garlic Mushrooms

Servings: 4
Cooking Time: 20 Min
Ingredients:
- 12 oz. button mushrooms /360g
- 2 rosemary sprigs
- 3 garlic cloves, minced
- ¼ cup melted butter /62.5ml
- ½ tsp salt /2.5g
- ¼ tsp black pepper /1.25g

Directions:
1. Wash and pat dry the mushrooms and cut them in half. Place in a large bowl. Add the remaining Ingredients to the bowl and toss well to combine.
2. Transfer the mushrooms to the basket of the Ninja Foodi. Close the crisping lid and cook for 12 minutes on Air Crisp mode, shaking once halfway through; at 350 °F or 175°C.

Cauliflower Gratin

Servings: 6
Cooking Time: 28 Minutes
Ingredients:
- 2 cups water
- 1 large head cauliflower, cut into 1-inch florets
- 3 tablespoons unsalted butter
- 3 tablespoons all-purpose flour
- 1½ cups whole milk
- 1 cup heavy (whipping) cream
- 2 tablespoons capers, drained
- 1 tablespoon fresh thyme
- Kosher salt
- Freshly ground black pepper
- ¾ cup shredded Swiss cheese
- ¼ cup grated Parmesan cheese

Directions:
1. Pour the water in the pot. Place the Reversible Rack in the lower position in the pot. Place the cauliflower on the rack. Assemble pressure lid, making sure the pressure release valve is in the SEAL position.
2. Select PRESSURE and set to HI. Set time to 5 minutes. Select START/STOP to begin.
3. When pressure cooking is complete, quick release the pressure by turning the pressure release valve to the VENT position. Carefully remove lid when the unit has finished releasing pressure.
4. Remove rack and place the cauliflower in the Ninja Multi-Purpose Pan or 8-inch baking dish. Drain the water from the pot and wipe it dry. Reinsert pot into base.
5. Select SEAR/SAUTÉ and set temperature to HI. Select START/STOP to begin. Let preheat for 5 minutes.
6. Add the butter. Once melted, add the onion and cook 3 minutes. Add the flour and cook, stirring constantly, 1 minute.
7. Add the milk, cream, capers, and thyme. Season with salt and pepper. Bring to a boil and cook, about 4 minutes.
8. Pour the sauce over the cauliflower. Place the pan onto the Reversible Rack, making sure the rack is in the lower position. Place the rack with pan in the pot. Close crisping lid.
9. Select BAKE/ROAST, set temperature to 400°F (205°C), and set time to 20 minutes. Select START/STOP to begin.
10. After 15 minutes, open lid and sprinkle the cauliflower with the Swiss and Parmesan cheeses. Close lid and continue cooking.
11. Once cooking is complete, open lid. Let the gratin sit for 10 minutes before serving.

Nutrition:
- InfoCalories: 341,Total Fat: 27g,Sodium: 263mg,Carbohydrates: 16g,Protein: 11g.

Mini Steak Kebabs

Servings: 12
Cooking Time: 10 Minutes
Ingredients:
- 1 lb. flank steak, cut in 24 thin slices
- ½ cup peanut butter, reduced fat
- 2 tbsp. light soy sauce
- 2 tsp sesame oil
- 1 tbsp. butter
- 1 tsp red pepper flakes

Directions:
1. Soak 24 6-inch wood skewers in water for 15 minutes.
2. Set cooker to air fryer function on 350°F (175°C). Lightly spray the fryer basket with cooking spray.
3. Thread sliced beef on prepared skewers.
4. In a small saucepan over low heat, combine remaining ingredients. Cook, stirring frequently, until butters are melted and sauce is smooth.
5. Place skewers in fryer basket in single layer, these will need to be cooked in batches. Brush sauce over them, making sure to coat them all.
6. Add tender-crisp lid and bake 8-10 minutes, turning over halfway through cooking time and brushing with sauce again. Repeat with remaining skewers. Serve.

Nutrition:
- InfoCalories 131,Total Fat 8g,Total Carbs 4g,Protein 11g,Sodium 178mg.

Spicy Turkey Meatballs

Servings: 8
Cooking Time: 15 Minutes
Ingredients:
- 1 lb. lean ground turkey
- 1 onion, chopped fine
- ¼ cup shredded wheat cereal, crushed
- 2 egg whites
- ½ tsp garlic powder
- ½ tsp salt
- ¼ tsp pepper
- Nonstick cooking spray
- ¼ cup jalapeno pepper jelly

Directions:
1. In a large bowl, combine all ingredients, except pepper jelly, and mix well. Form into 24 1-inch meatballs.
2. Lightly spray the fryer basket with cooking spray. Place meatballs in a single layer in the basket, these will need to be cooked in batches.
3. Add the basket to the cooking pot and secure the tender crisp lid. Set to air fry on 400°F (205°C). Cook meatballs 12-15 minutes, until no longer pink inside, turning halfway through cooking time.
4. Place the pepper jelly in a medium, microwave safe bowl. Microwave in 30 second intervals until the jelly is melted.
5. Toss cooked meatballs in the melted pepper jelly and serve immediately.
6. In a medium bowl, combine the turkey, onion, cereal, egg whites, garlic powder, salt, and black pepper. Shape into 24 one-inch meatballs.

Nutrition:
- InfoCalories 113,Total Fat 5g,Total Carbs 6g,Protein 12g,Sodium 199mg.

Teriyaki Chicken Wings

Servings: 6
Cooking Time: 30 Min
Ingredients:
- 2 lb. chicken wings /900g
- 1 cup teriyaki sauce /250ml
- 1 tbsp honey /15ml
- 2 tbsp cornstarch 30g
- 2 tbsp cold water /30ml
- 1 tsp finely ground black pepper /5g
- 1 tsp sesame seeds /5g

Ninja Foodi Cookbook Guide

Directions:
1. In the pot, combine honey, teriyaki sauce and black pepper until the honey dissolves completely; toss in chicken to coat. Seal the pressure lid, choose Pressure, set to High, and set the timer to 10 minutes. Press Start.
2. When ready, release the pressure quickly. Transfer chicken wings to a platter. Mix cold water with the cornstarch.
3. Press Sear/Sauté and stir in cornstarch slurry into the sauce and cook for 3 to 5 minutes until thickened. Top the chicken with thickened sauce. Add a garnish of sesame seeds, and serve.

Butter-flower Medley

Servings: 10
Cooking Time: 15 Minutes
Ingredients:
- 3 cups butternut squash, peel & cut in 1-inch cubes
- 1 head cauliflower, separated into florets
- 2 cloves garlic
- 1 tbsp. skim milk
- ½ tsp onion powder
- ¼ tsp thyme
- 1/8 tsp salt
- 1/8 tsp black pepper
- 1 tbsp. butter
- 1 tbsp. parmesan cheese, reduced fat

Directions:
1. Add the squash, cauliflower, and garlic to the cooking pot. Pour in ½ cup water. Add the lid and select pressure cooking on high. Set the timer for 8 minutes.
2. When timer goes off use natural release to remove the lid. Drain the vegetables and place in a large bowl.
3. Add remaining ingredients, except parmesan, and beat until smooth.
4. Transfer the squash mixture back to the cooking pot and sprinkle top with parmesan cheese. Add the tender-crisp lid and select air fry on 400°F (205°C). Cook 5-6 minutes or until top is lightly browned. Serve.

Nutrition:
- InfoCalories 47, Total Fat 1g, Total Carbs 8g, Protein 2g, Sodium 68mg.

Shallots With Mushrooms

Servings: 7
Cooking Time: 30 Minutes
Ingredients:
- 9 ounces shallot
- 8 ounces mushrooms
- ½ cup chicken stock
- 1 tablespoon paprika
- ½ tablespoon salt
- ¼ cup cream
- 1 teaspoon coriander
- ½ cup dill, chopped
- ½ cup parsley
- 1 tablespoon Erythritol

Directions:
1. Slice the shallot and chop the mushrooms.
2. Combine the chicken stock, salt, paprika, cream, coriander, and Erythritol in a mixing bowl.
3. Blend the mixture well. Chop the dill and parsley.
4. Pour the cream mixture in the Ninja Foodi's insert.

5. Set the Ninja Foodi's insert to "Sauté" mode and add sliced shallot and chopped mushrooms.
6. Blend the mixture using a wooden spoon. Close the Ninja Foodi's lid and sauté the mixture for 30 minutes.
7. Chop the parsley and dill. Once the dish is done, transfer it to serving plates.
8. Sprinkle the cooked dish with the chopped parsley and dill.
9. Do not stir again before serving it.

Nutrition:
- InfoCalories: 52; Fat: 1g; Carbohydrates: 10.2g; Protein: 3g

Loaded Potato Skins

Servings: 4
Cooking Time: 45 Minutes
Ingredients:
- 2 large Russet potatoes, cleaned
- 1 tablespoon extra-virgin olive oil
- Kosher salt
- Freshly ground black pepper
- ¾ cup shredded sharp Cheddar cheese
- 3 tablespoons unsalted butter
- ¼ cup milk
- ¼ cup sour cream, plus more for serving
- 1 bunch chives, sliced
- 4 slices of ham, cubed

Directions:
1. Using a fork, poke holes in each potato. Rub each potato with the olive oil and season the skin with salt and pepper. Place the potatoes on the Reversible Rack in the lower position and place in the pot. Close the crisping lid.
2. Select AIR CRISP, set temperature to 390°F (200°C), and set time to 35 minutes. Select START/STOP to begin.
3. When cooking is complete, open lid and use tongs to transfer the potatoes to a cutting board.
4. Cut the potatoes in half lengthwise. Using a spoon, scoop out the flesh into a large bowl, leaving about ¼ inch of flesh on the skins. Set aside.
5. Sprinkle the hollowed-out potato skins with ¼ cup of cheese and place them back in the pot on the rack. Close crisping lid.
6. Select BROIL and set time to 5 minutes. Select START/STOP to begin.
7. Add the butter, milk, and sour cream to the bowl with the flesh. Season with salt and pepper and mash together. Use a spatula to fold in ¼ cup of cheese, one-quarter of the chives, and ham into the potato mixture.
8. When cooking is complete, open lid. Using tongs, carefully transfer the potato skins to the cutting board. Evenly distribute the mashed potato mixture into each potato skin and top with the remaining ¼ cup of cheese. Return the loaded potato skins to the rack. Close crisping lid.
9. Select BROIL and set time to 5 minutes. Select START/STOP to begin.
10. When cooking is complete, open lid. Carefully remove the potatoes. Cut them in half and garnish with the remaining chives. Serve with additional sour cream, if desired.

Nutrition:
- InfoCalories: 402, Total Fat: 24g, Sodium: 561mg, Carbohydrates: 32g, Protein: 14g.

Cheesy Chicken Dip

Servings: 6
Cooking Time: 2 Hours
Ingredients:
- 1 lb. cheddar cheese, cubed
- 2 cups chicken, cooked & shredded
- 4 oz. cream cheese, cubed
- 1 cup tomatoes, diced
- 1 cup black beans, drained & rinsed
- ½ cup black olives, pitted & sliced
- 1 jalapeno, seeded & diced
- 2 tbsp. taco seasoning

Directions:
1. Place all ingredients in the cooking pot and stir to mix.
2. Add the lid and set to slow cooking on low heat. Set timer for 2 hours. Let dip cook, stirring occasionally until hot and bubbly and the cheese has melted.
3. Stir well then transfer to a serving dish and serve warm.

Nutrition:
- InfoCalories 507,Total Fat 35g,Total Carbs 12g,Protein 35g,Sodium 1022mg.

Scalloped Potatoes

Servings: 6
Cooking Time: 5 Minutes
Ingredients:
- 5 potatoes, sliced thin
- 5 tbsp. butter
- 2 cloves garlic, diced fine
- 1 cup vegetable broth
- ¾ tsp salt
- ½ tsp pepper
- 1 ½ tsp fresh parsley, diced fine
- ¼ cup cheddar cheese, grated

Directions:
1. Place potatoes in the cooking pot. Sprinkle with salt, pepper, and parsley, toss to coat.
2. Add butter, garlic, and broth to the potatoes.
3. Add the lid and select pressure cooking on high. Set timer to 5 minutes. When timer goes off use natural release to remove the lid.
4. Transfer potatoes to serving dish and top with grated cheese to garnish. Serve.

Nutrition:
- InfoCalories 415,Total Fat 17g,Total Carbs 55g,Protein 12g,Sodium 587mg.

Chili Chicken Dip

Servings: 8
Cooking Time: 20 Minutes
Ingredients:
- 1 tbsp. olive oil
- 1 sweet onion, chopped fine
- 2 cloves garlic, chopped fine
- 2 jalapeño peppers, seeded & chopped
- 1 Poblano pepper, seeded & chopped
- 1 cup Greek yogurt
- 8 oz. cream cheese, fat free, soft
- ½ cup cheddar cheese, reduced fat, grated
- 4 oz. green chilies, diced
- 1 tsp salt
- 2 cups chicken breasts, cooked & shredded
- 1 tbsp. chili powder
- 2 tsp cumin
- ½ tsp pepper
- 1 tsp oregano
- Nonstick cooking spray
- ¼ cup cilantro, chopped

Directions:
1. Set the cooker to sauté on medium heat. Add oil and let it get hot.
2. Add the onion, garlic, jalapeno, and poblano peppers. Cook, stirring frequently, until vegetables are tender, about 3-5 minutes. Transfer to a bowl and let cool completely.
3. In a medium bowl, beat together yogurt, and cream cheese until smooth.
4. Turn the mixer to low and add onion mixture along with remaining ingredients, except cilantro. Beat until all ingredients are combined.
5. Spray a casserole dish with cooking spray. Spread dip evenly in the dish.
6. Place the rack in the cooking pot and put the dish on it. Add the tender-crisp lid and select bake on 400°F (205°C). Bake 15 minutes until bubbly. Sprinkle with cilantro and serve.

Nutrition:
- InfoCalories 189,Total Fat 7g,Total Carbs 15g,Protein 19g,Sodium 1004mg.

Three-layer Taco Dip

Servings:6
Cooking Time: 15 Minutes
Ingredients:
- 2 cans pinto beans, rinsed and drained
- 1 white onion, chopped
- 8 garlic cloves, chopped
- 1 can diced tomatoes
- 1 serrano chile, seeded and chopped
- 1 teaspoon kosher salt
- 2 teaspoons ground cumin
- 2 teaspoons chili powder
- 2 cups shredded Mexican blend cheese
- 1 cup shredded iceberg lettuce

Directions:
1. Place the beans, onions, garlic, tomatoes, chile, salt, cumin, and chili powder in the pot. Assemble pressure lid, making sure the pressure release valve is in the SEAL position.
2. Select PRESSURE and set to HI. Set time to 5 minutes. Select START/STOP to begin.
3. When pressure cooking is complete, quick release the pressure by moving the pressure release valve to the VENT position. Carefully remove lid when unit has finished releasing pressure.
4. Using a silicone spatula, stir the mixture in the pot. Sprinkle shredded cheese across the top of the bean mixture. Close crisping lid.
5. Select BROIL and set time to 10 minutes. Select STOP/START to begin.
6. When cooking is complete, open lid. Let cool for 5 minutes, then add the shredded lettuce. Serve immediately.

Nutrition:
- InfoCalories: 327,Total Fat: 14g,Sodium: 612mg,Carbohydrates: 33g,Protein: 19g.

Mushrooms Stuffed With Veggies

Servings: 6
Cooking Time: 25 Minutes
Ingredients:
- 12 large mushrooms, washed
- 1 tbsp. olive oil
- 1 zucchini, grated
- ½ onion, chopped fine
- ½ red bell pepper, chopped fine
- ¼ cup bread crumbs
- ½ tsp garlic powder
- ¼ tsp salt
- ¼ tsp pepper

Directions:
1. Remove stems from mushroom and finely chop them.
2. Add oil to the cooking pot and set to sauté on medium heat.
3. Once oil is hot, add mushroom stems, zucchini, onion, and bell pepper. Cook, stirring occasionally, about 5 minutes or until vegetables are tender.
4. Stir in bread crumbs, garlic powder, salt, and pepper. Transfer mixture to a bowl.
5. Place the rack in the cooking pot and top with parchment paper.
6. Stuff each mushroom cap with vegetable mixture and place on the parchment.
7. Add the tender-crisp lid and set to air fry on 350°F (175°C). Bake 15-20 minutes or until mushrooms are tender. Serve immediately.

Nutrition:
- InfoCalories 56,Total Fat 3g,Total Carbs 6g,Protein 2g,Sodium 134mg.

Mexican Street Corn Queso Dip

Servings: 8
Cooking Time: 20 Minutes
Ingredients:
- 1 package cream cheese, quartered
- 6 ounces cotija cheese, crumbled, 2 ounces reserved for topping
- 1 can fire-roasted tomatoes with chiles
- ½ cup mayonnaise
- Zest of 2 limes
- Juice of 2 limes
- 2 packages shredded Mexican cheese blend, divided
- 1 garlic clove, grated
- 1 can cream corn
- 1 cup frozen corn
- Kosher salt
- Freshly ground black pepper

Directions:
1. Pour the cream cheese, 4 ounces of cotija cheese, tomatoes with chiles, mayonnaise, lime zest and juice, one 8-ounce package Mexican cheese blend, garlic, cream corn, and frozen corn in the pot. Season with salt and pepper and stir. Close crisping lid.
2. Select BAKE/ROAST, set temperature to 375°F (190°C), and set time to 20 minutes. Select START/STOP to begin.
3. After 10 minutes, open lid and sprinkle the dip with the remaining 2 ounces of cotija cheese and remaining 8-ounce package of Mexican blend cheese. Close crisping lid and continue cooking.
4. When cooking is complete, the cheese will be melted and the dip hot and bubbling at the edges. Open lid and let the dip cool for 5 to 10 minutes before serving. Serve topped with chopped cilantro, hot sauce, and chili powder, if desired.

Nutrition:
- InfoCalories: 538,Total Fat: 45g,Sodium: 807mg,Carbohydrates: 18g,Protein: 20g.

Nutmeg Peanuts

Servings: 8
Cooking Time: 1.5 Hour
Ingredients:
- 3 cups peanuts in shells
- 1 tablespoon salt
- 4 cups of water
- ½ teaspoon nutmeg

Directions:
1. Combine the water, nutmeg, and salt together.
2. Stir the mixture well until salt is dissolved.
3. Transfer the water in the Ninja Foodi's insert.
4. Add peanuts in shells and Close the Ninja Foodi's lid.
5. Cook the dish on the "Pressure" mode for 90 minutes.
6. Once done, remove the peanuts from the Ninja Foodi's insert.
7. Let the peanuts cool before serving.

Nutrition:
- InfoCalories: 562; Fat: 36.8g; Carbohydrates: 8.57g; Protein: 28g

Cashew Cream

Servings: 10
Cooking Time: 10 Minutes
Ingredients:
- 3 cups cashew
- 2 cups chicken stock
- 1 teaspoon salt
- 1 tablespoon butter
- 2 tablespoons ricotta cheese

Directions:
1. Combine the cashews with the chicken stock in the Ninja Foodi's insert.
2. Add salt and close the Ninja Foodi's lid.
3. Cook the dish in the "Pressure" mode for 10 minutes.
4. Remove the cashews from the Ninja Foodi's insert and drain the nuts from the water.
5. Transfer the cashews to a blender, and add the ricotta cheese and butter.
6. Blend the mixture until it is smooth. When you get the texture you want, remove it from a blender.
7. Serve it immediately, or keep the cashew butter in the refrigerator.

Nutrition:
- InfoCalories: 252; Fat: 20.6g; Carbohydrates: 13.8g; Protein: 6.8 g

Cheesy Stuffed Onions

Servings: 6
Cooking Time: 1 Hour
Ingredients:
- 3 onions, peeled & cut in half horizontally
- 1 tbsp. olive oil
- ¼ cup cream cheese, reduced fat, soft
- 2 tbsp. sour cream, fat free
- 1 clove garlic, diced fine
- 1 tsp fresh rosemary, diced fine
- 1/8 tsp salt
- 1/8 tsp pepper
- 2 tbsp. panko bread crumbs
- 1 tbsp. butter, melted
- 1 tsp bacon bits

Directions:
1. Place onions, cut side up, in the cooking pot. Drizzle with oil.
2. Add the tender-crisp lid and select air fry on 400°F (205°C). Cook onions for 40 minutes. Transfer to wire rack and let cool enough to handle.
3. Carefully remove the center of the onion so you have a shell.
4. In a small bowl, combine cream cheese, sour cream, garlic, rosemary, salt, and pepper. Spread over and into the onions.
5. In a separate small bowl, combine bread crumbs, butter, and bacon.
6. Place the rack in the cooking pot and top with a sheet of parchment paper. Place the onions back in the pot and sprinkle the tops with bacon mixture.
7. Add the tender-crisp lid and set to bake on 400°F (205°C). Bake onions another 10-15 minutes or until golden brown. Serve.

Nutrition:
- InfoCalories 93,Total Fat 6g,Total Carbs 8g,Protein 2g,Sodium 127mg.

Pork Shank

Servings: 6
Cooking Time: 45 Minutes
Ingredients:
- 1-pound pork shank
- ½ cup parsley, chopped
- 4 garlic cloves
- 1 teaspoon salt
- ½ teaspoon paprika
- 2 tablespoons olive oil
- 1 teaspoon cilantro, chopped
- 1 tablespoon celery
- 1 carrot, grated
- 1 cup of water
- 1 red onion, chopped
- ⅓ cup wine
- 2 tablespoons lemon juice

Directions:
1. Chop the parsley and slice the garlic cloves.
2. Combine the vegetables together and add salt, paprika, cilantro, wine, and lemon juice and stir the mixture.
3. Combine the pork shank and marinade together and leave the mixture.
4. Combine the sliced onion and grated carrot together.
5. Add celery and blend well. Add the vegetables to the pork shank mixture and stir using your hands.
6. Place the meat in the Ninja Foodi's insert and add water.
7. Close the Ninja Foodi's lid, and set the Ninja Foodi to" Pressure."
8. Cook for 45 minutes. Once done, remove the meat from the Ninja Foodi's insert and chill the dish well.
9. Slice the pork shank and serve.

Nutrition:
- InfoCalories: 242; Fat: 19.8g; Carbohydrates: 5.38g; Protein: 11g

Cheesy Fried Risotto Balls

Servings: 6
Cooking Time: 45 Minutes
Ingredients:
- ½ cup extra-virgin olive oil, plus 1 tablespoon
- 1 small yellow onion, diced
- 2 garlic cloves, minced
- 5 cups vegetable broth
- ½ cup white wine
- 2 cups arborio rice
- ½ cup shredded mozzarella cheese
- ½ cup shredded fontina cheese
- ½ cup grated Parmesan cheese, plus more for garnish
- 2 tablespoons chopped fresh parsley
- 1 teaspoon sea salt
- 1 teaspoon freshly ground black pepper
- 2 cups fresh bread crumbs
- 2 large eggs

Directions:
1. Select SEAR/SAUTÉ and set to MD:HI. Select START/STOP to begin. Allow the pot to preheat for 5 minutes.
2. Add 1 tablespoon of oil and the onion to the preheated pot. Cook until soft and translucent, stirring occasionally. Add the garlic and cook for 1 minute.
3. Add the broth, wine, and rice to the pot; stir to incorporate. Assemble the pressure lid, making sure the pressure release valve is in the SEAL position.
4. Select PRESSURE and set to HI. Set the time to 7 minutes. Press START/STOP to begin.
5. When pressure cooking is complete, allow pressure to naturally release for 10 minutes. After 10 minutes, quick release any remaining pressure by turning the pressure release valve to the VENT position. Carefully remove the lid when the unit has finished releasing pressure.
6. Add the mozzarella, fontina, and Parmesan cheeses, the parsley, salt, and pepper. Stir vigorously until the rice begins to thicken. Transfer the risotto to a large mixing bowl and let cool.
7. Meanwhile, clean the pot. In a medium mixing bowl, stir together the bread crumbs and the remaining ½ cup of olive oil. In a separate mixing bowl, lightly beat the eggs.
8. Divide the risotto into 12 equal portions and form each one into a ball. Dip each risotto ball in the beaten eggs, then coat in the breadcrumb mixture.
9. Arrange half of the risotto balls in the Cook & Crisp Basket in a single layer.
10. Close the crisping lid. Select AIR CRISP, set the temperature to 400°F (205°C), and set the time to 10 minutes. Select START/STOP to begin.
11. Repeat steps 9 and 10 to cook the remaining risotto balls.

Nutrition:
- InfoCalories: 722,Total Fat: 33g,Sodium: 1160mg,Carbohydrates: 81g,Protein: 23g.

Ninja Foodi Cookbook Guide

Sweet Potato Gratin

Servings: 6
Cooking Time: 15 Minutes

Ingredients:
- 2 tablespoons unsalted butter
- 3 tablespoons all-purpose flour
- 2 cups heavy (whipping) cream, warmed in microwave
- 2 teaspoons kosher salt
- 1 teaspoon pumpkin pie spice
- ¼ cup water
- 3 large sweet potatoes, peeled and cut in half, then cut into half-moons ¼-inch thick
- 1¼ cups shredded Cheddar cheese, divided
- ½ cup chopped walnuts or pecans, or slivered almonds

Directions:
1. Select SEAR/SAUTÉ and set to MD:HI. Select START/STOP to begin. Let preheat for 5 minutes.
2. Add the butter. Once melted, add the flour and stir together until a thick paste forms, about 1 minute. (The combination of butter and flour is called a roux). Continue cooking the roux for 2 minutes, stirring frequently with a rubber-coated whisk. Slowly add the warm cream while continuously whisking so there are no lumps, about 3 minutes. The cream should be thickened.
3. Add the salt and pumpkin pie spice and whisk to incorporate. Whisk in the water and let the mixture simmer for 3 minutes.
4. Place the potatoes in the pot. Assemble pressure lid, making sure the pressure release valve is in the SEAL position.
5. Select PRESSURE and set to LO. Set time to 1 minute. Select START/STOP to begin.
6. When pressure cooking is complete, quick release pressure by moving the pressure release valve to the VENT position. Carefully remove lid when unit has finished releasing pressure.
7. Add ¼ cup of cheese and stir gently to incorporate, being careful not to break up the cooked potatoes. Ensure mixture is flat, then cover top with remaining 1 cup of cheese. Sprinkle the nuts over the cheese. Close crisping lid.
8. Select BROIL and set time to 5 minutes. Select START/STOP to begin.
9. When cooking is complete, open lid and let the gratin cool for 10 minutes before serving.

Nutrition:
- InfoCalories: 536, Total Fat: 47g, Sodium: 409mg, Carbohydrates: 20g, Protein: 10g.

Breakfast

Carrot Cake Oats

Servings: 8
Cooking Time: 13 Minutes
Ingredients:
- 2 cups oats
- 1 cup water
- 4 cups unsweetened vanilla almond milk
- 2 apples, diced
- 2 cups shredded carrot
- 1 cup dried cranberries
- ½ cup maple syrup
- 2 teaspoons cinnamon
- 2 teaspoons vanilla extract

Directions:
1. Place all the ingredients in the pot. Assemble pressure lid, making sure the pressure release valve is in the SEAL position.
2. Select PRESSURE and set to LO. Set time to 3 minutes. Select START/STOP to begin.
3. When pressure cooking is complete, allow pressure to naturally release for 10 minutes. Then quick release remaining pressure by moving the pressure release valve to the VENT position. Carefully remove lid when unit has finished releasing pressure.
4. Stir oats, allowing them to cool, and serve with toppings such as chopped walnuts, diced pineapple, or shredded coconut, if desired.

Nutrition:
- InfoCalories: 252,Total Fat: 3g,Sodium: 112mg,Carbohydrates: 54g,Protein: 4g.

Ham & Spinach Breakfast Bake

Servings: 6
Cooking Time: 30 Minutes
Ingredients:
- Nonstick cooking spray
- 10 eggs
- 1 cup spinach, chopped
- 1 cup ham, chopped
- 1 cup red peppers, chopped
- 1 cup onion, chopped
- 1 tsp garlic powder
- ½ tsp onion powder
- ¼ tsp salt
- ¼ tsp pepper
- 1 cup Swiss cheese, grated

Directions:
1. Select the bake function and heat cooker to 350°F (175°C). Spray the cooking pot with cooking spray.
2. In a large bowl, whisk eggs together.
3. Add remaining ingredients and mix well.
4. Pour into cooking pot and secure the tender-crisp lid. Cook 25-30 minutes, or until eggs are set and top has started to brown.
5. Let cool 5 minutes before serving.

Nutrition:
- InfoCalories 287,Total Fat 18g,Total Carbs 7g,Protein 23g,Sodium 629mg.

Zucchini Pancakes

Servings: 6
Cooking Time: 10 Minutes
Ingredients:
- 1 cup almond milk, unsweetened
- 1 egg
- 2 tbsp. honey
- 1 tbsp. coconut oil, melted
- 1 tsp vanilla
- ½ cup zucchini, grated
- 1 ½ cup oat flour
- 2 tsp cinnamon
- 1 tsp baking powder
- ¼ tsp salt
- Nonstick cooking spray

Directions:
1. In a large bowl, combine milk, egg, honey, oil, vanilla, and zucchini.
2. In a separate bowl, stir together remaining ingredients. Add to zucchini mixture and mix just until combined.
3. Spray the cooking pot with cooking spray. Set to sauté on medium heat.
4. Pour batter, ¼ cup at a time, into cooking pot. Cook 3-4 minutes or until bubble form in the middle. Flip and cook another 2-3 minutes. Repeat with remaining batter. Serve immediately with your favorite toppings.

Nutrition:
- InfoCalories 188,Total Fat 7g,Total Carbs 27g,Protein 6g,Sodium 132mg.

Chocolate Hazelnut Toaster Pastries

Servings: 4
Cooking Time: 14 Minutes
Ingredients:
- All-purpose flour
- 1 refrigerated piecrust, at room temperature
- ¼ cup chocolate hazelnut spread
- Cooking spray
- Vanilla icing, for frosting
- Chocolate sprinkles, for topping

Directions:
1. Place the Cook & Crisp Basket in the pot and close crisping lid. Select AIR CRISP, set temperature to 350°F (175°C), and set time to 5 minutes. Press START/STOP to preheat.
2. On a lightly floured surface, roll out the piecrust into a large rectangle. Cut the dough into 8 rectangles.
3. Spoon 1 tablespoon of chocolate hazelnut spread into the center of each of 4 dough rectangles, leaving a ½-inch border. Brush the edges of the filled dough rectangles with water. Top each with one of the remaining 4 dough rectangles. Press the edges with a fork to seal.
4. Once unit is preheated, carefully place two pastries in the basket in a single layer. Coat each pastry well with cooking spray. Close crisping lid.
5. Select AIR CRISP, set temperature to 350°F (175°C), and set time to 7 minutes. Select START/STOP to begin.

Ninja Foodi Cookbook Guide

6. Once cooking is complete, check for your desired crispiness. Place the pastries on a wire rack to cool. Repeat steps 4 and 5 with the remaining 2 pastries.
7. Frost the pastries with vanilla icing, then top with sprinkles.
Nutrition:
- InfoCalories: 334,Total Fat: 17g,Sodium: 271mg,Carbohydrates: 43g,Protein: 1g.

Blueberry Muffins

Servings: 12
Cooking Time: 20 Minutes
Ingredients:
- 2 ½ cups oats
- 1 ½ cups almond milk, unsweetened
- Nonstick cooking spray
- 1 egg, lightly beaten
- 1/3 cup pure maple syrup
- 2 tbsp. coconut oil, melted
- 1 tsp vanilla
- 1 tsp cinnamon
- 1 tsp baking powder
- ¼ tsp salt
- 1 tsp lemon zest, grated
- 1 cup fresh blueberries

Directions:
1. In a large bowl, combine oats and milk. Cover and refrigerate overnight.
2. Select bake function and heat to 375°F (190°C). Spray 2 6-cup muffin tins with cooking spray.
3. Stir remaining ingredients into the oat mixture. Spoon into muffin tins.
4. Place the rack in the cooking pot and place muffin tin on it, these will need to be baked in 2 batches.
5. Secure the tender crisp lid and bake 20 minutes or until tops are golden brown. Serve warm.
Nutrition:
- InfoCalories 122,Total Fat 4g,Total Carbs 19g,Protein 3g,Sodium 108mg.

Prosciutto, Mozzarella Egg In A Cup

Servings: 2
Cooking Time: 20 Min
Ingredients:
- 2 slices bread
- 4 tomato slices
- 2 prosciutto slices; chopped
- 2 eggs
- 2 tbsp mayonnaise /30ml
- 2 tbsp grated mozzarella /30g
- Salt and pepper, to taste
- Cooking spray

Directions:
1. Preheat the Ninja Foodi to 320 °F or 160°C. Grease two large ramekins with cooking spray. Place one bread slice in the bottom of each ramekin.
2. Arrange 1 prosciutto slice and 2 tomato slices on top of each bread slice. Divide the mozzarella between the ramekins.
3. Crack the eggs over the mozzarella. Season with salt and pepper. Close the crisping lid and cook for 10 minutes on Air Crisp mode. Top with mayonnaise.

Spanish Potato And Chorizo Frittata

Servings:4
Cooking Time: 20 Minutes
Ingredients:
- 4 eggs
- 1 cup milk
- Sea salt
- Freshly ground black pepper
- 1 potato, diced
- ½ cup frozen corn
- 1 chorizo sausage, diced
- 8 ounces feta cheese, crumbled
- 1 cup water

Directions:
1. In a medium bowl, whisk together the eggs and milk. Season with salt and pepper.
2. Place the potato, corn, and chorizo in the Multi-Purpose Pan or an 8-inch baking pan. Pour the egg mixture and feta cheese over top. Cover the pan with aluminum foil and place on the Reversible Rack. Make sure it's in the lower position.
3. Pour the water into the pot. Assemble pressure lid, making sure the pressure release valve is in the SEAL position.
4. Select PRESSURE and set to HI. Set time to 20 minutes. Select START/STOP to begin.
5. When pressure cooking is complete, quick release the pressure by moving the pressure release valve to the VENT position. Carefully remove lid when unit has finished releasing pressure.
6. Remove the pan from pot and place it on a cooling rack for 5 minutes, then serve.
Nutrition:
- InfoCalories: 361,Total Fat: 24g,Sodium: 972mg,Carbohydrates: 17g,Protein: 21g.

Pumpkin Coconut Breakfast Bake

Servings: 8
Cooking Time: 1 Hour 15 Minutes
Ingredients:
- Butter flavored cooking spray
- 5 eggs
- ½ cup coconut milk
- 2 cups pumpkin puree
- 1 banana, mashed
- 2 dates, pitted & chopped
- 1 tsp cinnamon
- 1 cup raspberries
- ¼ cup coconut, unsweetened & shredded

Directions:
1. Lightly spray an 8-inch baking dish with cooking spray.
2. In a large bowl, whisk together eggs and milk.
3. Whisk in pumpkin until combined.
4. Stir in banana, dates, and cinnamon. Pour into prepared dish.
5. Sprinkle berries over top.
6. Place the rack in the cooking pot and place the dish on it. Add the tender-crisp lid and select bake on 350°F (175°C). Bake 20 minutes.
7. Sprinkle coconut over the top and bake another 20-25 minutes until top is lightly browned and casserole is set. Slice and serve warm.
Nutrition:
- InfoCalories 113,Total Fat 5g,Total Carbs 14g,Protein 6g,Sodium 62mg.

Nutmeg Pumpkin Porridge

Servings: 8
Cooking Time: 5 Hours
Ingredients:
- 1 cup unsweetened almond milk
- 2 pounds pumpkin, peeled and cubed into ½-inch size
- 6-8 drops liquid stevia
- ½ teaspoon ground allspice
- 1 tablespoon ground cinnamon
- 1 teaspoon ground nutmeg
- ¼ teaspoon ground cloves
- ½ cup walnuts, chopped

Directions:
1. In the Ninja Foodi's insert, place ½ cup of almond milk and remaining ingredients and stir to combine.
2. Close the Ninja Foodi's lid with a crisping lid and select "Slow Cooker."
3. Set on "Low" for 4-5 hours.
4. Press the "Start/Stop" button to initiate cooking.
5. Open the Ninja Foodi's lid and stir in the remaining almond milk.
6. With a potato masher, mash the mixture completely.
7. Divide the porridge into serving bowls evenly.
8. Serve warm with the topping of walnuts.

Nutrition:
- InfoCalories: 96; Fat: 5.5g; Carbohydrates: 11.2g; Protein: 3.3g

Pumpkin Breakfast Bread

Servings: 14
Cooking Time: 3 Hours
Ingredients:
- Nonstick cooking spray
- 2 cups whole wheat pastry flour
- 1 ½ tsp baking soda
- 2 tsp pumpkin pie spice
- ½ cup coconut oil, melted
- ¾ cup honey
- 2 eggs
- 3 cups pumpkin puree
- 1 tsp. vanilla extract
- 1 banana, mashed
- ½ cup walnuts, chopped & divided

Directions:
1. Spray the cooking pot with cooking spray.
2. In a large bowl, combine flour, baking soda, and pumpkin spice.
3. Make a "well" in the middle of the dry ingredients and add oil, honey, eggs, pumpkin, vanilla, and banana, and ¼ cup of the walnuts. Mix well to thoroughly combine all ingredients.
4. Pour batter into cooking pot and sprinkle remaining walnuts over the top. Place two paper towels over the top of the pot and secure the lid. Select slow cooking function on high. Set timer for 2 hours.
5. When timer goes off check bread, it should pass the toothpick test. If it is not done, continue cooking another 30-60 minutes.
6. When bread is done, transfer to a wire rack to cool.

Nutrition:
- InfoCalories 207,Total Fat 9g,Total Carbs 30g,Protein 4g,Sodium 130mg.

Baked Eggs In Mushrooms

Servings: 4
Cooking Time: 15 Minutes
Ingredients:
- 4 large Portobello mushrooms, rinse & remove stems
- 4 eggs
- 1 ½ tbsp. extra virgin olive oil
- ½ tsp salt, divided
- ½ tsp black pepper, divided

Directions:
1. Set to bake function on 450°F (230°C).
2. Rub mushrooms with oil and half the salt and pepper. Place on a small baking sheet, cap side down.
3. Carefully crack an egg into each mushroom and season with remaining salt and pepper.
4. Place sheet in the cooker and secure the tender-crisp lid. Bake 12-15 minutes, or until whites of the eggs are cooked through. Serve immediately.

Nutrition:
- InfoCalories 122,Total Fat 10g,Total Carbs 2g,Protein 7g,Sodium 363mg.

Pancetta Hash With Baked Eggs

Servings: 4
Cooking Time: 50 Min
Ingredients:
- 6 slices pancetta; chopped
- 2 potatoes, peeled and diced
- 4 eggs
- 1 white onion; diced
- 1 tsp freshly ground black pepper /5g
- 1 tsp garlic powder /5g
- 1 tsp sweet paprika /5g
- 1 tsp salt /5g

Directions:
1. Choose Sear/Sauté, set to Medium High, and choose Start/Stop to preheat the pot for 5 minutes.
2. Once heated, lay the pancetta in the pot, and cook, stirring occasionally; for 5 minutes, or until the pancetta is crispy.
3. Stir in the onion, potatoes, sweet paprika, salt, black pepper, and garlic powder. Close the crisping lid; choose Bake/Roast, set the temperature to 350°F or 175°C, and the time to 25 minutes. Cook until the turnips are soft and golden brown while stirring occasionally.
4. Crack the eggs on top of the hash, close the crisping lid, and choose Bake/Roast. Set the temperature to 350°F or 175°C, and the time to 10 minutes.
5. Cook the eggs and check two or three times until your desired crispiness has been achieved. Serve immediately.

Curried Chickpea And Roasted Tomato Shakshuka

Servings:6
Cooking Time: 30 Minutes
Ingredients:
- 2 tablespoons extra-virgin olive oil
- 2 red bell peppers, diced
- 1 small onion, diced
- 2 garlic cloves, minced
- 1 tablespoon red curry paste
- 1 tablespoon tomato paste

Ninja Foodi Cookbook Guide

- 1 can crushed fire-roasted tomatoes
- 1 can chickpeas, rinsed and drained
- Kosher salt
- Freshly ground black pepper
- 6 large eggs
- 2 tablespoons chopped cilantro

Directions:
1. Select SEAR/SAUTÉ and set to HI. Select START/STOP to begin. Add the olive oil and let preheat for 5 minutes.
2. Add the bell peppers, onion, and garlic and cook for 3 minutes, stirring occasionally.
3. Add the curry and tomato pastes and cook for 2 minutes, stirring occasionally.
4. Add the crushed tomatoes, chickpeas, and season with salt and pepper and stir. Assemble pressure lid, making sure the pressure release valve is in the SEAL position.
5. Select PRESSURE and set to HI. Set time to 10 minutes. Select START/STOP to begin.
6. When pressure cooking is complete, quick release the pressure by turning the pressure release valve to the VENT position. Carefully remove the lid when the unit has finished releasing pressure.
7. With the back of a spoon, make six indents in the sauce. Crack an egg into each indent. Close crisping lid.
8. Select BAKE/ROAST, set temperature to 350°F (175°C), and set time to 10 minutes (or until eggs are cooked to your liking). Select START/STOP to begin.
9. When cooking is complete, open lid. Let cool 5 to 10 minutes, then garnish with the cilantro and serve. If desired, serve with crusty bread, chopped scallions, feta cheese, and/or pickled jalapeños.

Nutrition:
- InfoCalories: 258,Total Fat: 12g,Sodium: 444mg,Carbohydrates: 27g,Protein: 11g.

Double Chocolate Quinoa Bowl

Servings: 2
Cooking Time: 15 Minutes
Ingredients:
- ½ cup quinoa
- 1 cup water
- 1 cup coconut milk
- 2 tsp honey
- 2 tsp chia seeds
- 2 tsp cocoa powder
- 1 oz. dark chocolate, chopped
- 1 tbsp. pecans, chopped
- 1 tbsp. coconut flakes

Directions:
1. Place quinoa and water in the cooking pot, stir.
2. Add the lid and select pressure cooker on high. Set timer for 10 minutes. When timer goes off, use quick release to remove the lid.
3. Set to sauté on med-low. Cook, stirring until all liquid is absorbed.
4. Stir in milk, honey, chia seeds, and cocoa powder. Cook, stirring, until heated through.
5. Ladle into bowls and top with chocolate, nuts, and coconut. Serve warm.

Nutrition:
- InfoCalories 456,Total Fat 24g,Total Carbs 50g,Protein 13g,Sodium 66mg.

Breakfast Burritos

Servings:4
Cooking Time: 30 Minutes
Ingredients:
- 1 pound ground chorizo
- ½ onion, diced
- ½ red bell pepper, diced
- 1 small jalapeño, minced
- ½ cup canned black beans, rinsed and drained
- Kosher salt
- Freshly ground black pepper
- 6 eggs, beaten
- 4 flour tortillas
- 1 cup shredded Mexican blend cheese
- 1 cup cilantro, minced
- Guacamole, for serving
- Pico de gallo, for serving

Directions:
1. Select SEAR/SAUTÉ and set temperature to MED. Let preheat for 5 minutes.
2. Add the chorizo, breaking up the meat with a silicone spatula until cooked through, 3 to 5 minutes. Add the onions, bell pepper, jalapeño, black beans, and season with salt and pepper. Cook until onions are translucent, about 3 minutes.
3. Add the eggs and cook, stirring frequently, until they have reached your desired consistency. When cooking is complete, transfer the mixture to a large bowl.
4. Lay a tortilla on a flat surface and load with ¼ cup of cheese, ¾ cup of egg mixture, and ¼ cup of cilantro. Roll the burrito by folding the right and left sides over the filling, then roll the tortilla over itself from the bottom forming a tight burrito. Repeat this step three more times with the remaining tortillas, cheese, egg mixture, and cilantro.
5. Place two burritos seam-side down in the Cook & Crisp Basket and place basket in pot. Close crisping lid.
6. Select AIR CRISP, set temperature to 390°F (200°C), and set time to 16 minutes. Select START/STOP to begin.
7. After 8 minutes, open lid and remove the burritos from basket. Place the remaining two burritos seam-side down in the basket. Close lid and continue cooking for the remaining 8 minutes.
8. When cooking is complete, let the burritos cool for a few minutes. Serve with the guacamole and pico de gallo.

Nutrition:
- InfoCalories: 693,Total Fat: 36g,Sodium: 1732mg,Carbohydrates: 48g,Protein: 44g.

Southwest Tofu Scramble

Servings: 4
Cooking Time: 10 Minutes
Ingredients:
- 1 tbsp. olive oil
- 4 oz. extra firm tofu, cut in small cubes
- ¼ cup red bell pepper, diced fine
- ¼ cup red onion, diced fine
- 1 cup kale, chopped
- ½ tsp cumin
- 1 tsp chili powder
- 6 egg whites, lightly beaten
- 2 tbsp. cilantro, chopped

Directions:
1. Select sauté function on med-high heat. Add oil and heat until hot.
2. Add the tofu, pepper, onion, and kale and cook, stirring frequently, until onion is soft and kale has wilted.
3. Stir in spices. Slowly add egg whites, stirring frequently to scramble. Cook until egg whites are set, but not brown. Sprinkle with cilantro and serve immediately.

Nutrition:
- InfoCalories 91,Total Fat 5g,Total Carbs 3g,Protein 10g,Sodium 97mg.

Spinach & Sausage Casserole

Servings: 8
Cooking Time: 7 Hours
Ingredients:
- Nonstick cooking spray
- 1 lb. pork breakfast sausage
- 1 yellow onion, diced
- 1 ½ tsp oregano
- 5 cups baby spinach, packed
- 4 cups potatoes, diced
- 1 ¼ cups Swiss cheese, grated
- ¼ cup Parmesan cheese
- 8 eggs
- 2 cups milk
- 2 tsp Dijon mustard
- 1 ½ tsp salt
- ¼ tsp black pepper

Directions:
1. Spray the cooking pot with cooking spray. Select the sauté function on med-high.
2. Add the sausage, onion, and oregano and cook, stirring to break up the sausage until no longer pink, about 8-10 minutes.
3. Stir in the spinach and cook until wilted, about 2 minutes.
4. Set the cooker to the slow cooker function on low heat.
5. Add the potatoes, 1 cup of Swiss cheese, and the parmesan cheese and mix well.
6. In a large bowl, whisk eggs, milk, mustard, salt, and pepper until smooth. Pour over ingredients in the cooking pot and stir to combine.
7. Secure the lid and set the timer for 6 hours. Casserole is done when the edges start to brown and the eggs are set. If it is not done, recover and cook another 60 minutes or until done.
8. When the casserole is set, top with remaining cheese and cover. Cook just until the cheese melts, about 5 minutes.

Nutrition:
- InfoCalories 439,Total Fat 29g,Total Carbs 18g,Protein 27g,Sodium 1098mg.

Plum Breakfast Clafoutis

Servings: 4
Cooking Time: 60 Min
Ingredients:
- 2 large eggs
- ⅓ cup half and half /84ml
- ⅓ cup sugar /44g
- ½ cup flour /65g
- 1 cup plums; chopped /130g
- ⅔ cup whole milk /168ml
- 2 tbsps confectioners' sugar /30g
- ¼ tsp cinnamon /1.25g
- 2 tsp s butter, softened /30g
- ½ tsp vanilla extract /2.5ml
- A pinch of salt

Directions:
1. Grease four ramekins with the butter and divide the plums into each cup. Pour the milk, half and half, sugar, flour, eggs, cinnamon, vanilla, and salt in a bowl and use a hand mixer to whisk the Ingredients on medium speed until the batter is smooth, about 2 minutes. Pour the batter over the plums two-third way up.
2. Pour 1 cup of water into the inner pot. Fix the reversible rack at the bottom of the pot and put the ramekins on the rack. Lay a square of aluminium foil on the ramekins but don't crimp.
3. Put the pressure lid together and lock in Seal position. Choose Pressure, set to high, and set the time to 11 minutes; press Start.
4. When ready, perform a quick pressure release and carefully open the lid. Use tongs to remove the foil. Close the crisping lid and choose Bake/Roast. Adjust the temperature to 400°F or 205°C and the time to 6 minutes. Press Start to brown the top of the clafoutis.
5. Check after about 4 minutes to ensure the clafoutis are lightly browned; otherwise bake for a few more minutes. Remove the ramekins onto a flat surface. Cool for 5 minutes, and then dust with the confectioners' sugar. Serve warm.

Banana Coconut Loaf

Servings: 8
Cooking Time: 35 Minutes
Ingredients:
- Nonstick cooking spray
- 1 ¼ cup whole wheat flour
- ½ cup coconut flakes, unsweetened
- 2 tsp baking powder
- ½ tsp baking soda
- ½ tsp salt
- 1 cup banana, mashed
- ¼ cup coconut oil, melted
- 2 tbsp. honey

Directions:
1. Select the bake function on heat cooker to 350°F (175°C). Spray an 8-inch loaf pan with cooking spray.
2. In a large bowl, combine flour, coconut, baking powder, baking soda, and salt.
3. In a separate bowl, combine banana, oil, and honey. Add to dry ingredients and mix well. Spread batter in prepared pan.
4. Secure the tender-crisp lid and bake 30-35 minutes or until loaf passes the toothpick test.
5. Remove pan from the cooker and let cool 10 minutes. Invert loaf to a wire rack and cool completely before slicing.

Nutrition:
- InfoCalories 201,Total Fat 11g,Total Carbs 26g,Protein 3g,Sodium 349mg.

Prosciutto Egg Bake

Servings: 4
Cooking Time: 45 Min
Ingredients:
- 8 ounces prosciutto; chopped /240g
- 1 cup shredded Monterey Jack cheese /130g
- 1 cup water /250ml
- 1 cup whole milk /250ml
- 1 orange bell pepper, seeded and chopped
- 4 eggs
- 1 tsp salt /5g
- 1 tsp freshly ground black pepper /5g

Directions:
1. Break the eggs into a bowl, pour in the milk, salt, and black pepper and whisk until combined. Stir in the Monterey Jack Cheese.
2. Put the bell pepper and prosciutto in the cake pan. Then, pour over the egg mixture, cover the pan with aluminum foil and put on the reversible rack.
3. Put the rack in the pot and pour in the water. Seal the pressure lid, choose pressure and set to High. Set the time to 20 minutes and choose Start/Stop.
4. When done cooking, do a quick pressure release and carefully remove the lid that is after the pressure has completely escaped.
5. When baking is complete, take the pan out of the pot and set it on a heatproof surface, and cool for 5 minutes.

Bacon And Gruyère Egg Bites

Servings: 6
Cooking Time: 26 Minutes
Ingredients:
- 5 slices bacon, cut into ½-inch pieces
- 5 eggs
- 1 teaspoon kosher salt
- ¼ cup sour cream
- 1 cup shredded Gruyère cheese, divided
- Cooking spray
- 1 cup water
- 1 teaspoon chopped parsley, for garnish

Directions:
1. Select SEAR/SAUTÉ and set temperature to HI. Select START/STOP and let preheat for 5 minutes.
2. Add the bacon and cook, stirring frequently, about 5 minutes, or until the fat is rendered and bacon starts to brown. Transfer the bacon to a paper towel-lined plate to drain. Wipe the pot clean of any remaining fat.
3. In a medium bowl, whisk together the eggs, salt, and sour cream until well combined. Fold in ¾ of cheese and the bacon.
4. Spray egg molds or Ninja Silicone Mold with the cooking spray. Ladle the egg mixture into each mold, filling them halfway.
5. Pour the water in the pot. Carefully place the egg molds in the pot. Assemble pressure lid, making sure the pressure release valve is in the SEAL position.
6. Select PRESSURE and set to LO. Set time to 10 minutes. Select START/STOP to begin.
7. When pressure cooking is complete, natural release the pressure for 6 minutes, then quick release the remaining pressure by moving the pressure release valve to the VENT position.
8. Carefully remove the lid. Using mitts or a towel, carefully remove egg molds. Top with the remaining ¼ cup of cheese, then place the mold back into the pot. Close the crisping lid.
9. Select AIR CRISP, set temperature to 390°F (200°C), and set time to 5 minutes. Select START/STOP to begin.
10. Once cooking is complete, carefully remove the egg molds and set aside to cool for 5 minutes. Using a spoon, carefully remove the egg bites from the molds. Top with chopped parsley and serve immediately.

Nutrition:
- InfoCalories: 230, Total Fat: 18g, Sodium: 557mg, Carbohydrates: 2g, Protein: 16g.

Butternut Squash Cake Oatmeal

Servings: 4
Cooking Time: 35 Min
Ingredients:
- 1 cup steel-cut oats /130g
- ⅓ cup honey /84ml
- 3 ½ cups coconut milk /875ml
- ¼ cup toasted walnuts; chopped /32.5g
- 1 cup shredded Butternut Squash /250ml
- ½ cup sultanas /65g
- ¼ tsp ground nutmeg /1.25g
- 1 tsp ground cinnamon /5g
- ½ tsp vanilla extract /2.5ml
- ½ tsp fresh orange zest /2.5g
- ¾ tsp ground ginger /3.75g
- ½ tsp salt /2.5g
- ½ tsp sugar /2.5g

Directions:
1. In the pressure cooker, mix sultanas, orange zest, ginger, milk, honey, squash, salt, oats, and nutmeg.
2. Seal the pressure lid, choose Pressure, set to High, and set the timer to 12 minutes; press Start. When ready, do a natural pressure release for 10 minutes. Into the oatmeal, stir in the vanilla extract and sugar. Top with walnuts and serve.

Crustless Quiche

Servings: 2
Cooking Time: 40 Min
Ingredients:
- 4 eggs
- ¼ cup chopped kalamata olives /32.5g
- ¼ cup chopped onion /32.5g
- ½ cup milk /125ml
- ½ cup chopped tomatoes /65g
- 1 cup crumbled feta cheese /130g
- 1 tbsp chopped basil /15g
- 1 tbsp chopped oregano /15g
- 2 tbsp olive oil /30ml
- Salt and pepper to taste

Directions:
1. Brush a pie pan with the olive oil. Beat the eggs along with the milk, salt, and pepper. Stir in all of the remaining Ingredients.
2. Pour the egg mixture into the pan. Close the crisping lid and cook for 30 minutes on Air Crisp mode at 340 °F or 170°C. Leave to cool before serving.

Waffle Bread Pudding With Maple-jam Glaze

Servings: 6
Cooking Time: 25 Minutes
Ingredients:
- 2 whole eggs
- 4 egg yolks
- 1 cup heavy (whipping) cream
- ½ teaspoon ground cinnamon
- ¼ cup granulated sugar
- 1 teaspoon vanilla extract
- 20 waffles, cut in sixths
- 1 cup water
- ⅓ cup desired jam
- raspberry)
- ⅓ cup maple syrup

Directions:
1. In a large mixing bowl, combine the eggs, egg yolks, cream, cinnamon, sugar, and vanilla. Whisk well to combine. Add the waffle pieces and toss very well to incorporate. The waffles should be completely soaked through with cream sauce, with some extra residual cream sauce at the bottom of the bowl.
2. Place the waffle mixture in the Ninja Multi-Purpose Pan or 8-inch round baking dish. Press down gently to ensure ingredients are well packed into the pan. Cover the pan tightly with plastic wrap.
3. Add the water to the pot. Place the pan on the Reversible Rack and place rack in pot. Assemble pressure lid, making sure the pressure release valve is in the SEAL position.
4. Select PRESSURE and set to HI. Set time to 15 minutes. Select START/STOP to begin.
5. Place the jam and maple syrup in a small bowl and mix well to combine.
6. When pressure cooking is complete, quick release the pressure by moving the pressure release valve to the VENT position. Carefully remove lid when unit has finished releasing pressure.
7. Remove rack from pot, then remove the plastic wrap from the pan. Pour the jam and syrup mixture over top of waffles. Place rack and pan back in pot. Close crisping lid.
8. Select BROIL and set time to 10 minutes. Select START/STOP to begin.
9. When cooking is complete, open lid and remove rack from pot. Serve the bread pudding warm.

Nutrition:
- InfoCalories: 640, Total Fat: 30g, Sodium: 765mg, Carbohydrates: 82g, Protein: 12g.

Broccoli, Ham, And Cheddar Frittata

Servings: 6
Cooking Time: 40 Minutes
Ingredients:
- 1 head broccoli, cut into 1-inch florets
- 1 tablespoon canola oil
- Kosher salt
- Freshly ground black pepper
- 12 large eggs
- ¼ cup whole milk
- 1½ cups shredded white Cheddar cheese, divided
- 3 tablespoons unsalted butter
- ½ medium white onion, diced
- 1 cup diced ham

Directions:
1. Place Cook & Crisp Basket in the pot. Close crisping lid. Select AIR CRISP, setting temperature to 390°F (200°C), and set time to 5 minutes. Select START/STOP to begin preheating.
2. In a large bowl, toss the broccoli with the oil and season with salt and pepper.
3. Once unit is preheated, open lid and add the broccoli to basket. Close crisping lid.
4. Select AIR CRISP, set temperature to 390°F (200°C), and set time to 15 minutes. Select START/STOP to begin.
5. In a separate large bowl, whisk together the eggs, milk, and 1 cup of cheese.
6. After 7 minutes, open lid. Remove basket and shake the broccoli. Return basket to pot and close lid to continue cooking.
7. After 8 minutes, check the broccoli for desired doneness. When cooking is complete, remove broccoli and basket from pot.
8. Select SEAR/SAUTÉ and set to HI. Select START/STOP to begin.
9. After 5 minutes, add the butter. Melt for 1 minute, then add the onion and cook for 3 minutes, stirring occasionally.
10. Add the ham and broccoli and cook, stirring occasionally, for 2 minutes.
11. Add the egg mixture, season with salt and pepper, and stir. Close crisping lid.
12. Select BAKE/ROAST, set temperature to 400°F (205°C), and set time to 15 minutes. Select STOP/START to begin.
13. After 5 minutes, open lid and sprinkle the remaining ½ cup of cheese on top. Close lid to continue cooking.
14. When cooking is complete, remove pot from unit and let the frittata sit for 5 to 10 minutes before serving.

Nutrition:
- InfoCalories: 404, Total Fat: 30g, Sodium: 671mg, Carbohydrates: 10g, Protein: 27g.

Egg Spinach Bites

Servings: 6
Cooking Time: 27 Minutes
Ingredients:
- 4 slices of bacon
- 1/2 cup lite coconut milk
- 1 cup Spinach cut up
- 6 eggs

Directions:
1. Place air crisper basket in the Ninja Foodi and place the bacon in it.
2. Secure the Ninja Foodi lid and Air Fry them for 10 minutes.
3. Transfer the cooked crispy bacon to a plate and keep them aside.
4. Whisk egg with spinach, coconut milk and crispy bacon in a bowl.
5. Divide this batter in a silicone muffin tray.
6. Set the trivet in the Ninja Food then place the muffin pan over the trivet and seal the lid.
7. Secure the Ninja Foodi lid and turn the pressure valve to the 'closed' position.
8. Cook the egg bites for 17 minutes for 325 °F (160°C) on Bake/Roast mode.
9. Once done, remove the lid and remove the bites from the muffin tray.
10. Serve warm.

Nutrition:
- InfoCalories 211; Total Fat 18.5 g; Total Carbs 0.5 g; Protein 11.5 g

Baked Eggs In Spinach

Servings: 4
Cooking Time: 20 Minutes
Ingredients:
- 2 tsp olive oil
- 2 cloves garlic, diced fine
- 4 cups baby spinach
- ½ cup parmesan cheese, reduced fat
- 4 eggs
- 1 tomato, diced fine

Directions:
1. Select sauté function on medium heat. Add oil to the pot and heat.
2. Add the spinach and garlic and cook, stirring, about 2 minutes, or until spinach has wilted. Drain off excess liquid.
3. Stir in parmesan cheese. Make 4 small indents in the spinach. Crack an egg into each indent.
4. Set to air fryer function at 350°F (175°C). Secure the tender-crisp lid and bake 15-20 minutes or until egg whites are cooked and yolks are still slightly runny.
5. Let cool 5 minutes, serve topped with tomatoes.

Nutrition:
- InfoCalories 139, Total Fat 10g, Total Carbs 3g, Protein 12g, Sodium 280mg.

Carrot Cake Muffins

Servings: 12
Cooking Time: 30 Minutes
Ingredients:
- ¾ cup almond flour, sifted
- ½ cup coconut flour
- 1 tsp baking soda
- ½ tsp baking powder
- 1 tsp cinnamon
- ¼ tsp salt
- ¼ tsp cloves
- ¼ tsp nutmeg
- 2 eggs
- ½ cup honey
- 1 tsp vanilla
- ¼ cup coconut milk, unsweetened
- 2 tbsp. coconut oil, melted
- 1 banana, mashed
- 1 ½ cups carrots, grated

Directions:
1. Select the bake function and heat cooker to 350°F (175°C). Line 2 6-cup muffin tins with liners.
2. In a medium bowl, combine flours, baking soda, baking powder, cinnamon, salt, cloves, and nutmeg.
3. In a large bowl, beat eggs, honey, vanilla, and milk together until thoroughly combined.
4. Add the melted oil and mix well.
5. Add the banana and beat to combine. Stir in dry ingredients until mixed in. Fold in carrots.
6. Spoon into prepared muffin tins about ¾ full.
7. Place muffin tin, one at a time on the rack in the cooker and secure the tender-crisp lid. Bake 25-30 minutes, or until muffins pass the toothpick test.

Nutrition:
- InfoCalories 113, Total Fat 4g, Total Carbs 16g, Protein 1g, Sodium 196mg.

Glazed Lemon Muffins

Servings: 12
Cooking Time: 20 Minutes
Ingredients:
- 1 cup flour
- 1 tsp baking powder
- ½ tsp baking soda
- ¼ tsp salt
- ½ cup of coconut oil, melted
- 2 eggs
- 2 tbsp. Stevia
- ¼ cup honey
- 1 cup Greek yogurt, low-fat
- 1 ¼ tsp vanilla, divided
- 3 tbsp. + 2 tsp fresh lemon juice, divided
- 1 ½ tsp lemon zest
- 2 tbsp. Stevia powdered sugar

Directions:
1. Select bake function and heat to 350°F (175°C). Line 2 6- cup muffin tins with paper liners.
2. In a medium bowl, stir together flour, baking powder, baking soda, and salt.
3. In a large bowl, whisk together oil and eggs until smooth.
4. Add Stevia, honey, and yogurt and mix until combined.
5. Whisk in 1 teaspoon vanilla, 3 tablespoons lemon juice, and 1 teaspoon zest. Fold in dry ingredients just until combined.
6. Pour batter evenly into prepared muffin tins. Place tins, one at a time in the cooker. Secure the tender-crisp lid and bake 20 minutes or until muffins pass the toothpick test. Remove to wire rack to cool.
7. In a small bowl, whisk together Stevia confectioner's sugar and remaining vanilla, lemon juice, and zest until smooth. Drizzle over the tops of the muffins and serve.

Nutrition:
- InfoCalories 164, Total Fat 10g, Total Carbs 15g, Protein 4g, Sodium 120mg.

Stuffed Baked Potatoes

Servings: 4
Cooking Time: 20 Minutes
Ingredients:
- 4 large baked potatoes
- 2 tbsp. butter, melted
- 1 tsp salt
- 1 tsp black pepper
- 1 cup cheddar cheese, grated
- 6 slices bacon, cook crisp & chop
- 4 large eggs
- 2 tbsp. chives, chop

Directions:
1. Select bake function and heat cooker to 350°F (175°C).
2. Cut an opening in the top of the potatoes. With a spoon, scoop out most of the center.
3. Brush with melted butter and sprinkle with salt and pepper.
4. Divide ¾ of the cheese evenly among the potatoes. Top with ¾ of the bacon.
5. Crack one egg into each potato then top with remaining bacon, cheese and chives.
6. Place on the rack of the cooker and secure the tender-crisp lid. Set the timer for 20 minutes. Egg whites should be cooked completely but the yolk should still be soft. Serve immediately.

Nutrition:
- InfoCalories 389, Total Fat 31g, Total Carbs 6g, Protein 20g, Sodium 1052mg.

Cheesy Meat Omelet

Servings: 2
Cooking Time: 20 Min
Ingredients:
- 1 beef sausage; chopped
- 4 slices prosciutto; chopped
- 1 cup grated mozzarella cheese /130g
- 4 eggs
- 3 oz. salami; chopped /90g
- 1 tbsp chopped onion /15g
- 1 tbsp ketchup /15ml

Directions:
1. Preheat the Ninja Foodi to 350 °F or 175°C on Air Crisp mode. Whisk the eggs with the ketchup, in a bowl. Stir in the onion. Spritz the inside of the Ninja Foodi basket with a cooking spray. Add and brown the sausage for about 2 minutes.
2. Meanwhile, combine the egg mixture, mozzarella cheese, salami and prosciutto. Pour the egg mixture over the sausage and stir it. Close the crisping lid and cook for 10 minutes. Once the timer beeps, ensure the omelet is just set. Serve immediately.

Broccoli Egg Scramble

Servings: 4
Cooking Time: 5 Minutes
Ingredients:
- 1 pack, 12 ounces frozen broccoli florets
- 2 tablespoons butter
- Black pepper and salt, to taste
- 8 whole eggs
- 2 tablespoons milk
- ¾ cup white cheddar cheese, shredded
- Crushed red pepper to taste
- Optional bacon strips

Directions:
1. Open your Ninja Foodi lid and add butter, broccoli, and stir.
2. Season the mix with black pepper and salt, adjust according to your taste.
3. Lock and secure the Ninja Foodi's lid, then cook on "HIGH" pressure for 10 minutes.
4. Release pressure naturally.
5. Take a medium-sized bowl and crack an egg, beat well, add milk to the eggs and stir.
6. Add egg mixture into the Ninja Foodi over the broccoli mix, gently stir.
7. Set your pot to "Sauté" mode and let it cook for 2 minutes.
8. Once the egg has settled in, add cheese, sprinkle red and black pepper.
9. Season with salt.
10. Serve and enjoy with some bacon.

Nutrition:
- InfoCalories: 184; Fat: 12g; Carbohydrates: 5 g; Protein: 12 g

Cinnamon Crumb Donuts

Servings: 6
Cooking Time: 10 Minutes
Ingredients:
- Butter flavored cooking spray
- ¼ cup Stevia, granulated
- 1 cup + 3 ½ tbsp. flour, divided
- ¼ tsp cinnamon
- ¼ cup butter, cut in cubes
- ½ cup Stevia brown sugar, packed
- ½ tsp salt
- 1 tsp baking powder
- ½ cup sour cream
- 2 ½ tbsp. butter, melted
- 1 egg, room temperature
- ½ cup Stevia confectioners' sugar
- ½ tbsp. milk
- ½ tsp vanilla

Directions:
1. Select air fryer function and heat cooker to 350°F (175°C). Spray a 6 mold donut pan with cooking spray.
2. In a small bowl, combine ¼ cup granulated Stevia, 3 ½ tablespoons flour, and ¼ teaspoon cinnamon.
3. With a pastry cutter, or fork, cut in the cold butter until mixture resembles coarse crumbs. Cover and chill until ready to use.
4. In a large bowl, stir together 1 cup flour, the Stevia brown sugar, salt, and baking powder.
5. In a separate bowl, whisk together sour cream, melted butter, and egg. Stir into dry ingredients just until combined.
6. Spoon dough into prepared pan. Sprinkle chilled crumb topping evenly over the tops.
7. Place the pan in the cooker and secure the tender-crisp lid. Cook 10-11 minutes or donuts pass the toothpick test. Cool in the pan 10 minutes then transfer to a wire rack.
8. In a small bowl, whisk together Stevia powdered sugar substitute, milk, and vanilla. Drizzle donuts with glaze and serve.

Nutrition:
- InfoCalories 250,Total Fat 18g,Total Carbs 21g,Protein 4g,Sodium 366mg.

Poached Egg Heirloom Tomato

Servings: 4
Cooking Time: 10 Min
Ingredients:
- 4 large eggs
- 2 large Heirloom ripe tomatoes; halved crosswise
- 4 small slices feta cheese
- 1 cup water /250ml
- 2 tbsp grated Parmesan cheese /30g
- 1 tsp chopped fresh herbs, of your choice /5g
- Salt and black pepper to taste
- Cooking spray

Directions:
1. Pour the water into the Ninja Foodi and fit the reversible rack. Grease the ramekins with the cooking spray and crack each egg into them.
2. Season with salt and pepper. Cover the ramekins with aluminum foil. Place the cups on the trivet. Seal the lid.
3. Select Steam mode for 3 minutes on High pressure. Press Start/Stop.Once the timer goes off, do a quick pressure release. Use a napkin to remove the ramekins onto a flat surface.
4. In serving plates, share the halved tomatoes, feta slices, and toss the eggs in the ramekin over on each tomato half. Sprinkle with salt and pepper, parmesan, and garnish with chopped herbs.

Bacon And Sausage Cheesecake

Servings: 6
Cooking Time: 25 Min
Ingredients:
- 8 eggs, cracked into a bowl
- 8 oz. breakfast sausage; chopped /240g
- 4 slices bread, cut into ½-inch cubes
- 1 large green bell pepper; chopped
- 1 large red bell pepper; chopped
- 1 cup chopped green onion /130g
- ½ cup milk /125ml
- 2 cups water /500ml
- 1 cup grated Cheddar cheese /130g
- 3 bacon slices; chopped
- 1 tsp red chili flakes /5g
- Salt and black pepper to taste

Directions:
1. Add the eggs, sausage chorizo, bacon slices, green and red bell peppers, green onion, chili flakes, cheddar cheese, salt, pepper, and milk to a bowl and use a whisk to beat them together.
2. Grease a bundt pan with cooking spray and pour the egg mixture into it. After, drop the bread slices in the egg mixture all around while using a spoon to push them into the mixture.
3. Open the Ninja Foodi, pour in water, and fit the rack at the center of the pot. Place bundt pan on the rack and seal the pressure lid. Select Pressure mode on High pressure for 6 minutes, and press Start/Stop.
4. Once the timer goes off, press Start/Stop, do a quick pressure release. Run a knife around the egg in the bundt pan, close the crisping lid and cook for another 4 minutes on Bake/Roast on 380 °F or 195°C.
5. When ready, place a serving plate on the bundt pan, and then, turn the egg bundt over. Use a knife to cut the egg into slices. Serve with a sauce of your choice.

Sausage & Egg Stuffed Peppers

Servings: 4
Cooking Time: 6 Hours
Ingredients:
- ½ lb. breakfast sausage
- 4 bell peppers
- ½ cup water
- 6 eggs
- ½ cup cheddar Jack cheese, grated
- 4 oz. green chilies, diced
- ¼ tsp salt
- 1/8 tsp pepper
- 2 tbsp. green onion, diced

Directions:
1. Set cooker to sauté on med-high heat.
2. Add sausage and cook, breaking up with spatula, until no longer pink. Transfer to a bowl and drain off the grease.
3. Cut the tops off the peppers and remove the seeds and ribs. Place in the cooking pot and pour the water around them.
4. In a medium bowl, whisk eggs until smooth. Stir in cheese, chilies, salt, and pepper until combined. Fill the peppers with the egg mixture.
5. Secure the lid and set to slow cooker function on high. Set the timer for 4 hours.
6. Casserole is done when the eggs are set, if not done when the timer goes off, cook another 1-2 hours. Garnish with green onions and serve.

Nutrition:
- InfoCalories 364,Total Fat 22g,Total Carbs 15g,Protein 27g,Sodium 874mg.

Walnut Orange Coffee Cake

Servings: 8
Cooking Time: 25 Minutes
Ingredients:
- Butter flavor cooking spray
- 1 cup Stevia
- 1/4 cup butter, unsalted, soft
- 1 egg
- 2 tsp orange zest, grated
- ½ tsp vanilla
- 1/8 tsp cinnamon
- 2 cups whole wheat flour
- 1 tsp baking soda
- ½ cup orange juice, fresh squeezed
- ½ cup water
- ½ cup walnuts, chopped

Directions:
1. Select bake function and heat cooker to 350°F (175°C). Spray a 7-inch round pan with cooking spray.
2. In a medium bowl, beat Stevia and butter until smooth.
3. Add egg, zest, vanilla, and cinnamon and mix until combined.
4. In a separate bowl, combine dry ingredients. Add to butter mixture and mix until thoroughly combined. Stir in nuts.
5. Spread batter in prepared pan and place in the cooker. Secure the tender-crisp lid and bakke 20-25 minutes, or until it passes the toothpick test.
6. Let cool in pan 10 minutes, then invert onto wire rack. Serve warm.

Nutrition:
- InfoCalories 203,Total Fat 10g,Total Carbs 53g,Protein 6g,Sodium 170mg.

Double Berry Dutch Baby

Servings: 6
Cooking Time: 25 Minutes
Ingredients:
- 1 tbsp. butter, melted
- 2 eggs
- ½ cup skim milk
- 1 tsp vanilla
- ½ cup flour
- ¼ tsp cinnamon
- 1/8 tsp salt
- 2 tbsp. sugar
- 2 tsp cornstarch
- 1/3 cup water
- ½ cup strawberries, sliced

- ½ cup blueberries

Directions:
1. Select air fryer function and heat cooker to 400°F (205°C). Pour melted butter in an 8-inch round pan and swirl to coat bottom.
2. In a medium bowl, whisk together eggs, milk, and vanilla.
3. In a small bowl, combine flour, cinnamon, and salt. Whisk into egg mixture until smooth. Pour into prepared pan.
4. Place in the cooker and secure the tender-crisp lid. Bake 18-20 minutes until golden brown and set in the center.
5. Remove pancake from the cooker and set to sauté on medium heat.
6. Add sugar, cornstarch, and water to the cooking pot and stir until smooth.
7. Stir in both berries and bring to a boil. Cook about 5 minutes, stirring frequently, until berries have softened and mixture has thickened. Spoon into pancake, slice and serve.

Nutrition:
- InfoCalories 125,Total Fat 4g,Total Carbs 17g,Protein 4g,Sodium 100mg.

Flaxseeds Granola

Servings: 16
Cooking Time: 2½ Hours
Ingredients:
- ½ cup sunflower kernels
- 5 cups mixed nuts, crushed
- 2 tablespoons ground flax seeds
- ¼ cup olive oil
- ½ cup unsalted butter
- 1 teaspoon ground cinnamon
- 1 cup choc zero maple syrup

Directions:
1. Grease the Ninja Foodi's insert.
2. In the greased Ninja Foodi's insert, add sunflower kernels, nuts, flax seeds, oil, butter, and cinnamon and stir to combine.
3. Close the Ninja Foodi's lid with a crisping lid and select "Slow Cooker."
4. Set on "High" for 2½ hours.
5. Press the "Start/Stop" button to initiate cooking.
6. Stir the mixture after every 30 minutes.
7. Open the Ninja Foodi's lid and transfer the granola onto a large baking sheet.
8. Add the maple syrup and stir to combine.
9. Set aside to cool completely before serving.
10. You can preserve this granola in an airtight container.

Nutrition:
- InfoCalories: 189; Fat: 10 g; Carbohydrates: 7.7 g; Protein: 4.6 g

Breakfast Souffles

Servings: 6
Cooking Time: 20 Minutes
Ingredients:
- 1 lb. thick cut bacon, chopped
- 8 oz. pork sausage links, chopped
- Nonstick cooking spray
- 5 eggs, separated
- 1/3 cup heavy cream
- ½ cup cheddar cheese, grated
- ½ tsp salt
- ¼ tsp thyme

Directions:
1. Set cooker to sauté function on med-high.
2. Add the bacon and cook until almost crisp. Transfer to a paper towel lined plate.
3. Add the sausage and cook until done. Transfer to a separate paper towel lined plate.
4. Drain off fat and set cooker to air fry setting. Preheat to 350°F (175°C).
5. Spray 6 ramekins with cooking spray.
6. In a large bowl, beat egg whites until stiff peaks form.
7. In a medium bowl, whisk the yolks, cream, cheese, and seasonings together. Stir in the meats and mix well.
8. Gently fold the yolk mixture into the egg whites. Spoon the mixture into the prepared ramekins.
9. Place the rack in the cooker and place the ramekins on top. Secure the tender-crisp lid and bake 20 minutes, or until the soufflés have puffed up. Serve immediately.

Nutrition:
- InfoCalories 565,Total Fat 50g,Total Carbs 2g,Protein 24g,Sodium 1134mg.

Ricotta Raspberry Breakfast Cake

Servings: 12
Cooking Time: 40 Minutes
Ingredients:
- Nonstick cooking spray
- 1 ¼ cups oat flour
- ½ tsp xanthan gum
- ¼ cup cornstarch
- ¼ tsp baking soda
- 1 ½ tsp baking powder
- ½ tsp salt
- ½ cup sugar
- 4 tbsp. butter, unsalted, soft
- 1 cup ricotta cheese, room temperature
- 3 eggs, room temperature, beaten
- 1 tsp vanilla
- 1 cup fresh raspberries

Directions:
1. Set to bake function on 350°F (175°C). Lightly spray an 8-inch round baking pan with cooking spray.
2. In a large bowl, combine dry ingredients.
3. Make a well in the center and add butter, ricotta, eggs, and vanilla and mix just until combined.
4. Gently fold in half the berries, being careful not to crush them.
5. Pour batter into prepared pan and sprinkle remaining berries on the top. Add the tender-crisp lid and bake 40 minutes, or until a light brown and only a few moist crumbs show on a toothpick when inserted in the center.
6. Let cool in the pan 10 minutes then transfer to a wire rack to cool completely before serving.

Nutrition:
- InfoCalories 170,Total Fat 8g,Total Carbs 20g,Protein 6g,Sodium 164mg.

Banana Custard Oatmeal

Servings: 6
Cooking Time: 40 Minutes
Ingredients:
- Butter flavored cooking spray
- 1 2/3 cups vanilla almond milk, unsweetened

- 2 large bananas, mashed
- 1 cup bananas, sliced
- 1 cup steel cut oats
- 1/3 cup maple syrup
- 1/3 cup walnuts, chopped
- 2 eggs, beaten
- 1 tbsp. butter, melted
- 1 ½ tsp cinnamon
- 1 tsp baking powder
- 1 tsp vanilla extract
- ½ tsp nutmeg
- ¼ teaspoon salt
- 2 ½ cups water

Directions:
1. Spray a 1 1/2 –quart baking dish with cooking spray.
2. In a large bowl, combine all ingredients thoroughly. Transfer to prepared baking dish.
3. Pour 1 ½ cups water into the cooking pot and add the trivet. Place dish on the trivet and secure the lid.
4. Select pressure cooking on high and set timer for 40 minutes.
5. When timer goes off, release pressure naturally for 10 minutes, then use quick release. Stir oatmeal well then serve.

Nutrition:
- InfoCalories 349,Total Fat 10g,Total Carbs 56g,Protein 10g,Sodium 281mg.

Raspberry And Vanilla Pancake

Servings: 4
Cooking Time: 15 Min
Ingredients:
- ½ cup frozen raspberries, thawed /65g
- 3 eggs, beaten
- 1 cup brown sugar /130g
- 2 cups all-purpose flour /260g
- 1 cup milk /250ml
- 2 tbsp maple syrup /30ml
- 1 tsp baking powder /5g
- 1 ½ tsp vanilla extract /7.5g
- Pinch of salt
- Cooking spray

Directions:
1. In a bowl, mix the sifted flour, baking powder, salt, milk, eggs, vanilla extract, sugar, and maple syrup, until smooth. Gently stir in the raspberries.
2. Grease the basket of your Ninja Foodi with cooking spray. Drop the batter into the basket. Close the crisping lid and cook for 10 minutes on Air Crisp mode at 390 °F or 200°C. Serve the pancake right away.

Bell Pepper Frittata

Servings: 2
Cooking Time: 18 Minutes
Ingredients:
- 1 tablespoon olive oil
- 1 chorizo sausage, sliced
- 1½ cups bell peppers, seeded and chopped
- 4 large eggs
- Black pepper and salt, as required
- 2 tablespoons feta cheese, crumbled
- 1 tablespoon fresh parsley, chopped

Directions:
1. Select the "Sauté/Sear" setting of Ninja Foodi and place the butter into the pot.
2. Press the "Start/Stop" button to initiate cooking and heat for about 2-3 minutes.
3. Add the sausage and bell peppers and cook for 6-8 minutes or until golden brown.
4. Meanwhile, in a suitable bowl, add the eggs, salt, and black pepper and beat well.
5. Press the "Start/Stop" button to pasue cooking and place the eggs over the sausage mixture, followed by the cheese and parsley.
6. Close the Ninja Foodi's lid with a crisping lid and select "Air Crisp."
7. Set its cooking temperature to 355 °F (180°C) for 10 minutes.
8. Press the "Start/Stop" button to initiate cooking.
9. Open the Ninja Foodi's lid and transfer the frittata onto a platter.
10. Cut into equal-sized wedges and serve hot.

Nutrition:
- InfoCalories: 398; Fat: 31g; Carbohydrates: 8g; Protein: 22.9g

Savory Oatmeal

Servings: 2
Cooking Time: 10 Minutes
Ingredients:
- 2 cups chicken broth, low sodium
- ¾ cup old-fashioned oats
- ¼ tsp salt, divided
- 1 tbsp. olive oil
- 1 tbsp. butter, unsalted
- 8 oz. baby bella mushrooms, sliced
- ¼ tsp pepper
- 1 cup fresh baby spinach
- 2 eggs
- ½ cup cherry tomatoes, halved

Directions:
1. Add the broth, oats, and 1/8 teaspoon salt to the cooking pot, stir to combine.
2. Secure the lid and select pressure cooking function on high. Set timer to 5 minutes.
3. Heat oil and butter in a medium skillet over low heat until butter has melted.
4. Add mushrooms and season with salt and pepper. Cook 4-5 minutes, or until mushrooms are tender.
5. Stir in spinach and cook until it wilts, about 2 minutes. Transfer to a plate.
6. In the same skillet, crack 2 eggs and fry them the way you like them.
7. When the timer goes off, use quick release to remove the lid. Stir the oatmeal and ladle into bowls.
8. Top each bowl with spinach mixture, an egg, and tomatoes. Serve immediately.

Nutrition:
- InfoCalories 511,Total Fat 21g,Total Carbs 59g,Protein 25g,Sodium 1268mg.

Fish & Seafood

Fish Broccoli Stew

Servings: 4
Cooking Time: 20 Minutes
Ingredients:
- 1-pound white fish fillets, chopped
- 1 cup broccoli, chopped
- 3 cups fish stock
- 1 onion, diced
- 2 cups celery stalks, chopped
- 1 cup heavy cream
- 1 bay leaf
- 1 and 1/2 cups cauliflower, diced
- 1 carrot, sliced
- 2 tablespoons butter
- 1/4 teaspoon garlic powder
- 1/2 teaspoon salt
- 1/4 teaspoon black pepper

Directions:
1. Select "Sauté" mode on your Ninja Foodi.
2. Add butter, and let it melt.
3. Stir in onion and carrots, cook for 3 minutes.
4. Stir in remaining ingredients.
5. Close the Ninja Foodi's lid.
6. Cook for 4 minutes on High.
7. Release the pressure naturally over 10 minutes.
8. Remove the bay leave once cooked.
9. Serve and enjoy.

Nutrition:
- InfoCalories: 298g; Fat: 18g; Carbohydrates: 6g; Protein: 24g

Blackened Tilapia With Cilantro-lime Rice And Avocado Salsa

Servings: 4
Cooking Time: 12 Minutes
Ingredients:
- 2 cups white rice, rinsed
- 2 cups water
- ¼ cup blackening seasoning
- 4 tilapia fillets
- 2 tablespoons freshly squeezed lime juice, divided
- 1 bunch cilantro, minced
- 1 tablespoon extra-virgin olive oil
- 2 avocados, diced
- 1 large red onion, diced
- 2 Roma tomatoes, diced
- Kosher salt
- Freshly ground black pepper

Directions:
1. Place the rice and water in the pot and stir. Assemble pressure lid, making sure the pressure release valve is in the SEAL position.
2. Select PRESSURE and set to HI. Set time to 2 minutes. Select START/STOP to begin.
3. Place the blackening seasoning on a plate. Dredge the tilapia fillets in the seasoning.
4. When pressure cooking is complete, allow pressure to naturally release for 10 minutes. After 10 minutes, quick release remaining pressure by turning the pressure release valve to the VENT position. Carefully remove lid when unit has finished releasing pressure.
5. Transfer the rice to a large bowl and stir in 1 tablespoon of lime juice and half the cilantro. Cover the bowl with aluminum foil and set aside.
6. Place the Reversible Rack in the pot and arrange tilapia fillets on top. Close crisping lid.
7. Select BROIL and set time to 10 minutes. Select START/STOP to begin.
8. In a medium bowl, stir together the remaining cilantro, remaining 1 tablespoon of lime juice, olive oil, avocado, onion, tomato, and season with salt and pepper.
9. When cooking is complete, open lid and lift the rack out of the pot. Serve the fish over the rice and top with avocado salsa.

Nutrition:
- InfoCalories: 637, Total Fat: 19g, Sodium: 108mg, Carbohydrates: 89g, Protein: 30g.

Tuna Zoodle Bake

Servings: 4
Cooking Time: 20 Minutes
Ingredients:
- Nonstick cooking spray
- 2 zucchini, cut in noodles with a spiralizer
- 1tsp olive oil
- ¼ cup onion, chopped fine
- 6 oz. tuna, drained
- ½ tbsp. tomato paste
- ½ cup tomatoes, diced & drained
- ¼ cup skim milk
- ½ tsp thyme
- ¼ tsp salt
- ¼ tsp pepper
- 1/8 cup parmesan cheese, fat free
- 1/4 cup cheddar cheese, reduced fat, grated

Directions:
1. Spray an 8x8-inch baking pan with cooking spray.
2. Place the zucchini in an even layer in the prepared pan.
3. Add the oil to the cooking pot and set to sauté on med-high heat. Once the oil is hot, add the onion and cook 2 minutes, or until soft.
4. Stir in the tuna and tomato paste and cook 1 minute more. Add the tomatoes, milk, thyme, salt, and pepper and bring to a low simmer. Stir in parmesan cheese and cook until it melts.
5. Pour the tuna mixture over the zucchini and sprinkle cheddar cheese over the top. Wipe out the pat and place the baking pan in it.
6. Add the tender-crisp lid and set to bake on 400°F (205°C). Bake 15 minutes until cheese is melted and bubbly. Serve.

Nutrition:
- InfoCalories 80, Total Fat 3g, Total Carbs 2g, Protein 11g, Sodium 371mg.

Coconut Curried Mussels

Servings: 4
Cooking Time: 20 Minutes
Ingredients:
- 2 tbsp. water
- ½ cup onion, chopped fine
- ½ cup red bell pepper, seeded & chopped fine
- 3 cloves garlic, chopped fine
- ½ tsp pepper
- 2 tbsp. curry powder
- 1 cup coconut milk, unsweetened
- ½ cup vegetable broth
- 2 lbs. mussels, washed & cleaned
- ¼ cup cilantro, chopped

Directions:
1. Add the water, onion, bell pepper, and garlic to the cooking pot. Set to sauté on medium heat and cook, stirring occasionally until onions are soft, about 5-8 minutes, add more water if needed to prevent vegetables from sticking.
2. Stir in pepper, curry powder, coconut milk, and broth, stir well until smooth. Bring up to a simmer and add the mussels.
3. Add the lid and cook 5-6 minutes, or until all the mussels have opened. Discard any that do not open. Ladle into bowls and garnish with cilantro. Serve.

Nutrition:
- InfoCalories 331,Total Fat 18g,Total Carbs 15g,Protein 29g,Sodium 664mg.

Shrimp & Asparagus Risotto

Servings: 4
Cooking Time: 25 Minutes
Ingredients:
- 1 tbsp. butter
- ½ onion, chopped fine
- 1 clove garlic, chopped fine
- 1 cup Arborio rice
- 5 cups water, divided
- 1 cup clam juice
- 1 tbsp. olive oil
- ½ lb. small shrimp, peeled & deveined
- ½ bunch asparagus, cut in 1-inch pieces
- ¼ cup parmesan cheese

Directions:
1. Add butter to cooking pot and set to sauté on medium heat. Once butter melts, add onion and garlic and cook 5 minutes, stirring frequently.
2. Add the rice and stir to coat with butter mixture. Transfer mixture to a 1-quart baking dish.
3. Pour 1 cup water and clam juice over rice mixture and cover tightly with foil.
4. Pour 2 cups water in the cooking pot and add the rack. Place the rice mixture on the rack, secure the lid and set to pressure cooking on high. Set timer for 10 minutes.
5. When timer goes off release the pressure quickly and remove the baking dish carefully. Drain out any remaining water.
6. Set the cooker back to sauté on med-high and heat the oil. Add the shrimp and asparagus and cook, stirring, just until shrimp start to turn pink.
7. Add the shrimp and asparagus to the rice and stir to mix well. Recover tightly with foil. Pour 2 cups water back in the pot and add the rack.
8. Place the rice mixture back on the rack and secure the lid. Set to pressure cooking on high and set the timer for 4 minutes.
9. When the timer goes off, release the pressure quickly. Remove the foil and stir. Serve immediately sprinkled with parmesan cheese.

Nutrition:
- InfoCalories 362,Total Fat 11g,Total Carbs 45g,Protein 20g,Sodium 623mg.

Penne All Arrabbiata With Seafood And Chorizo

Servings: 4
Cooking Time: 50 Min
Ingredients:
- 16 ounces penne /480g
- 8 ounces shrimp, peeled and deveined /240g
- 8 ounces scallops /240g
- 12 clams, cleaned and debearded
- 1 jar Arrabbiata sauce /720ml
- 1 onion; diced
- 3 cups fish broth /750ml
- 1 chorizo; sliced
- 1 tbsp olive oil /15ml
- ½ tsp freshly ground black pepper /2.5g
- ½ tsp salt /2.5g

Directions:
1. Choose Sear/Sauté on the pot and set to Medium High. Choose Start/Stop to preheat the pot. Heat the oil and add the chorizo, onion, and garlic; sauté them for about 5 minutes. Stir in the penne, Arrabbiata sauce, and broth.
2. Season with the black pepper and salt and mix. Seal the pressure lid, choose Pressure, set to High and set the time to 2 minutes; press Start. When the time is over, do a quick pressure release and carefully open the lid.
3. Choose Sear/Sauté and set to Medium High. Choose Start/Stop. Stir in the shrimp, scallops, and clams. Put the pressure lid together and set to the Vent position.
4. Cover and cook for 5 minutes, until the clams have opened and the shrimp and scallops are opaque and cooked through.
5. Discard any unopened clams. Spoon the seafood and chorizo pasta into serving bowls and serve warm.

New England Lobster Rolls

Servings:4
Cooking Time: 20 Minutes
Ingredients:
- 4 lobster tails
- ¼ cup mayonnaise
- 1 celery stalk, minced
- Zest of 1 lemon
- Juice of 1 lemon
- ¼ teaspoon celery seed
- Kosher salt
- Freshly ground black pepper
- 4 split-top hot dog buns
- 4 tablespoons unsalted butter, at room temperature
- 4 leaves butter lettuce

Directions:
1. Insert Cook & Crisp Basket into the pot and close the crisping lid. Select AIR CRISP, set temperature to 375°F

Ninja Foodi Cookbook Guide

(190°C), and set time to 15 minutes. Select START/STOP to begin. Let preheat for 5 minutes.
2. Once unit has preheated, open lid and add the lobster tails to the basket. Close the lid and cook for 10 minutes.
3. In a medium bowl, mix together the mayonnaise, celery, lemon zest and juice, and celery seed, and add salt and pepper.
4. Fill a large bowl with a tray of ice cubes and enough water to cover the ice.
5. When cooking is complete, open lid. Transfer the lobster into the ice bath for 5 minutes. Close lid to keep unit warm.
6. Spread butter on the hot dog buns. Open lid and place the buns in the basket. Close crisping lid.
7. Select AIR CRISP, set temperature to 375°F (190°C), and set time to 4 minutes. Select START/STOP to begin.
8. Remove the lobster meat from the shells and roughly chop. Place in the bowl with the mayonnaise mixture and stir.
9. When cooking is complete, open lid and remove the buns. Place lettuce in each bun, then fill with the lobster salad.
Nutrition:
- InfoCalories: 408,Total Fat: 24g,Sodium: 798mg,Carbohydrates: 22g,Protein: 26g.

Herb Salmon With Barley Haricot Verts

Servings: 4
Cooking Time: 50 Min
Ingredients:
- 4 salmon fillets
- 8 ounces green beans haricot verts, trimmed /240g
- 2 garlic cloves, minced
- 1 cup pearl barley /130g
- 2 cups water /500ml
- ½ tbsp brown sugar /65g
- ½ tbsp freshly squeezed lemon juice /7.5ml
- 1 tbsp olive oil /15ml
- 4 tbsps melted butter/60ml
- ½ tsp dried thyme /2.5g
- ½ tsp dried rosemary /2.5g
- 1 tsp salt; divided /5g
- 1 tsp freshly ground black pepper; divided /5g

Directions:
1. Pour the barley and water in the pot and mix to combine. Place the reversible rack in the pot. Lay the salmon fillets on the rack. Seal the pressure lid, choose Pressure, set to High and set the time to 2 minutes. Press Start.
2. In a bowl, toss the green beans with olive oil, ½ tsp or 5g of black pepper, and ½ tsp or 2.5g of salt.
3. Then, in another bowl, mix the remaining black pepper and salt, the butter, brown sugar, lemon juice, rosemary, garlic, and rosemary.
4. When done cooking the rice and salmon, perform a quick pressure release. Gently pat the salmon dry with a paper towel, then coat with the buttery herb sauce.
5. Position the haricots vert around the salmon. Close the crisping lid; choose Broil and set the time to 7 minutes; press Start/Stop. When ready, remove the salmon from the rack, and serve with the barley and haricots vert.

Steamed Sea Bass With Turnips

Servings: 4
Cooking Time: 15 Min
Ingredients:
- 4 sea bass fillets
- 4 sprigs thyme
- 1 lemon; sliced
- 2 turnips; sliced
- 1 white onion; sliced into thin rings
- 1½ cups water /375ml
- 2 tsp olive oil /30ml
- 2 pinches salt
- 1 pinch ground black pepper

Directions:
1. Add water to the Foodi. Set a reversible rack into the pot. Line a parchment paper to the bottom of steamer basket. Place lemon slices in a single layer on the reversible rack.
2. Arrange fillets on the top of the lemons, cover with onion and thyme sprigs and top with turnip slices.
3. Drizzle pepper, salt, and olive oil over the mixture. Put steamer basket onto the reversible rack. Seal lid and cook on Low for 8 minutes; press Start.
4. When ready, release pressure quickly. Serve over the delicate onion rings and thinly sliced turnips.

Salmon Kale Meal

Servings: 4
Cooking Time: 4 Minutes
Ingredients:
- 1 lemon, juiced
- 2 salmon fillets
- 1/4 cup extra virgin olive oil
- 1 teaspoon Dijon mustard
- 4 cups kale, sliced, ribs removed
- 1 teaspoon salt
- 1 avocado, diced
- 1 cup pomegranate seeds
- 1 cup walnuts, toasted
- 1 cup goat parmesan cheese, shredded

Directions:
1. Season salmon with salt and keep it on the side.
2. Place a trivet in your Ninja Foodi.
3. Place salmon over the trivet.
4. Release pressure naturally over 10 minutes.
5. Transfer salmon to a serving platter.
6. Take a suitable and stir in kale, season with salt.
7. Season kale with dressing and add diced avocado, pomegranate seeds, walnuts and cheese.
8. Toss and serve with the fish.
9. Enjoy.

Nutrition:
- InfoCalories: 234; Fat: 14g; Carbohydrates: 12g; Protein: 16g

Pepper Smothered Cod

Servings: 4
Cooking Time: 20 Minutes
Ingredients:
- ¼ cup olive oil
- ½ cup red onion, chopped
- 2 tsp garlic, chopped
- ½ cup red bell pepper, chopped

- ½ cup green bell pepper, chopped
- Salt and pepper, to taste
- 4 tbsp. flour
- 2 cups chicken broth, low sodium
- ½ cup tomato, seeded & chopped
- 2 tsp fresh thyme, chopped
- 4 cod filets

Directions:
1. Set to sauté on med-high heat and add oil to the cooking pot.
2. Add the onion and garlic and cook, stirring, 1 minute.
3. Add the peppers, salt, and pepper and cook, stirring frequently about 2-3 minutes, or until peppers start to get tender.
4. Stir in the flour and cook until it turns a light brown.
5. Pour in the broth and cook, stirring, until smooth and the sauce starts to thicken. Stir in tomato and thyme.
6. Season the fish with salt and pepper. Place in the pot and add the lid. Cook 3-4 minutes, then turn the fish over and cook another 3-4 minute or until fish flakes easily with a fork. Transfer the fish to serving plates and top with sauce. Serve immediately.

Nutrition:
- InfoCalories 249,Total Fat 14g,Total Carbs 11g,Protein 19g,Sodium 1107mg.

Mussel Chowder With Oyster Crackers

Servings: 4
Cooking Time: 75 Min
Ingredients:
- 1 pound parsnips, peeled and cut into chunks /450g
- 3 cans chopped mussels, drained, liquid reserved /180g
- 1½ cups heavy cream /375ml
- 2 cups oyster crackers /260g
- ¼ cup white wine /62.5ml
- ¼ cup finely grated Pecorino Romano cheese/32.5g
- 1 cup clam juice /130g
- 2 thick pancetta slices, cut into thirds
- 1 bay leaf
- 2 celery stalks; chopped
- 1 medium onion; chopped
- 1 tbsp flour /15g
- 2 tbsps chopped fresh chervil/30g
- 2 tbsps melted ghee /30g
- ½ tsp garlic powder /2.5g
- 1 tsp salt; divided /5g
- 1 tsp dried rosemary /5g

Directions:
1. To preheat the Foodi, close the crisping lid and Choose Air Crisp; adjust the temperature to 375°F or 190°C and the time to 2 minutes; press Start. In a bowl, pour in the oyster crackers. Drizzle with the melted ghee, add the cheese, garlic powder, and ½ tsp or 2.5g of salt. Toss to coat the crackers. Transfer to the crisping basket.
2. Once the pot is ready, open the pressure lid and fix the basket in the pot. Close the lid and Choose Air Crisp; adjust the temperature to 375°F or 190°C and the cook time to 6 minutes; press Start.
3. After 3 minutes, carefully open the lid and mix the crackers with a spoon. Close the lid and resume cooking until crisp and lightly browned. Take out the basket and set aside to cool.
4. On the pot, choose Sear/Sauté and adjust to Medium. Press Start. Add the pancetta and cook for 5 minutes, turning once or twice, until crispy.
5. Remove the pancetta to a paper towel-lined plate to drain fat; set aside.
6. Sauté the celery and onion in the pancetta grease for 1 minute or until the vegetables start softening. Mix the flour into the vegetables to coat evenly and pour the wine over the veggies. Cook for about 1 minute or until reduced by about one-third.
7. Pour in the clam juice, the reserved mussel liquid, parsnips, remaining salt, rosemary, and bay leaf. Seal the pressure lid, choose Pressure; adjust the pressure to High and the cook time to 4 minutes. Press Start.
8. After cooking, perform a natural pressure release for 5 minutes. Stir in the mussels and heavy cream. Choose Sear/Sauté and adjust to Medium. Press Start to simmer to the chowder and heat the mussels. Carefully remove and discard the bay leaf after.
9. Spoon the soup into bowls and crumble the pancetta over the top. Garnish with the chervil and a handful of oyster crackers, serving the remaining crackers on the side.

Caramelized Salmon

Servings: 4
Cooking Time: 10 Minutes
Ingredients:
- 1 tbsp. coconut oil, melted
- 1/3 cup Stevia brown sugar, packed
- 3 tbsp. fish sauce
- 1 ½ tbsp. soy sauce
- 1 tsp fresh ginger, peeled & grated
- 2 tsp lime zest, finely grated
- 1 tbsp. fresh lime juice
- ½ tsp pepper
- 4 salmon fillets
- 1 tbsp. green onions, sliced
- 1 tbsp. cilantro chopped

Directions:
1. Add the oil, brown sugar, fish sauce, soy sauce, ginger, zest, juice, and pepper to the cooking pot. Stir to mix.
2. Set to sauté on medium heat and bring mixture to a simmer, stirring frequently. Turn heat off.
3. Add the fish to the sauce making sure it is covered. Add the lid and set to pressure cooking on low. Set the timer for 1 minute.
4. When the timer goes off let the pressure release naturally for 5 minutes, the release it manually. Fish is done when it flakes with a fork.
5. Transfer fish to a serving dish with the caramelized side up.
6. Set cooker back to sauté on medium and cook sauce 3-4 minutes until it's thickened. Spoon over fish and garnish with chopped green onions and scallions. Serve.

Nutrition:
- InfoCalories 316,Total Fat 18g,Total Carbs 5g,Protein 35g,Sodium 1514mg.

Panko Crusted Cod

Servings: 4
Cooking Time: 15 Minutes
Ingredients:
- 2 uncooked cod fillets
- 3 teaspoons kosher salt
- ¾ cup panko bread crumbs
- 2 tablespoons butter, melted
- 1/4 cup fresh parsley, minced
- 1 lemon. Zested and juiced

Directions:
1. Pre-heat your Ninja Foodi at 390 °F (200°C) and place the Air Crisper basket inside.
2. Season cod and salt.
3. Take a suitable and stir in bread crumbs, parsley, lemon juice, zest, butter, and mix well.
4. Coat fillets with the bread crumbs mixture and place fillets in your Air Crisping basket.
5. Lock Air Crisping lid and cook on Air Crisp mode for 15 minutes at 360 °F (180°C).
6. Serve and enjoy.

Nutrition:
- InfoCalories: 554; Fat: 24g; Carbohydrates: 5g; Protein: 37g

Swordfish With Caper Sauce

Servings: 4
Cooking Time: 8 Minutes
Ingredients:
- 4 swordfish steaks, about 1-inch thick
- 4 tablespoons unsalted butter
- 1 lemon, sliced into 8 slices
- 1 tablespoon lemon juice
- 1 tablespoon olive oil
- 2 tablespoons capers, drained
- Sea salt, to taste
- Black pepper, to taste

Directions:
1. Take a large shallow bowl and whisk together the lemon juice and oil.
2. Season with swordfish steaks with black pepper and salt on each side, place in the oil mixture.
3. Turn to coat both sides and refrigerate for 15 minutes.
4. Preheat Ninja Foodi by pressing the "GRILL" option and setting it to "MAX" and timer to 8 minutes.
5. Let it preheat until you hear a beep.
6. Set the swordfish over the grill grate, Lock and secure the Ninja Foodi's lid and cook for 9 minutes.
7. Then turn off the heat.
8. Enjoy.

Nutrition:
- InfoCalories: 472; Fat: 31g; Carbohydrates: 2g; Protein: 48g

Air Fried Scallops

Servings: 4
Cooking Time: 5 Minutes
Ingredients:
- 12 scallops
- 3 tablespoons olive oil
- Black pepper and salt, to taste

Directions:
1. Rub the scallops with salt, pepper and olive oil.
2. Transfer it to Ninja foodi.
3. Place the insert in your Ninja foodi.
4. Close the air crisping lid.
5. Cook for 4 minutes to 390°F (200°C).
6. Flip them after 2 minutes.
7. Serve and enjoy.

Nutrition:
- InfoCalories: 372g; Fat: 11g; Carbohydrates: 0.9g; Protein: 63g

Italian Flounder

Servings: 4
Cooking Time: 70 Min
Ingredients:
- 4 flounder fillets
- 3 slices prosciutto; chopped
- 2 bags baby kale /180g
- ½ small red onion; chopped
- ½ cup whipping cream /125ml
- 1 cup panko breadcrumbs /130g
- 2 tbsps chopped fresh parsley /30g
- 3 tbsps unsalted butter, melted and divided /45g
- ¼ tsp fresh ground black pepper /1.25g
- ½ tsp salt; divided /2.5g

Directions:
1. On the Foodi, choose Sear/Sauté and adjust to Medium. Press Start to preheat the inner pot. Add the prosciutto and cook until crispy, about 6 minutes. Stir in the red onions and cook for about 2 minutes or until the onions start to soften. Sprinkle with half of the salt.
2. Fetch the kale into the pot and cook, stirring frequently until wilted and most of the liquid has evaporated, about 4-5 minutes. Mix in the whipping cream.
3. Lay the flounder fillets over the kale in a single layer. Brush 1 tbsp or 15ml of the melted butter over the fillets and sprinkle with the remaining salt and black pepper.
4. Close the crisping lid and choose Bake/Roast. Adjust the temperature to 300°F or 150°C and the cook time to 3 minutes. Press Start.
5. Combine the remaining butter, the parsley and breadcrumbs in a bowl.
6. When done cooking, open the crisping lid. Spoon the breadcrumbs mixture on the fillets.
7. Close the crisping lid and Choose Bake/Roast. Adjust the temperature to 400°F or 205°C and the cook time to 6 minutes. Press Start.
8. After about 4 minutes, open the lid and check the fish. The breadcrumbs should be golden brown and crisp. If not, close the lid and continue to cook for an additional two minutes.

Lemon Cod Goujons And Rosemary Chips

Servings: 4
Cooking Time: 100 Min
Ingredients:
- 4 cod fillets, cut into strips
- 2 potatoes, cut into chips
- 4 lemon wedges to serve
- 2 eggs
- 1 cup arrowroot starch /130g
- 1 cup flour /130g
- 2 tbsps olive oil /30ml

Ninja Foodi Cookbook Guide

- 3 tbsp fresh rosemary; chopped /45g
- 1 tbsp cumin powder /15g
- ½ tbsp cayenne powder /7.5g
- 1 tsp black pepper, plus more for seasoning /5g
- 1 tsp salt, plus more for seasoning /5g
- Zest and juice from 1 lemon
- Cooking spray

Directions:
1. Fix the Crisping Basket in the pot and close the crisping lid. Choose Air Crisp, set the temperature to 375°F or 190°C, and the time to 5 minutes. Choose Start/Stop to preheat the pot.
2. In a bowl, whisk the eggs, lemon zest, and lemon juice. In another bowl, combine the arrowroot starch, flour, cayenne powder, cumin, black pepper, and salt.
3. Coat each cod strip in the egg mixture, and then dredge in the flour mixture, coating well on all sides. Grease the preheated basket with cooking spray. Place the coated fish in the basket and oil with cooking spray.
4. Close the crisping lid. Choose Air Crisp, set the temperature to 375°F or 190°C, and the time to 15 minutes; press Start/Stop. Toss the potatoes with oil and season with salt and pepper.
5. After 15 minutes, check the fish making sure the pieces are as crispy as desired. Remove the fish from the basket.
6. Pour the potatoes in the basket. Close the crisping lid; choose Air Crisp, set the temperature to 400°F or 205°C, and the time to 24 minutes; press Start/Stop.
7. After 12 minutes, open the lid, remove the basket and shake the fries. Return the basket to the pot and close the lid to continue cooking until crispy.
8. When ready, sprinkle with fresh rosemary. Serve the fish with the potatoes and lemon wedges.

Paella Señorito

Servings: 5
Cooking Time: 25 Min
Ingredients:
- 1 pound frozen shrimp, peeled and deveined /450g
- 2 garlic cloves, minced
- 1 onion; chopped
- 1 lemon, cut into wedges
- 1 red bell pepper; diced
- 2 cups fish broth /500ml
- ¼ cup olive oil /62.5ml
- 1 cup bomba rice /130g
- ¼ cup frozen green peas /32.5g
- 1 tsp paprika /5g
- 1 tsp turmeric /5g
- salt and ground white pepper to taste
- chopped fresh parsley

Directions:
1. Warm oil on Sear/Sauté. Add in bell pepper and onions and cook for 5 minutes until fragrant. Mix in garlic and cook for one more minute until soft.
2. Add paprika, ground white pepper, salt and turmeric to the vegetables and cook for 1 minute.
3. Stir in fish broth and rice. Add shrimp in the rice mixture. Seal the pressure lid, choose Pressure, set to High, and set the timer to 5 minutes; press Start. When ready, release the pressure quickly.
4. Stir in green peas and let sit for 5 minutes until green peas are heated through. Serve warm garnished with parsley and lemon wedges.

Potato Chowder With Peppery Prawns

Servings: 4
Cooking Time: 80 Min
Ingredients:
- 4 slices serrano ham; chopped
- 16 ounces frozen corn /500g
- 16 prawns, peeled and deveined
- 1 onion; chopped
- 2 Yukon Gold potatoes; chopped
- ¾ cup heavy cream /188ml
- 2 cups vegetable broth /500ml
- 2 tbsps olive oil /30ml
- 4 tbsps minced garlic; divided /60g
- 1 tsp dried rosemary /5g
- 1 tsp salt; divided /5g
- 1 tsp freshly ground black pepper; divided /5g
- ½ tsp red chili flakes /2.5g

Directions:
1. Choose Sear/Sauté on the pot and set to Medium High. Choose Start/Stop to preheat the pot. Add 1 tbsp or 15ml of the olive oil and cook the serrano ham, 2 tbsps of garlic, and onion, stirring occasionally; for 5 minutes. Fetch out one-third of the serrano ham into a bowl for garnishing.
2. Add the potatoes, corn, vegetable broth, rosemary, half of the salt, and half of the black pepper to the pot.
3. Seal the pressure lid, hit Pressure and set to High. Set the time to 10 minutes, and press Start.
4. In a bowl, toss the prawns in the remaining garlic, salt, black pepper, the remaining olive oil, and the red chili flakes. When done cooking, do a quick pressure release and carefully open the pressure lid.
5. Stir in the heavy cream and fix the reversible rack in the pot over the chowder.
6. Spread the prawn in the rack. Close the crisping lid. Choose Broil and set the time to 8 minutes. Choose Start/Stop. When the timer has ended, remove the rack from the pot.
7. Ladle the corn chowder into serving bowls and top with the prawns. Garnish with the reserved ham and serve immediately.

Haddock With Sanfaina

Servings: 4
Cooking Time: 40 Min
Ingredients:
- 4 haddock fillets
- 1 can diced tomatoes, drained /435g
- ½ small onion; sliced
- 1 small jalapeño pepper, seeded and minced
- 2 large garlic cloves, minced
- 1 eggplant; cubed
- 1 bell pepper; chopped
- 1 bay leaf
- ⅓ cup sliced green olives /44g
- ¼ cup chopped fresh chervil; divided /32.5g
- 3 tbsps olive oil /45ml
- 3 tbsps capers; divided/45g
- ½ tsp dried basil /2.5g

Ninja Foodi Cookbook Guide

- ¼ tsp salt /1.25g

Directions:
1. Season the fish on both sides with salt, place in the refrigerator, and make the sauce. Press Sear/Sauté and set to Medium. Press Start. Melt the butter until no longer foaming. Add onion, eggplant, bell pepper, jalapeño, and garlic; sauté for 5 minutes.
2. Stir in the tomatoes, bay leaf, basil, olives, half of the chervil, and half of the capers. Remove the fish from the refrigerator and lay on the vegetables in the pot.
3. Seal the pressure lid, choose Pressure; adjust the pressure to Low and the cook time to 3 minutes; press Start. After cooking, do a quick pressure release and carefully open the lid. Remove and discard the bay leaf.
4. Transfer the fish to a serving platter and spoon the sauce over. Sprinkle with the remaining chervil and capers. Serve.

Salmon With Dill Chutney

Servings: 2
Cooking Time: 15 Min
Ingredients:
- 2 salmon fillets
- Juice from ½ lemon
- 2 cups water /500ml
- ¼ tsp paprika /1.25g
- salt and freshly ground pepper to taste
- For Chutney:
- ¼ cup extra virgin olive oil /62.5ml
- ¼ cup fresh dill /32.5g
- Juice from ½ lemon
- Sea salt to taste

Directions:
1. In a food processor, blend all the chutney Ingredients until creamy. Set aside. To your Foodi, add the water and place a reversible rack.
2. Arrange salmon fillets skin-side down on the steamer basket. Drizzle lemon juice over salmon and apply a seasoning of paprika.
3. Seal the pressure lid, choose Pressure, set to High, and set the timer to 3 minutes; press Start. When ready, release the pressure quickly. Season the fillets with pepper and salt, transfer to a serving plate and top with the dill chutney.

Shrimp Etouffee

Servings: 6
Cooking Time: 30 Minutes
Ingredients:
- ¼ cup olive oil
- ¼ cup flour
- 1 stalk celery, chopped
- 1 green bell pepper, chopped
- 2 jalapeno peppers, chopped
- ½ onion, chopped
- 4 cloves garlic, chopped
- 2 cups clam juice
- 1 tbsp. Cajun seasoning
- ½ tsp celery seed
- 1 tbsp. paprika
- 2 pounds shrimp, shell on, deveined
- 3 green onions, chopped
- Hot sauce to taste

Directions:
1. Add the oil to the cooking pot and set to sauté on medium heat. Whisk in the flour until smooth. Cook until a deep brown, whisking frequently, about 10 minutes.
2. Add celery, bell pepper, jalapeno, and onion and cook 4 minutes, stirring occasionally. Add the garlic and cook 2 minutes more.
3. Slowly stir in clam juice, a little at a time, until combined. The sauce should resemble syrup, add more juice if needed.
4. Add Cajun seasoning, celery seed, and paprika and mix well. Add the shrimp. Cover, reduce heat to low and cook 10 minutes.
5. Stir in green onions and hot sauce. Serve over rice.

Nutrition:
- InfoCalories 83,Total Fat 3g,Total Carbs 6g,Protein 7g,Sodium 395mg.

Shrimp Fried Rice

Servings: 6
Cooking Time: 15 Minutes
Ingredients:
- 2 tbsp. sesame oil
- 2 tbsp. olive oil
- 1 lb. medium shrimp, peeled & deveined
- 1 cup frozen peas & carrots
- 1/2 cup corn
- 3 cloves garlic, chopped fine
- ½ tsp ginger
- 3 eggs, lightly beaten
- 4 cups brown rice, cooked
- 3 green onions, sliced
- 3 tbsp. tamari
- ½ tsp salt
- ½ tsp pepper

Directions:
1. Add the sesame and olive oils to the cooking pot and set to sauté on med-high heat.
2. Add the shrimp and cook 3 minutes, or until they turn pink, turning shrimp over halfway through. Use a slotted spoon to transfer shrimp to a plate.
3. Add the peas, carrots, and corn to the pot and cook 2 minutes until vegetables start to soften, stirring occasionally. Add the garlic and ginger and cook 1 minute more.
4. Push the vegetables to one side and add the eggs, cook to scramble, stirring frequently. Add the shrimp, rice, and onions and stir to mix all ingredients together.
5. Drizzle with tamari and season with salt and pepper, stir to combine. Cook 2 minutes or until everything is heated through. Serve immediately.

Nutrition:
- InfoCalories 361,Total Fat 13g,Total Carbs 38g,Protein 24g,Sodium 1013mg.

Sweet & Spicy Shrimp

Servings: 4
Cooking Time: 5 Minutes
Ingredients:
- ¾ cup pineapple juice, unsweetened
- 1 red bell pepper, sliced
- 1 ½ cups cauliflower, grated
- ¼ cup dry white wine
- ½ cup water
- 2 tbsp. soy sauce

Ninja Foodi Cookbook Guide

- 2 tbsp. Thai sweet chili sauce
- 1 tbsp. chili paste
- 1 lb. large shrimp, frozen
- 4 green onions, chopped, white & green separated
- 1 ½ cups pineapple chunks, drained

Directions:
1. Add ¾ cup pineapple juice along with remaining ingredients, except the pineapple chunks and green parts of the onion, to the cooking pot. Stir to mix.
2. Add the lid and set to pressure cook on high. Set timer for 2 minutes. When the timer goes off, release pressure 10 minutes before opening the pot.
3. Add the green parts of the onions and pineapple chunks and stir well. Serve immediately.

Nutrition:
- InfoCalories 196,Total Fat 1g,Total Carbs 22g,Protein 26g,Sodium 764mg.

Easy Clam Chowder

Servings: 6
Cooking Time: 3 Hours
Ingredients:
- 5 slices bacon, chopped
- 2 cloves garlic, chopped fine
- ½ onion, chopped
- ½ tsp thyme
- 1 cup chicken broth, low sodium
- 4 oz. cream cheese
- 18 oz. clams, chopped & drained
- 1 bay leaf
- 3 cups cauliflower, separated in florets
- 1 cup almond milk, unsweetened
- 1 cup heavy cream
- 2 tbsp. fresh parsley, chopped

Directions:
1. Add the bacon to the cooking pot and set to sauté on med-high heat. Cook until crisp, transfer to a paper-towel lined plate. Pour out all but 3 tablespoons of the fat.
2. Add the onion and garlic and cook 2-3 minutes until onion is translucent. Add the thyme and cook 1 minute more.
3. Add the broth, cream cheese, clams, bay leaf, and cauliflower, mix until combined. Add the lid and set to slow cook on low. Cook 2-3 hours until cauliflower is tender. Stir in the milk and cream and cook until heated through.
4. Ladle into bowls and top with bacon and parsley. Serve warm.

Nutrition:
- InfoCalories 377,Total Fat 24g,Total Carbs 13g,Protein 27g,Sodium 468mg.

Glazed Salmon

Servings: 4
Cooking Time: 25 Minutes
Ingredients:
- 1-2 Coho salmon filets
- 1 cup of water
- 1/4 cup of soy sauce
- 1/4 cup brown erythritol
- 1 tablespoon choc zero maple syrup
- 1 and 1/2 tablespoons ginger roots, minced
- 1/2 teaspoon white pepper
- 2 tablespoons cornstarch
- 1/4 cup of cold water

Directions:
1. Preheat Ninja Foodi by pressing the "GRILL" option and setting it to "HIGH" for 15 minutes.
2. Take a medium saucepan over medium heat, combine sauce ingredients. except for salmon, cornstarch and cold water and bring to a low boil.
3. Then add cornstarch and water in another bowl, whisk cornstarch mixture slowly into sauce until it thickens.
4. Stir in one chunk of pecan wood to the hot coal of your grill.
5. Brush sauce onto the salmon filet.
6. Place on the grill grate, then close the hood.
7. Cook for 15 minutes.
8. Brush the salmon with another coat of sauce.
9. Serve and enjoy.

Nutrition:
- InfoCalories: 163; Fat: 0g; Carbohydrates: 15g; Protein: 0g

Buttered Fish

Servings: 4
Cooking Time: 6 Minutes
Ingredients:
- 1-pound fish chunks
- 1 tablespoon vinegar
- 2 drops liquid stevia
- 1/4 cup butter
- Black pepper and salt to taste

Directions:
1. Select "Sauté" mode on your Ninja Foodi.
2. Stir in butter and melt it.
3. Add fish chunks, Sauté for 3 minutes.
4. Stir in stevia, salt, pepper, stir it.
5. Close the crisping lid.
6. Cook on "Air Crisp" mode for 3 minutes to 360 °F (180°C).
7. Serve and enjoy.

Nutrition:
- InfoCalories: 274g; Fat: 15g; Carbohydrates: 2g; Protein: 33g

Awesome Shrimp Roast

Servings: 2
Cooking Time: 7 Minutes
Ingredients:
- 3 tablespoons chipotle in adobo sauce, minced
- ¼ teaspoon salt
- 1/4 cup BBQ sauce
- ½ orange, juiced
- ½ pound large shrimps

Directions:
1. Preheat Ninja Foodi by pressing the "Bake/Roast" mode and setting it to "400 °F (205°C)" and timer to 7 minutes.
2. Let it preheat until you hear a beep.
3. Set shrimps over Grill Grate and lock lid, cook until the timer runs out.
4. Serve and enjoy.

Nutrition:
- InfoCalories: 173; Fat: 2g; Carbohydrates: 21g; Protein: 17g

Flounder Veggie Soup

Servings: 10
Cooking Time: 20 Minutes
Ingredients:
- 2 cups water, divided
- 14 oz. chicken broth, low sodium
- 2 lbs. potatoes, peeled & cubed
- 1 onion, chopped
- 2 stalks celery, chopped
- 1 carrot, chopped
- 1 bay leaf
- 2 12 oz. cans evaporated milk, fat free
- 4 tbsp. butter
- 1 lb. flounder filets, cut in 1/2-inch pieces
- ½ tsp thyme
- ¼ tsp salt
- ¼ tsp pepper

Directions:
1. Add 1 ½ cups water, broth, potatoes, onion, celery, carrot, and the bay leaf to the cooking pot. Stir to mix.
2. Add the lid and set to pressure cooker on high. Set the timer for 8 minutes. When the timer goes off, use quick release to remove the lid.
3. Set cooker to sauté on med-low. Stir in milk, butter, fish, thyme, salt and pepper and bring to a boil.
4. In a small bowl, whisk together remaining water and cornstarch until smooth. Add to the soup and cook, stirring, until thickened. Discard the bay leaf and serve.

Nutrition:
- InfoCalories 213,Total Fat 6g,Total Carbs 25g,Protein 14g,Sodium 649mg.

Baked Cod Casserole

Servings: 6
Cooking Time: 20 Minutes
Ingredients:
- Nonstick cooking spray
- 1 lb. mushrooms, chopped
- 1 onion, chopped
- ½ cup fresh parsley, chopped
- ½ tsp salt, divided
- ½ tsp pepper, divided
- 6 cod fillets
- ¾ cup dry white wine
- ¾ cup plain bread crumbs
- 2 tbsp. butter, melted
- 1 cup Swiss cheese, grated

Directions:
1. Spray the cooking pot with cooking spray.
2. In a medium bowl, combine mushrooms, onion, parsley, ¼ teaspoon salt, and ¼ teaspoon pepper and mix well. Spread evenly on the bottom of the cooking pot.
3. Place the fish on top of the mushroom mixture and pour the wine over them.
4. In a separate medium bowl, combine remaining ingredients and mix well. Sprinkle over the fish.
5. Add the tender-crisp lid and set to bake on 450°F (230°C). Bake 15-20 minutes or until golden brown and fish flakes easily with a fork. Serve immediately.

Nutrition:
- InfoCalories 284,Total Fat 10g,Total Carbs 16g,Protein 27g,Sodium 693mg.

Coconut Shrimp

Servings: 2
Cooking Time: 30 Min
Ingredients:
- 8 large shrimp
- ½ cup orange jam /65g
- ½ cup shredded coconut /65g
- ½ cup breadcrumbs /65g
- 8 oz. coconut milk /240ml
- 1 tbsp honey /15ml
- ½ tsp cayenne pepper/2.5g
- ¼ tsp hot sauce /1.25ml
- 1 tsp mustard /5g
- ¼ tsp salt /1.25g
- ¼ tsp pepper /1.25g

Directions:
1. Combine the breadcrumbs, cayenne pepper, shredded coconut, salt, and pepper in a small bowl. Dip the shrimp in the coconut milk, first, and then in the coconut crumbs.
2. Arrange in the lined Ninja Foodi basket, close the crisping lid and cook for 20 minutes on Air Crisp mode at 350 °F or 175°C.
3. Meanwhile whisk the jam, honey, hot sauce, and mustard. Serve the shrimp with the sauce.

Oyster Stew

Servings: 4
Cooking Time: 12 Min
Ingredients:
- 3 jars shucked oysters in liqueur /300g
- 3 Shallots, minced
- 3 cloves garlic, minced
- 2 cups chopped celery /260g
- 2 cups bone broth /500ml
- 2 cups heavy cream /500ml
- 3 tbsp olive oil /45ml
- 3 tbsp chopped parsley /45g
- Salt and white pepper to taste

Directions:
1. Add oil, garlic, shallot, and celery. Stir-fry them for 2 minutes on Sear/Sauté mode, and add the heavy cream, broth, and oysters. Stir once or twice.
2. Close the lid, secure the pressure valve, and select Steam mode on High pressure for 3 minutes. Press Start/Stop. Once the timer has stopped, do a quick pressure release, and open the lid.
3. Season with salt and white pepper. Close the crisping lid and cook for 5 minutes on Broil mode. Stir and dish the oyster stew into serving bowls. Garnish with parsley and top with some croutons.

Crab Cakes With Spicy Dipping Sauce

Servings: 4
Cooking Time: 20 Minutes
Ingredients:
- Nonstick cooking spray
- 1/3 cup + ¼ cup mayonnaise, divided
- 1 tbsp. + 2 tsp spicy brown mustard, divided
- 1 tsp hot sauce
- ¼ cup + 1 tbsp. celery, chopped fine, divided
- ¼ cup + 1 tbsp. red bell pepper, chopped fine, divided
- 4 tsp Cajun seasoning, divided
- 2 tbsp. fresh parsley, chopped, divided

- 8 oz. jumbo lump crab meat
- ¼ cup green bell pepper, chopped fine
- 2 tbsp. green onions, chopped fine
- ¼ cup bread crumbs

Directions:
1. Spray the fryer basket with cooking spray.
2. In a small bowl, combine 1/3 cup mayonnaise, 2 teaspoons mustard, hot sauce, 1 tablespoon celery, 1 tablespoon red bell pepper, 2 teaspoons Cajun seasoning, and 1 tablespoon parsley, mix well. Cover and refrigerate until ready to use.
3. In a large bowl, combine all remaining ingredients with the crab, green bell pepper, onions, and bread crumbs, mix well. Form into 8 patties.
4. Place the patties in the fryer basket and add the tender-crisp lid. Set to air fry on 400 °F (205°C). Cook 20 minutes, or until golden brown, turning over halfway through cooking time.
5. Serve with prepared sauce for dipping.

Nutrition:
- InfoCalories 166,Total Fat 8g,Total Carbs 11g,Protein 11g,Sodium 723mg.

Smoked Salmon Pilaf With Walnuts

Servings: 4
Cooking Time: 60 Min

Ingredients:
- 4 green onions; chopped (white part separated from the green part)
- 1 smoked salmon fillet, flaked
- 1 medium tomato, seeded and diced
- 1 cup basmati rice /130g
- 1 cup frozen corn, thawed /130g
- 2 cups water /500ml
- ½ cup walnut pieces /65g
- 1 tbsp ghee /15g
- 1 tsp salt /5g
- 2 tsp s prepared horseradish /10g

Directions:
1. Pour the walnuts into a heatproof bowl. Put the Crisping basket in the inner pot and the bowl in the basket.
2. Close the crisping lid and Choose Air Crisp; adjust the temperature to 375°F (190°C) and the time to 5 minutes. Press Start to begin toasting the walnuts.
3. After the cooking time is over, carefully take the bowl and basket out of the pot and set aside.
4. On the Foodi, choose Sear/Sauté and adjust to Medium to preheat the inner pot. Add the ghee to melt and sauté the white part of the green onions for about a minute, or until starting to soften.
5. Stir in the rice and corn, stirring occasionally for 2 to 3 minutes, or until starting to be fragrant. Add the water and salt.
6. Seal the pressure lid, choose Pressure; adjust the pressure to High and the cook time to 3 minutes; press Start.
7. After cooking, perform a natural pressure release for 5 minutes, then a quick pressure and carefully open the lid.
8. Fluff the rice gently with a fork. Stir in the flaked salmon, green parts of the green onions, and the horseradish.
9. Add the tomato and allow sitting a few minutes to warm through. Spoon the pilaf into serving bowls and top with the walnuts. Serve.

Pistachio Crusted Salmon

Servings: 1
Cooking Time: 15 Min

Ingredients:
- 1 salmon fillet
- 3 tbsp pistachios /45g
- 1 tsp grated Parmesan cheese /5g
- 1 tsp lemon juice /5ml
- 1 tsp mustard /5g
- 1 tsp olive oil /5ml
- Pinch of sea salt
- Pinch of garlic powder
- Pinch of black pepper

Directions:
1. Whisk the mustard and lemon juice together. Season the salmon with salt, pepper, and garlic powder. Brush the olive oil on all sides.
2. Brush the mustard-lemon mixture on top of the salmon. Chop the pistachios finely, and combine them with the Parmesan cheese.
3. Sprinkle them on top of the salmon. Place the salmon in the Ninja Foodi basket with the skin side down.
4. Close the crisping lid and cook for 10 minutes on Air Crisp mode at 350 °F or 175°C.

Shrimp And Chorizo Potpie

Servings:6
Cooking Time: 23 Minutes

Ingredients:
- ¼ cup unsalted butter
- ½ large onion, diced
- 1 celery stalk, diced
- 1 carrot, peeled and diced
- 8 ounces chorizo, fully cooked, cut into ½-inch wheels
- ¼ cup all-purpose flour
- 16 ounces frozen tail-off shrimp, cleaned and deveined
- ¾ cup chicken stock
- 1 tablespoon Cajun spice mix
- ½ cup heavy (whipping) cream
- Sea salt
- Freshly ground black pepper
- 1 refrigerated store-bought pie crust, at room temperature

Directions:
1. Select SEAR/SAUTÉ and set to MD:HI. Select START/STOP to begin. Let preheat for 5 minutes.
2. Add the butter. Once melted, add the onion, celery, carrot, and sausage, and cook until softened, about 3 minutes. Stir in the flour and cook 2 minutes, stirring occasionally.
3. Add the shrimp, stock, Cajun spice mix, and cream and season with salt and pepper. Stir until sauce thickens and bubbles, about 3 minutes.
4. Lay the pie crust evenly on top of the filling, folding over the edges if necessary. Make a small cut in center of pie crust so that steam can escape during baking. Close crisping lid.
5. Select BROIL and set time to 10 minutes. Select START/STOP to begin.
6. When cooking is complete, open lid and remove pot from unit. Let rest 10 to 15 minutes before serving.

Nutrition:
- InfoCalories: 528,Total Fat: 37g,Sodium: 776mg,Carbohydrates: 19g,Protein: 28g.

Coconut Cilantro Shrimp

Servings: 4
Cooking Time: 4 ½ Hours
Ingredients:
- 3 ¾ cups coconut milk, unsweetened
- 1 ¾ cups water
- 2 tbsp. red curry paste
- 2 ½ tsp lemon garlic seasoning
- 1 lb. shrimp, peeled & deveined
- ¼ cup cilantro, chopped

Directions:
1. Place all ingredients, except shrimp and cilantro, in the cooking pot and stir to well to mix.
2. Add the lid and set to slow cook on low heat. Cook 4 hours, stirring occasionally.
3. Stir in shrimp and continue cooking another 15-30 minutes until shrimp turn pink and tender.
4. Transfer mixture to a serving plate and garnish with cilantro. Serve immediately.

Nutrition:
- InfoCalories 525,Total Fat 46g,Total Carbs 8g,Protein 28g,Sodium 168mg.

Farfalle Tuna Casserole With Cheese

Servings: 4
Cooking Time: 60 Min
Ingredients:
- 6 ounces farfalle /180g
- 1 can full cream milk; divided /360ml
- 2 cans tuna, drained /180g
- 1 medium onion; chopped
- 1 large carrot; chopped
- 1 cup vegetable broth /250ml
- 2 cups shredded Monterey Jack cheese /260g
- 1 cup chopped green beans /130g
- 2½ cups panko bread crumbs /325g
- 3 tbsps butter, melted /45ml
- 1 tbsp olive oil/ 15ml
- 1 tsp salt/ 5g
- 2 tsp s corn starch /10g

Directions:
1. On the Foodi, Choose Sear/Sauté and adjust to Medium. Press Start to preheat the pot.
2. Heat the oil until shimmering and sauté the onion and carrots for 3 minutes, stirring, until softened.
3. Add the farfalle, ¾ cup or 188ml of milk, broth, and salt to the pot. Stir to combine and submerge the farfalle in the liquid with a spoon.
4. Seal the pressure lid, choose pressure; adjust the pressure to Low and the cook time to 5 minutes; press Start. After cooking, do a quick pressure release and carefully open the pressure lid.
5. Choose Sear/Sauté and adjust to Less for low heat. Press Start. Pour the remaining milk on the farfalle.
6. In a medium bowl, mix the cheese and cornstarch evenly and add the cheese mixture by large handfuls to the sauce while stirring until the cheese melts and the sauce thickens. Add the tuna and green beans, gently stir. Heat for 2 minutes.
7. In another bowl, mix the crumbs and melted butter well. Spread the crumbs over the casserole. Close the crisping lid and press Broil. Adjust the cook time to 5 minutes; press Start. When ready, the topping should be crisp and brown. If not, broil for 2 more minutes. Serve immediately.

Cheesy Crab Pie

Servings: 8
Cooking Time: 40 Minutes
Ingredients:
- 1 cup cheddar cheese, grated
- 1 pie crust, uncooked
- 1 cup crab meat
- 3 eggs
- 1 cup half and half, fat free
- ½ tsp salt
- ¼ tsp pepper
- ½ tsp lemon zest

Directions:
1. Place the rack in the cooking pot.
2. Spread the cheese in an even layer in the bottom of the pie crust. Top with crab.
3. In a medium bowl, whisk together remaining ingredients until combined. Pour over crab.
4. Place the pie on the rack and add the tender-crisp lid. Set to bake on 325°F (160°C). Bake 40 minutes until filling is set and the top is lightly browned. Let cool 10 minutes before serving.

Nutrition:
- InfoCalories 246,Total Fat 14g,Total Carbs 18g,Protein 11g,Sodium 469mg.

Salmon & Quinoa Patties

Servings: 5
Cooking Time: 20 Minutes
Ingredients:
- 1 lb. salmon filets, skin removed
- 1 tbsp. olive oil
- Nonstick cooking spray
- 1 ½ cups quinoa, cooked
- 2 green onions, sliced
- ¼ cup fresh dill, chopped
- ¼ cup Greek yogurt
- 1 egg
- 1 tbsp. lemon juice
- 1 tsp Dijon mustard
- 1 tsp salt
- ½ tsp pepper

Directions:
1. Add the rack to the cooking pot and set to bake on 425°F (220°C).
2. Rub the salmon with oil and place in a baking pan. Place on the rack and add the tender-crisp lid. Bake 10 minutes. Remove from cooker and let cool 10-15 minutes.
3. Spray the fryer basket with cooking spray.
4. Add the salmon with the cooking juices to a large bowl. Add the remaining ingredients and mix well. Form into 10 patties.
5. Place the patties in the fryer basket, these will need to be cooked in 2 batches. Set to air fry on 350°F (175°C). Cook 10 minutes turning over halfway through cooking time. Serve.

Nutrition:
- InfoCalories 308,Total Fat 18g,Total Carbs 13g,Protein 23g,Sodium 470mg.

Mediterranean Cod

Servings: 4
Cooking Time: 20 Min
Ingredients:
- 4 fillets cod
- 1 bunch fresh thyme sprigs
- 1 pound cherry tomatoes, halved /450g
- 1 clove garlic, pressed
- 1 cup white rice /130g
- 2 cups water /500ml
- 1 cup Kalamata olives /130g
- 2 tbsp pickled capers /30g
- 1 tbsp olive oil; divided /15ml
- 1 tsp olive oil /15ml
- 1 pinch ground black pepper
- 3 pinches salt

Directions:
1. Line a parchment paper to the steamer basket of your Foodi. Place about half the tomatoes in a single layer on the paper. Sprinkle with thyme, reserving some for garnish. Arrange cod fillets on the top of tomatoes. Sprinkle with a little bit of olive oil.
2. Spread the garlic, pepper, salt, and remaining tomatoes over the fish. In the pot, mix rice and water. Lay a trivet over the rice and water. Lower steamer basket onto the trivet.
3. Seal the pressure lid, choose Pressure, set to High, and set the timer to 7 minutes. Press Start. When ready, release the pressure quickly.
4. Remove the steamer basket and trivet from the pot. Use a fork to fluff rice. Plate the fish fillets and apply a garnish of olives, reserved thyme, pepper, remaining olive oil, and capers. Serve with rice.

Clam Fritters

Servings: 4
Cooking Time: 10 Minutes
Ingredients:
- Nonstick cooking spray
- 1 1/3 cups flour
- 2 tsp baking powder
- 1 tsp Old Bay seasoning
- ¼ tsp cayenne pepper
- ¼ tsp salt
- ¼ tsp pepper
- 13 oz. clams, chopped
- 3 tbsp. clam juice
- 1 tbsp. lemon juice
- 2 eggs
- 1 ½ tbsp. chives, chopped
- 2 tbsp. milk

Directions:
1. Spray the fryer basket with cooking spray and add it to the cooking pot.
2. In a large bowl, combine flour, baking powder, Old Bay, cayenne pepper, salt, and pepper, mix well.
3. In a medium bowl, combine clams, clam juice, lemon juice, eggs, chives, and milk, mix well. Add the liquid ingredients to the dry ingredients and mix until combined.
4. Drop by spoonful into the fryer basket, don't over crowd them. Add the tender-crisp lid and set to air fry on 400°F (205°C). Cook 8-10 minutes until golden brown, turning over halfway through cooking time.

Nutrition:
- InfoCalories 276,Total Fat 4g,Total Carbs 37g,Protein 21g,Sodium 911mg.

Spicy "grilled" Catfish

Servings: 4
Cooking Time: 10 Minutes
Ingredients:
- Nonstick cooking spray
- 1 tbsp. fresh basil, chopped
- 1 tsp crushed red pepper flakes
- 1 tsp garlic powder
- ½ tsp salt
- ½ tsp pepper
- 4 catfish fillets
- 2 tbsp. olive oil

Directions:
1. Spray the rack with cooking spray and add to the cooking pot.
2. In a small bowl, combine all the spices and mix well.
3. Pat the fish dry with a paper towel. Rub both sides of the fish with the oil and coat with the seasoning mix.
4. Place the fish on the rack and add the tender-crisp lid. Set to roast on 350°F (175°C). Cook 7-9 minutes until fish flakes with a fork, turning over halfway through cooking time. Serve immediately.

Nutrition:
- InfoCalories 211,Total Fat 11g,Total Carbs 0g,Protein 26g,Sodium 359mg.

Sweet Sour Fish

Servings: 4
Cooking Time: 6 Minutes
Ingredients:
- 1-pound fish chunks
- 1 tablespoon vinegar
- 2 drops liquid stevia
- 1/4 cup butter
- Black pepper and salt to taste

Directions:
1. Select "Sauté" mode on your Ninja Foodi.
2. Stir in butter and melt it.
3. Add fish chunks, sauté for 3 minutes.
4. Stir in stevia, salt, pepper, stir it.
5. Close the crisping lid.
6. Cook on "Air Crisp" mode for 3 minutes to 360°F (180°C).
7. Serve and enjoy.

Nutrition:
- InfoCalories: 274g; Fat: 15g; Carbohydrates: 2g; Protein: 33g

Vegan & Vegetable

Okra Stew

Servings: 4
Cooking Time: 12 Minutes
Ingredients:
- 1-pound okra, trimmed
- 2 leeks, sliced
- Black pepper and salt to the taste
- 1 cup tomato sauce
- ¼ cup pine nuts, toasted
- 1 tablespoon cilantro, chopped

Directions:
1. In your Ninja Foodi, mix the okra with the leeks and the other ingredients except the cilantro.
2. Put the Ninja Foodi's lid on and cook on High for 12 minutes.
3. Release the pressure quickly for 5 minutes, divide the okra mix into bowls and serve with the cilantro sprinkled on top.

Nutrition:
- InfoCalories: 146; Fat: 3g; Carbohydrates: 4g; Protein: 3g

Pineapple Appetizer Ribs

Servings: 4
Cooking Time: 30 Min
Ingredients:
- 2 lb. cut spareribs /900g
- 2 cups water /500ml
- 5 oz. canned pineapple juice /150ml
- 7 oz. salad dressing /210g
- Garlic salt
- Salt and black pepper

Directions:
1. Sprinkle the ribs with salt and pepper and place them in a saucepan. Pour water and cook the ribs for around 12 minutes on high heat. Drain the ribs and arrange them in the Ninja Foodi.
2. Sprinkle with garlic salt. Close the crisping lid and cook for 15 minutes at 390 °F or 200°C on Air Crisp mode.
3. Meanwhile, prepare the sauce by combining the salad dressing and the pineapple juice. Serve the ribs with this delicious dressing sauce!

Balsamic Cabbage With Endives

Servings: 4
Cooking Time: 15 Minutes
Ingredients:
- 1 green cabbage head, shredded
- 2 endives, trimmed and sliced lengthwise
- Black pepper and salt to the taste
- 1 tablespoon olive oil
- 2 shallots, chopped
- ½ cup chicken stock
- 1 tablespoon sweet paprika
- 1 tablespoon balsamic vinegar

Directions:
1. Set the Foodi on Sauté mode, stir in the oil, heat it up, add the shallots and sauté for 2 minutes.
2. Add the cabbage, the endives and the other ingredients.
3. Put the Ninja Foodi's lid on and cook on High for 13 minutes.
4. Release the pressure quickly for 5 minutes, divide the mix between plates and serve.

Nutrition:
- InfoCalories: 120; Fat: 2g; Carbohydrates: 3.3g; Protein: 4

Veggie Potpie

Servings: 6
Cooking Time: 22 Minutes
Ingredients:
- Find Ginnie at Hellolittlehome.com
- 4 tablespoons unsalted butter
- ½ large onion, diced
- 1½ cups diced carrot
- 1½ cups diced celery
- 2 garlic cloves, minced
- 3 cups red potatoes, diced
- 1 cup vegetable broth
- ½ cup frozen peas
- ½ cup frozen corn
- 1 tablespoon chopped fresh Italian parsley
- 2 teaspoons fresh thyme leaves
- ¼ cup all-purpose flour
- ½ cup heavy (whipping) cream
- Salt
- Freshly ground black pepper
- 1 prepared piecrust

Directions:
1. Select SEAR/SAUTÉ and set temperature to MD:HI. Set the time to 5 minutes to preheat. Select START/STOP to begin.
2. Add the butter to the pot to melt. Add the onion, carrot, and celery to the melted butter. Sauté for about 3 minutes until softened.
3. Stir in the garlic and cook, stirring constantly, for about 30 seconds until fragrant. Select START/STOP to end the function.
4. Add the potatoes and vegetable broth to pot and stir to combine.
5. Assemble the pressure lid, making sure the pressure release valve is in the SEAL position.
6. Select PRESSURE and set to HI. Set the time to 5 minutes. Select START/STOP to begin.
7. When pressure cooking is complete, quick release the pressure by turning the pressure release valve to the VENT position. Carefully remove the lid when the unit has finished releasing pressure.
8. Add the peas, corn, parsley, and thyme to the pot. Season with salt and pepper. Sprinkle the flour over the top and stir to mix well. Stir in the heavy cream.
9. Select SEAR/SAUTÉ and set temperature to MD:HI. Select START/STOP to begin. Cook for 2 to 3 minutes, stirring constantly, until the sauce thickens and is hot. Select START/STOP to end the function.
10. Place the piecrust over the vegetable mixture. Fold over the edges of the crust to fit the pot. Make a small slit in the center of the crust for steam to release. Close the crisping lid.
11. Select BROIL. Set the time to 10 minutes. Select START/STOP to begin.

Ninja Foodi Cookbook Guide

12. After the cooking is complete, carefully transfer the inner pot to a heat-proof surface. Let the potpie sit for 10 minutes before serving.

Nutrition:
- InfoCalories: 361,Total Fat: 22g,Sodium: 339mg,Carbohydrates: 36g,Protein: 6g.

Southern Pineapple Casserole

Servings: 8
Cooking Time: 35 Minutes
Ingredients:
- Nonstick cooking spray
- 1/3 cup butter, soft
- 1/4 cup Stevia
- 2 eggs
- 2 egg whites
- 1 tsp vanilla
- 2 tbsp. flour
- 20 oz. crushed pineapple in juice, drained; reserve 1 cup liquid
- 5 slices whole-wheat bread, cubed

Directions:
1. Spray the cooking pot with cooking spray.
2. In a large bowl, beat butter and Stevia until smooth and creamy.
3. Beat in eggs, egg whites, and vanilla until combined.
4. Stir in flour, pineapple, and reserved juice and mix well.
5. Add bread and toss to coat. Pour into cooking pot.
6. Add tender-crisp lid and set to bake on 350°F (175°C). Bake 30-35 minutes or until a knife inserted in center comes out clean. Serve warm.

Nutrition:
- InfoCalories 191,Total Fat 10g,Total Carbs 29g,Protein 5g,Sodium 183mg.

Palak Paneer

Servings: 4
Cooking Time: 20 Min
Ingredients:
- 1 pound spinach; chopped /450g
- 1 tomato; chopped
- 2 cups paneer; cubed /260g
- 1 cup water /250ml
- ¼ cup milk /62.5ml
- 2 tbsp butter /30g
- 1 tsp minced fresh ginger /5g
- 1 tsp minced fresh garlic /5g
- 1 red onion; chopped
- 1 tsp cumin seeds /5g
- 1 tsp coriander seeds /5g
- 1 tsp salt, or to taste /5g
- 1 tsp chilli powder/5g

Directions:
1. Warm butter on Sear/Sauté, set to Medium High, and choose Start/Stop to preheat the pot. Press Start.
2. Add in garlic, cumin seeds, coriander seeds, chilli powder, ginger, and garlic and fry for 1 minute until fragrant; add onion and cook for 2 more minutes until crispy. Add in salt, water and chopped spinach.
3. Seal the pressure lid, choose Pressure, set to High, and set the timer to 1 minute. Press Start.
4. When ready, release the pressure quickly. Add spinach mixture to a blender and blend to obtain a smooth paste. Mix paneer and tomato with spinach mixture.

Italian Spinach & Tomato Soup

Servings: 6
Cooking Time: 4 Hours
Ingredients:
- 1 tsp olive oil
- 1 onion, chopped
- 3 cloves garlic, chopped fine
- 3 large tomatoes, chopped
- 2 tsp Italian seasoning
- 28 oz. vegetable broth, low sodium
- 10 oz. fresh spinach, trimmed
- ½ tsp pepper
- 2 tbsp. parmesan cheese

Directions:
1. Add the oil to the cooking pot and set to sauté on med-high.
2. Add the onion and garlic and cook, stirring occasionally, 5 minutes or until onion starts to brown.
3. Stir in remaining ingredients, except spinach and parmesan, and mix well. Add the lid and set to slow cook on high. Cook 3-4 hours until tomatoes are tender. Stir occasionally.
4. Add the spinach and cook until it wilts. Ladle into bowls and sprinkle with parmesan. Serve.

Nutrition:
- InfoCalories 60,Total Fat 2g,Total Carbs 10g,Protein 3g,Sodium 602mg.

Cheesy Green Beans With Nuts

Servings: 6
Cooking Time: 15 Min
Ingredients:
- 2 pounds green beans, trimmed /900g
- 1 cup chopped toasted pine nuts /130g
- 1 cup feta cheese, crumbled /130g
- 1½ cups water /375ml
- Juice from 1 lemon
- 6 tbsp olive oil /90ml
- ½ tsp salt /2.5g
- freshly ground black pepper to taste

Directions:
1. Add water to the pot. Set the reversible rack over the water. Loosely heap green beans into the reversible rack.
2. Seal lid and cook on High Pressure for 5 minutes. Press Start. When the cooking cycle is complete, When ready, release pressure quickly. Drop green beans into a salad bowl; top with the olive oil, feta cheese, pepper, and pine nuts.

Cauliflower Cakes

Servings: 6
Cooking Time: 15 Minutes
Ingredients:
- 1 cup water
- 1 head cauliflower, cut in florets
- ¼ cup onion, chopped
- ½ cup cheddar cheese, low fat, grated
- ½ cup panko bread crumbs

Ninja Foodi Cookbook Guide

- 2 eggs, lightly beaten
- ½ tsp salt
- ¼ tsp cayenne pepper
- Nonstick cooking spray

Directions:
1. Add water, cauliflower and onion to the cooking pot. Add the lid and set to pressure cook on high. Set the timer for 6 minutes. When the timer goes off, use quick release to remove the pressure. Drain and add the vegetables to a large bowl.
2. Mash the cauliflower with an electric mixer beating until smooth.
3. Stir in remaining ingredients. Form into 12 patties.
4. Spray the fryer basket with cooking spray. Place the patties in a single layer in the basket. Add the tender-crisp lid and set to air fry on 375°F (190°C). Cook cauliflower 4-5 minutes per side until golden brown. Serve immediately.

Nutrition:
- InfoCalories 102, Total Fat 3g, Total Carbs 12g, Protein 8g, Sodium 395mg.

Hearty Veggie Soup

Servings: 12
Cooking Time: 15 Minutes
Ingredients:
- 2 cups water
- 3 ½ cups vegetable broth, low sodium
- 15 oz. red kidney beans, drained & rinsed
- 16 oz. cannellini beans, drained & rinsed
- 28 oz. tomatoes, crushed
- 10 oz. spinach, chopped
- 1 onion, chopped
- 10 oz. mixed vegetables, frozen
- 1 tsp garlic powder
- ½ tsp pepper
- 1 cup elbow macaroni

Directions:
1. Set the cooker to sauté on med-high heat.
2. Add all the ingredients, except macaroni, and stir to combine. Bring to a boil.
3. Stir in macaroni. Add the lid and set to pressure cook on high. Set timer for 10 minutes. When timer goes off, use natural release to remove the pressure. Stir well and serve.

Nutrition:
- InfoCalories 181, Total Fat 1g, Total Carbs 34g, Protein 10g, Sodium 478mg.

Creamy Carrot Soup

Servings: 4
Cooking Time: 15 Minutes
Ingredients:
- 3 ½ cups chicken broth, low sodium
- 5 carrots, peeled & cut in 1-inch pieces
- 1 large parsnip, peeled & cut in 1-inch pieces
- 1 potato, peeled & cut in 1-inch pieces
- 1 onion, chopped
- 2 ½ cups skim milk
- ¼ tsp thyme
- ¼ tsp pepper

Directions:
1. Add the broth, carrots, parsnip, potato, and onion to the cooking pot and toss to mix.
2. Add the lid and set to pressure cook on high. Set the timer for 8 minutes. When timer goes off, use natural release to remove the pressure.
3. Use an immersion blender to process the vegetables until almost smooth.
4. Set to sauté on medium heat. Stir in remaining ingredients and cook 6-8 minutes or until heated through. Ladle into bowls and serve.

Nutrition:
- InfoCalories 226, Total Fat 2g, Total Carbs 42g, Protein 13g, Sodium 206mg.

Cheese And Mushroom Tarts

Servings: 4
Cooking Time: 75 Min
Ingredients:
- 1 small white onion; sliced
- 1 sheet puff pastry, thawed
- 5 ounces oyster mushrooms; sliced /150g
- 1 cup shredded Swiss cheese /130g
- ¼ cup dry white wine /62.5ml
- 1 tbsp thinly sliced fresh green onions /15ml
- 2 tbsps melted butter; divided /30ml
- ¼ tsp salt /1.25g
- ¼ tsp freshly ground black pepper /1.25g

Directions:
1. Choose Sear/Sauté, set to High, and set the time to 5 minutes. Choose Start/Stop to preheat the pot. Add 1 tbsp of butter, the onion, and mushrooms to the pot. Sauté for 5 minutes or until the vegetables are tender and browned.
2. Season with salt and black pepper, pour in the white wine, and cook until evaporated, about 2 minutes. Spoon the vegetables into a bowl and set aside.
3. Unwrap the puff pastry and cut into 4 squares. Pierce the dough with a fork and brush both sides with the remaining oil. Share half of the cheese evenly over the puff pastry squares, leaving a ½- inch border around the edges. Also, share the mushroom mixture over the pastry squares and top with the remaining cheese.
4. Put the Crisping Basket in the pot. Close the crisping lid, choose Air Crisp, set the temperature to 400°F (205°C), and the time to 5 minutes.
5. Once the pot has preheated, put 1 tart in the Crisping Basket. Close the crisping lid, choose Air Crisp, set the temperature to 360°F or 180°C, and set the time to 6 minutes; press Start.
6. After 6 minutes, check the tart for your preferred brownness. Take the tart out of the basket and transfer to a plate. Repeat the process with the remaining tarts. Garnish with the green onions and serve.

Colorful Vegetable Medley

Servings: 4
Cooking Time: 15 Min
Ingredients:
- 16 asparagus, trimmed
- 1 small head broccoli, broken into florets
- 1 small head cauliflower, broken into florets
- 5 ounces green beans /150g
- 2 carrots, peeled and cut on bias into 1/4-inch rounds
- 1 cup water /250ml
- salt to taste

Directions:

Ninja Foodi Cookbook Guide

1. Into the pot, add water and set trivet on top of water and place steamer basket on top of the trivet. In an even layer, spread green beans, broccoli, cauliflower, asparagus, and carrots in the steamer basket.
2. Seal the pressure lid, choose Pressure, set to High, and set the timer to 3 minutes on High. When ready, release the pressure quickly. Remove steamer basket from cooker and add salt to vegetables for seasoning. Serve immediately.

Pomegranate Radish Mix

Servings: 4
Cooking Time: 8 Minutes
Ingredients:
- 1-pound radishes, roughly cubed
- Black pepper and salt to the taste
- 2 garlic cloves, minced
- ½ cup chicken stock
- 2 tablespoons pomegranate juice
- ¼ cup pomegranate seeds

Directions:
1. In your Ninja Foodi, combine the radishes with the stock and the other ingredients.
2. Put the Ninja Foodi's lid on and cook on High for 8 minutes.
3. Release the pressure quickly for 5 minutes, divide everything between plates and serve.

Nutrition:
- InfoCalories: 133; Fat: 2.3g; Carbohydrates: 2.4g; Protein: 2g

Cheese Crusted Carrot Casserole

Servings: 6
Cooking Time: 40 Minutes
Ingredients:
- 1 ¼ lb. carrots, sliced
- Nonstick cooking spray
- ½ cup light mayonnaise
- ¼ cup onion, chopped fine
- 1 tsp horseradish
- ¼ cup cheddar cheese, reduced fat, grated
- 1 tbsp. whole wheat bread crumbs

Directions:
1. Add the carrots to the cooking pot with enough water to cover them. Set to sauté on high and bring to a boil. Reduce heat to med-low and simmer 7-9 minutes until carrots are tender-crisp. Drain.
2. Spray the cooking pot with cooking spray.
3. In a small bowl, combine mayonnaise, onion, and horseradish, mix well.
4. Return carrots to the cooking pot and spread mayonnaise mixture over the top. Sprinkle the cheese and bread crumbs over the top.
5. Add the tender-crisp lid and set to bake on 350°F (175°C). Bake 25-30 minutes until top is golden brown. Serve.

Nutrition:
- InfoCalories 121, Total Fat 7g, Total Carbs 12g, Protein 2g, Sodium 245mg.

Burrito Bowls

Servings: 4
Cooking Time: 30 Min
Ingredients:
- 1 can diced tomatoes /435g
- 1 can black beans, drained and rinsed /435g
- 1 ½ cups vegetable stock /375ml
- 1 cup frozen corn kernels /130g
- 1 cup quinoa, rinsed /130g
- 1 avocado; sliced
- 1 onion
- 2 garlic cloves, minced
- 2 tbsp chopped cilantro /30g
- 1 tbsp roughly chopped fresh coriander /15g
- 2 tbsp olive oil /30ml
- 1 tbsp chili powder /15g
- 2 tsp ground cumin /10g
- 2 tsp paprika /10g
- 1 tsp salt /5g
- ½ tsp black pepper /2.5g
- ¼ tsp cayenne pepper /1.25g
- Cheddar cheese, grated for garnish

Directions:
1. Warm oil on Sear/Sauté. Add in onion and cook for 3 to 5 minutes until fragrant. Add garlic and cook for 2 more minutes until soft and golden brown. Add in chili powder, paprika, cayenne pepper, salt, cumin, and black pepper and cook for 1 minute until spices are soft.
2. Pour quinoa into onion and spice mixture and stir to coat quinoa completely in spices. Add diced tomatoes, black beans, vegetable stock, and corn; stir to combine.
3. Seal the pressure lid, choose Pressure, set to High, and set the timer to 7 minutes. Press Start. When ready, release the pressure quickly. Open the lid and let sit for 6 minutes until flavors combine. Use a fork to fluff quinoa and season with pepper and salt if desired.
4. Into quinoa and beans mixture, stir in cilantro and divide among plates. Top with cheese and avocado slices.

Sesame Radish

Servings: 4
Cooking Time: 15 Minutes
Ingredients:
- 2 leeks, sliced
- ½ pound radishes, sliced
- 2 scallions, chopped
- 2 tablespoons black sesame seeds
- 1/3 cup chicken stock
- 1 tablespoon ginger, grated
- 1 tablespoon chives, minced

Directions:
1. In your Ninja Foodi, combine the leeks with the radishes and the other ingredients.
2. Put the Ninja Foodi's lid on and cook on High for 15 minutes more.
3. Release the pressure quickly for 5 minutes, divide everything between plates and serve.

Nutrition:
- InfoCalories: 112; Fat: 2g; Carbohydrates: 4.2g; Protein: 2g

Radish Apples Salad

Servings: 4
Cooking Time: 15 Minutes
Ingredients:
- 1-pound radishes, roughly cubed
- 2 apples, cored and cut into wedges
- ¼ cup chicken stock
- 2 spring onions, chopped
- 3 tablespoons tomato paste
- Juice of 1 lime
- Cooking spray
- 1 tablespoon cilantro, chopped

Directions:
1. In your Ninja Foodi, combine the radishes with the apples and the other ingredients.
2. Put the Ninja Foodi's lid on and cook on High for 15 minutes.
3. Release the pressure quickly for 5 minutes, divide everything between plates and serve.

Nutrition:
- InfoCalories: 122; Fat: 5g; Carbohydrates: 4.5g; Protein: 3g

Stuffed Summer Squash

Servings: 4
Cooking Time: 25 Minutes
Ingredients:
- 2 yellow squash, halved lengthwise & seeded
- 1 cup brown rice, cooked
- 2 tbsp. liquid egg substitute
- 2 tbsp. parmesan cheese, divided
- ½ tsp onion powder
- 2 tsp fresh parsley, chopped
- ¼ tsp pepper
- Nonstick cooking spray

Directions:
1. Add enough water to cover ½ inch up the sides of the cooking pot. Add the squash.
2. Add the lid and set to pressure cook on high. Set timer for 5 minutes. When timer goes off, use manual release to remove the pressure. Drain.
3. In a small bowl, combine rice, egg substitute, 1 tablespoon parmesan, parsley, onion powder, and pepper and mix well.
4. Place squash, cut side up, in the cooking pot. Divide the rice mixture evenly between the squash halves. Sprinkle remaining cheese over the top. Spray lightly with cooking spray.
5. Add the tender-crisp lid and set to bake on 350°F (175°C). Bake 15-20 minutes until cheese is melted and starting to brown. Serve.

Nutrition:
- InfoCalories 84,Total Fat 1g,Total Carbs 15g,Protein 3g,Sodium 66mg.

Cabbage With Carrots

Servings: 4
Cooking Time: 20 Minutes
Ingredients:
- 1 Napa cabbage, shredded
- 2 carrots, sliced
- 2 tablespoons olive oil
- 1 red onion, chopped
- Black pepper and salt to the taste
- 2 tablespoons sweet paprika
- ½ cup tomato sauce

Directions:
1. Set the Foodi on Sauté mode, stir in the oil, heat it up, add the onion and sauté for 5 minutes.
2. Add the carrots, the cabbage and the other ingredients, toss.
3. Put the Ninja Foodi's lid on and cook on High for 15 minutes.
4. Release the pressure quickly for 5 minutes, divide everything between plates and serve.

Nutrition:
- InfoCalories: 140; Fat: 3.4g; Carbohydrates: 1.2g; Protein: 3.5 g

Hot & Sour Soup

Servings: 5
Cooking Time: 20 Minutes
Ingredients:
- 3 ½ cups chicken broth, low sodium, divided
- ½ lb. firm tofu, cut in 1-inch cubes
- ¼ lb. mushrooms, sliced
- 3 tbsp. soy sauce, low sodium
- 3 tbsp. vinegar
- 1 tsp ginger
- ½ tsp pepper
- 2 tbsp. cornstarch
- 1 egg, lightly beaten
- ½ cup fresh bean sprouts
- ½ tsp sesame oil

Directions:
1. Add 3 ¼ cups broth, tofu, mushrooms, soy sauce, vinegar, ginger, and pepper to the cooking pot and stir well.
2. Set to sauté on medium heat and bring to a boil.
3. In a small bowl, whisk together remaining broth and cornstarch until smooth. Reduce heat to low and whisk in cornstarch mixture until thickened.
4. Slowly stir in egg to form egg "ribbons". Add bean sprouts and simmer 1-2 minutes or until heated through. Stir in sesame oil and serve immediately.
5. Slowly stir in egg to form egg strands. Add bean sprouts and simmer 1 to 2 minutes, or until heated through, stirring occasionally.

Nutrition:
- InfoCalories 123,Total Fat 6g,Total Carbs 8g,Protein 11g,Sodium 978mg.

Cheesy Baked Spinach

Servings: 8
Cooking Time: 30 Minutes
Ingredients:
- Nonstick cooking spray
- 15 oz. spinach, thawed, chopped & drained well
- 1 cup wild rice, cooked
- 1 ½ cup cheddar cheese, reduced fat, grated
- 10 ½ oz. cream of mushroom soup, low fat
- 1 tbsp. butter, melted
- 1 tsp onion powder
- ¼ tsp nutmeg

Directions:
1. Place the rack in the cooking pot. Spray a casserole dish with cooking spray.

2. In a large bowl, combine all ingredients and mix well. Spoon into prepared dish and place on the rack.
3. Add the tender-crisp lid and set to bake on 350°F (175°C). Bake 30 minutes or until heated through. Serve.
Nutrition:
- InfoCalories 113,Total Fat 5g,Total Carbs 10g,Protein 8g,Sodium 492mg.

Zucchinis Spinach Fry

Servings: 4
Cooking Time: 17 Minutes
Ingredients:
- 2 zucchinis, sliced
- 1-pound baby spinach
- ½ cup tomato sauce
- Black pepper and salt
- 1 tablespoon avocado oil
- 1 red onion, chopped
- 1 tablespoon sweet paprika
- ½ teaspoon garlic powder
- ½ teaspoon chilli powder

Directions:
1. Set the Foodi on Sauté, stir in the oil, heat it up, add the onion and sauté for 2 minutes.
2. Add the zucchinis, spinach, and the other ingredients Put the Ninja Foodi's lid on and cook on High for 15 minutes.
3. Release the pressure quickly for 5 minutes, divide everything between plates and serve.
Nutrition:
- InfoCalories: 130; Fat: 5.5g; Carbohydrates: 3.3g; Protein: 1g

Paneer Cutlet

Servings: 1
Cooking Time: 15 Min
Ingredients:
- 1 small onion, finely chopped
- 2 cup grated paneer /260g
- 1 cup grated cheese /130g
- ½ tsp chai masala /2.5g
- 1 tsp butter /5g
- ½ tsp garlic powder /2.5g
- ½ tsp oregano /2.5g
- ½ tsp salt /2.5g

Directions:
1. Preheat the Ninja Foodi to 350 °F or 175°C. Oil the Ninja Foodi basket. Mix all Ingredients in a bowl, until well incorporated.
2. Make cutlets out of the mixture and place them on the greased baking dish. Place the baking dish in the Ninja Foodi and cook the cutlets for 10 minutes.

Asparagus With Feta

Servings: 4
Cooking Time: 15 Min
Ingredients:
- 1-pound asparagus spears, ends trimmed /450g
- 1 lemon, cut into wedges
- 1 cup feta cheese; cubed /130g
- 1 cup water /250ml
- 1 tbsp olive oil /15ml
- salt and freshly ground black pepper to taste

Directions:
1. Into the pot, add water and set trivet over the water. Place steamer basket on the trivet. Place the asparagus into the steamer basket. Seal the pressure lid, choose Pressure, set to High, and set the timer to 1 minute. Press Start.
2. When ready, release the pressure quickly. Add olive oil in a bowl and toss in asparagus until well coated; season with pepper and salt. Serve alongside feta cheese and lemon wedges.

Quinoa Stuffed Butternut Squash

Servings:4
Cooking Time: 13 Minutes
Ingredients:
- 2 tablespoons extra-virgin olive oil
- 1 tablespoon minced garlic
- 1 small shallot, minced
- Kosher salt
- Freshly ground black pepper
- ½ cup dried cranberries
- 1 cup tri-colored quinoa
- 2¾ cups water, divided
- 2 cups roughly chopped kale
- 1 small butternut squash, top trimmed, halved lengthwise
- 1 tablespoon freshly squeezed orange juice
- Zest of 1 orange
- 1 jar pine nuts
- 1 can chickpeas, rinsed and drained

Directions:
1. Select SEAR/SAUTÉ and set to HI. Select START/STOP to begin. Let preheat for 5 minutes.
2. Add the olive oil, garlic, shallot, salt, and pepper. Cook until garlic and shallot have softened and turned golden brown, about 2 minutes.
3. Stir in the cranberries, quinoa, and 1¼ cups of water. Assemble pressure lid, making sure the pressure release valve is in the SEAL position.
4. Select PRESSURE and set to HI. Set time to 2 minutes. Select START/STOP to begin.
5. When pressure cooking is complete, allow pressure to naturally release for 10 minutes. After 10 minutes, quick release remaining pressure by turning the pressure release valve to the VENT position. Carefully remove lid when the unit has finished releasing pressure.
6. Place the quinoa in a large bowl. Stir in the kale. Cover the bowl with aluminum foil and set aside.
7. Pour the remaining 1½ cups of water into the pot. Place the butternut squash cut-side up on the Reversible Rack, then lower it into the pot. Assemble pressure lid, making sure the pressure release valve is in the SEAL position.
8. Select PRESSURE and set to HI. Set the time to 8 minutes. Select START/STOP to begin.
9. Mix the orange juice, orange zest, pine nuts, and chickpeas into the quinoa mixture.
10. When pressure cooking is complete, quick release the pressure by turning the pressure release valve to the VENT position. Carefully remove lid when unit has finished releasing pressure.
11. Carefully remove rack from pot. Using a spoon slightly hollow out the squash. Spoon the quinoa mixture into the squash. Cut in half and serve.
Nutrition:
- InfoCalories: 563,Total Fat: 21g,Sodium: 66mg,Carbohydrates: 83g,Protein: 16g.

Cauliflower Enchiladas

Servings: 5
Cooking Time: 25 Minutes
Ingredients:
- 2 tablespoons canola oil
- 1 large head cauliflower, cut into 1-inch florets
- 2 teaspoons ground cumin
- 1 teaspoon ground chili pepper
- 2 teaspoons kosher salt
- ½ teaspoon freshly ground black pepper
- 1 can diced tomatoes, drained
- 5 flour tortillas
- 1 can red enchilada sauce
- 1½ cups shredded Mexican blend cheese
- ½ cup chopped cilantro, for garnish

Directions:
1. In a medium bowl, toss together the oil, cauliflower, cumin, chili pepper, salt, and black pepper. Place the cauliflower in the Cook & Crisp Basket and place the basket in pot. Close crisping lid.
2. Select AIR CRISP, set temperature to 390°F (200°C), and set time to 15 minutes. Select START/STOP to begin.
3. After 8 minutes, open lid, then lift the basket and shake the cauliflower. Lower basket back into pot and close lid. Continue cooking, until the cauliflower reaches your desired crispiness.
4. When cooking is complete, remove basket from pot. Place the cauliflower in a bowl and mix with the tomatoes.
5. Lay the tortillas on a work surface. Divide the cauliflower-
6. tomato mixture between the tortillas and roll them up. Place the filled tortillas seam-side down in the pot. Pour the enchilada sauce on top.
7. Close crisping lid. Select BROIL and set time to 10 minutes. Select START/STOP to begin.
8. After 5 minutes, open lid and add the cheese on top. Close lid and continue cooking until cheese is golden brown.
9. When cooking is complete, add cilantro and serve.

Nutrition:
- InfoCalories: 315, Total Fat: 19g, Sodium: 822mg, Carbohydrates: 28g, Protein: 13g.

Cauliflower Chunks With Lemon Sauce

Servings: 4
Cooking Time: 15 Minutes
Ingredients:
- 1-pound cauliflower, cut into chunks
- 1 tablespoon dill, chopped
- 1 tablespoon lemon zest, grated
- Juice of ½ lemon
- 2 tablespoons butter, melted
- Black pepper and salt to the taste

Directions:
1. Set the Foodi on Sauté mode, stir in the butter, melt it, add the cauliflower chunks and brown for 5 minutes.
2. Add the lemon zest and the other ingredients set the machine on Air Crisp and cook at 390 °F (200°C) for 10 minutes.
3. Divide everything between plates and serve.

Nutrition:
- InfoCalories: 122; Fat: 3.3g; Carbohydrates: 3g; Protein: 2g

Potato Filled Bread Rolls

Servings: 4
Cooking Time: 25 Min
Ingredients:
- 8 slices of bread
- 2 green chilies, deseeded; chopped
- 5 large potatoes, boiled, mashed
- 2 sprigs curry leaf
- 1 medium onion; chopped
- 1 tbsp olive oil /15ml
- ½ tsp mustard seeds /2.5g
- ½ tsp turmeric /2.5g
- Salt, to taste

Directions:
1. Combine the olive oil, onion, curry leaves, and mustard seed, in the Ninja Foodi basket. Cook for 5 minutes. Mix the onion mixture with the mashed potatoes, chilies, turmeric, and some salt. Divide the dough into 8 equal pieces.
2. Trim the sides of the bread, and wet it with some water. Make sure to get rid of the excess water. Take one wet bread slice in your palm and place one of the potato pieces in the center.
3. Roll the bread over the filling, sealing the edges. Place the rolls onto a prepared baking dish, close the crisping lid and cook for 12 minutes on Air Crisp at 350 °F or 175°C.

Minestrone With Pancetta

Servings: 6
Cooking Time: 40 Min
Ingredients:
- 2 ounces pancetta; chopped /60g
- 1 can diced tomatoes/450g
- 1 can chickpeas, rinsed and drained /450g
- 1 onion; diced
- 1 parsnip, peeled and chopped
- 2 carrots, peeled and sliced into rounds
- 2 celery stalks,
- 2 garlic cloves, minced
- 6 cups chicken broth /1500ml
- ½ cup grated Parmesan cheese/65g
- 2 cups green beans, trimmed and chopped /260g
- 1½ cups small shaped pasta /195g
- 1 tbsp dried basil/ 15g
- 1 tbsp dried oregano/15g
- 2 tbsp olive oil /30ml
- 1 tbsp dried thyme /15g
- salt and ground black pepper to taste

Directions:
1. Warm oil on Sear/Sauté. Add onion, carrots, garlic, pancetta, celery, and parsnip, and cook for 5 minutes until they become soft.
2. Stir in basil, oregano, green beans, broth, tomatoes, pepper, salt, thyme, vegetable broth, chickpeas, and pasta.
3. Seal the pressure lid, choose Pressure, set to High, and set the timer to 6 minutes. Press Start.
4. Release pressure naturally for 10 minutes then release the remaining pressure quickly. Ladle the soup into bowls and serve garnished with grated parmesan cheese.

Ninja Foodi Cookbook Guide

Eggplant Lasagna

Servings: 4
Cooking Time: 25 Min
Ingredients:
- 3 large eggplants; sliced in uniform ¼ inches
- ¼ cup Parmesan cheese, grated /32.5g
- 4 ¼ cups Marinara sauce /1062.5ml
- 1 ½ cups shredded Mozzarella cheese /195g
- Cooking spray
- Chopped fresh basil to garnish

Directions:
1. Open the pot and grease it with cooking spray. Arrange the eggplant slices in a single layer on the bottom of the pot and sprinkle some cheese all over it.
2. Arrange another layer of eggplant slices on the cheese, sprinkle this layer with cheese also, and repeat the layering of eggplant and cheese until both Ingredients are exhausted.
3. Lightly spray the eggplant with cooking spray and pour the marinara sauce all over it. Close the lid and pressure valve, and select Pressure mode on High pressure for 8 minutes. Press Start/Stop.
4. Once the timer has stopped, do a quick pressure release, and open the lid. Sprinkle with grated parmesan cheese, close the crisping lid and cook for 10 minutes on Bake/Roast mode on 380 °F or 195°C.
5. With two napkins in hand, gently remove the inner pot. Allow cooling for 10 minutes before serving. Garnish the lasagna with basil and serve warm as a side dish.

Creamy Polenta & Mushrooms

Servings: 2
Cooking Time: 40 Minutes
Ingredients:
- 3 tbsp. olive oil
- 1 lb. assorted mushrooms, rinsed & chopped
- 1 clove garlic, chopped fine
- 1 tsp salt, divided
- 3/8 tsp pepper, divided
- 2 ½ cups water, divided
- 3 tbsp. butter
- 1 ½ tbsp. fresh lemon juice
- 1 tbsp. fresh parsley, chopped
- ½ cup stone-ground white grits
- 1/8 cup heavy cream
- 3 tbsp. parmesan cheese, grated, divided
- ¼ cup mascarpone

Directions:
1. Add oil to the cooking pot and set to sauté on medium heat.
2. Add mushrooms, garlic, ½ teaspoon salt, and ¼ teaspoon pepper and cook, stirring occasionally, until mushrooms are nicely browned and liquid has evaporated, about 6-8 minutes.
3. Add ¼ cup water, butter, lemon juice, and parsley and cook, stirring, until butter melts. Cook 1-2 minutes. Transfer to a large bowl and keep warm.
4. Add the remaining water to the pot and increase heat to med-high. Bring just to a boil.
5. Whisk in grits slowly until combined. Reduce heat to med-low and simmer, stirring occasionally, about 30 minutes, or until liquid is absorbed. Turn off the heat.
6. Stir in cream, 1 tablespoon cheese, and remaining salt and pepper and mix well. Ladle polenta onto serving plates. Top with mushrooms, mascarpone, and remaining parmesan cheese. Serve immediately.

Nutrition:
- InfoCalories 102,Total Fat 7g,Total Carbs 8g,Protein 2g,Sodium 215mg.

Eggplant With Kale

Servings: 4
Cooking Time: 15 Minutes
Ingredients:
- Juice of 1 lime
- 1-pound eggplant, roughly cubed
- 1 cup kale, torn
- A pinch of black pepper and salt
- ½ teaspoon chilli powder
- ½ cup chicken stock
- 3 tablespoons olive oil

Directions:
1. Set the Foodi on Sauté mode, stir in the oil, heat it up, add the eggplant and sauté for 2 minutes.
2. Stir in the kale and the rest of the ingredients.
3. Put the Ninja Foodi's lid on and cook on and cook on High for 13 minutes.
4. Release the pressure quickly for 5 minutes, divide the mix between plates and serve.

Nutrition:
- InfoCalories: 110; Fat: 3g; Carbohydrates: 4.3g; Protein: 1.1g

Broccoli Cauliflower

Servings: 4
Cooking Time: 15 Minutes
Ingredients:
- 2 cups broccoli florets
- 1 cup cauliflower florets
- 2 tablespoons lime juice
- 1 tablespoon avocado oil
- 1/3 cup tomato sauce
- 2 teaspoons ginger, grated
- 2 teaspoons garlic, minced
- 1 tablespoon chives, chopped

Directions:
1. Set the Foodi on Sauté mode, stir in the oil, heat it up, add the garlic and the ginger and sauté for 2 minutes.
2. Stir in the broccoli, cauliflower and the rest of the ingredients.
3. Put the Ninja Foodi's lid on and cook on High for 13 minutes.
4. naturally Release the pressure for 10 minutes, divide everything between plates and serve.

Nutrition:
- InfoCalories: 118; Fat: 1.5g; Carbohydrates: 4.3g; Protein: 6g

Beets And Carrots

Servings: 4
Cooking Time: 20 Minutes
Ingredients:
- 1-pound beets, peeled and roughly cubed
- 1-pound baby carrots, peeled
- Black pepper and salt to the taste
- 2 tablespoons olive oil

- 1 tablespoon chives, minced

Directions:
1. In a suitable, mix the beets with the carrots and the other ingredients and toss.
2. Put the beets and carrots in the Foodi's basket.
3. Cook on Air Crisp at 390 °F (200°C) for 20 minutes, divide between plates and serve.

Nutrition:
- InfoCalories: 150; Fat: 4.5g; Carbohydrates: 7.3g; Protein: 3.6g

Quick Indian-style Curry

Servings: 8
Cooking Time: 35 Minutes

Ingredients:
- 1 tablespoon vegetable oil
- 1 small onion, diced
- 1 small bell pepper, diced
- 1 large potato, cut into 1-inch cubes
- 1 teaspoon ground turmeric
- 1 teaspoon cumin seeds
- 1 teaspoon ground cumin
- 1 teaspoon garam masala (optional)
- 1 teaspoon curry powder
- 1 jar curry sauce, plus 1 jar water
- 1 can diced tomatoes
- 1 cup dried red lentils
- 8 ounces paneer, cubed (optional)
- 1 cup fresh cilantro, roughly chopped (optional)
- Salt
- Freshly ground black pepper

Directions:
1. Select SEAR/SAUTÉ and set temperature to HI. Select START/STOP to begin and allow to preheat for 5 minutes.
2. Add the oil to the pot and allow to heat for 1 minute. Add the onion and bell pepper and sauté for 3 to 4 minutes.
3. Add the potato, turmeric, cumin seeds, cumin, garam masala, and curry powder. Stir and cook for 5 minutes.
4. Stir in the curry sauce, water, tomatoes, and lentils.
5. Assemble the pressure lid, making sure the pressure release valve is in the SEAL position.
6. Select PRESSURE and set to HI. Set the time to 15 minutes. Select START/STOP to begin.
7. When pressure cooking is complete, allow the pressure to naturally release for 10 minutes. After 10 minutes, quick release any remaining pressure by moving the pressure release valve to the VENT position. Carefully remove the lid when the unit has finished releasing pressure.
8. Stir in the paneer (if using) and cilantro. Taste and season with salt and pepper, as needed.

Nutrition:
- InfoCalories: 217, Total Fat: 6g, Sodium: 27mg, Carbohydrates: 33g, Protein: 8g.

Artichoke With Mayo

Servings: 4
Cooking Time: 20 Min

Ingredients:
- 2 large artichokes
- 2 garlic cloves, smashed
- ½ cup mayonnaise /125ml
- 2 cups water /500ml
- Juice of 1 lime
- Salt and black pepper to taste

Directions:
1. Using a serrated knife, trim about 1 inch from the artichokes' top. Into the pot, add water and set trivet over. Lay the artichokes on the trivet. Seal lid and cook for 14 minutes. Press Start.
2. When ready, release the pressure quickly. Mix the mayonnaise with garlic and lime juice; season with salt and pepper. Serve artichokes in a platter with garlic mayo on the side.

Pepper And Sweet Potato Skewers

Servings: 1
Cooking Time: 20 Min

Ingredients:
- 1 large sweet potato
- 1 green bell pepper
- 1 beetroot
- 1 tbsp olive oil /15ml
- 1 tsp chili flakes /5g
- ¼ tsp black pepper /1.25g
- ½ tsp turmeric /2.5g
- ¼ tsp garlic powder /2.5g
- ¼ tsp paprika /2.5g

Directions:
1. Soak 3 to 4 skewers until ready to use. Peel the veggies and cut them into bite-sized chunks. Place the chunks in a bowl along with the remaining Ingredients Mix until fully coated. Thread the veggies in this order: potato, pepper, beetroot.
2. Place in the Ninja Foodi, close the crisping lid and cook for 15 minutes on Air Crisp mode at 350 °F or 175°C; flip skewers halfway through.

Garlic Potatoes

Servings: 4
Cooking Time: 30 Min

Ingredients:
- 1½ pounds potatoes /675g
- ½ cup vegetable broth /125ml
- 3 cloves garlic, thinly sliced
- 3 tbsp butter /45g
- 2 tbsp fresh rosemary; chopped /30g
- ½ tsp fresh parsley; chopped /2.5g
- ½ tsp fresh thyme; chopped /2.5g
- 1/4 tsp ground black pepper 1.25g

Directions:
1. Use a small knife to pierce each potato to ensure there are no blowouts when placed under pressure. Melt butter on Sear/Sauté. Add in potatoes, rosemary, parsley, pepper, thyme, and garlic, and cook for 10 minutes until potatoes are browned and the mixture is aromatic.
2. In a bowl, mix miso paste and vegetable stock; stir into the mixture in the pressure cooker.
3. Seal the pressure lid, choose Pressure, set to High, and set the timer to 5 minutes. Press Start. Do a pressure quickly.

Zucchini Quinoa Stuffed Red Peppers

Servings: 4
Cooking Time: 40 Min
Ingredients:
- 1 small zucchini; chopped
- 4 red bell peppers
- 2 large tomatoes; chopped
- 1 small onion; chopped
- 2 cloves garlic, minced
- 1 cup quinoa, rinsed /130g
- 1 cup grated Gouda cheese /130g
- ½ cup chopped mushrooms /65g
- 1 ½ cup water /375ml
- 2 cups chicken broth /500ml
- 1 tbsp olive oil /15ml
- ½ tsp smoked paprika /2.5g
- Salt and black pepper to taste

Directions:
1. Select Sear/Sauté mode on High. Once it is ready, add the olive oil to heat and then add the onion and garlic. Sauté for 3 minutes to soften, stirring occasionally.
2. Include the tomatoes, cook for 3 minutes and then add the quinoa, zucchinis, and mushrooms. Season with paprika, salt, and black pepper and stir with a spoon. Cook for 5 to 7 minutes, then, turn the pot off.
3. Use a knife to cut the bell peppers in halves (lengthwise) and remove their seeds and stems.
4. Spoon the quinoa mixture into the bell peppers. Put the peppers in a greased baking dish and pour the broth over.
5. Wipe the pot clean with some paper towels, and pour the water into it. After, fit the steamer rack at the bottom of the pot.
6. Place the baking dish on top of the reversible rack, cover with aluminum foil, close the lid, secure the pressure valve, and select Pressure mode on High pressure for 15 minutes. Press Start/Stop.
7. Once the timer has ended, do a quick pressure release and open the lid. Remove the aluminum foil and sprinkle with the gouda cheese.
8. Close the crisping lid, select Bake/Roast mode and cook for 10 minutes on 375 °F or 190°C. Arrange the stuffed peppers on a serving platter and serve right away or as a side to a meat dish.

Hawaiian Tofu

Servings: 6
Cooking Time: 3 Hours
Ingredients:
- 1 package extra firm tofu, cubed
- ¼ cup fresh pineapple, cubed
- ¼ cup tamari, low sodium
- 1 tbsp. sesame oil
- 1 tbsp. olive oil
- 1 tbsp. brown rice vinegar
- 2 cloves garlic, chopped
- 2 tsp fresh ginger, chopped
- 4 cups zucchini, chopped
- ¼ cup sesame seeds

Directions:
1. Add the tofu to the cooking pot.
2. Add the pineapple, soy sauce, sesame oil, olive oil, vinegar, garlic, and ginger to a food processor or blender. Process until smooth. Pour over tofu.
3. Add the lid and set to slow cook on low. Cook 3 hours, stirring occasionally.
4. During the last 15 minutes of cooking time, add the zucchini and sesame seeds to the pot and stir to combine. Serve over quinoa or rice.

Nutrition:
- InfoCalories 164,Total Fat 13g,Total Carbs 5g,Protein 10g,Sodium 680mg.

Carrot Gazpacho

Servings: 4
Cooking Time: 2 Hr 30 Min
Ingredients:
- 1 pound trimmed carrots /450g
- 1 pound tomatoes; chopped /450g
- 1 red onion; chopped
- 2 cloves garlic
- 1 cucumber, peeled and chopped
- 1/4 cup extra-virgin olive oil /62.5ml
- 1 pinch salt
- 2 tbsp lemon juice /30ml
- 2 tbsp white wine vinegar /30ml
- salt and freshly ground black pepper to taste

Directions:
1. To the Foodi add carrots, salt and enough water. Seal the pressure lid, choose Pressure, set to High, and set the timer to 20 minutes. Press Start.
2. Once ready, do a quick release. Set the beets to a bowl and place in the refrigerator to cool.
3. In a blender, add carrots, cucumber, red onion, pepper, garlic, olive oil, tomatoes, lemon juice, vinegar, and salt.
4. Blend until very smooth. Place gazpacho to a serving bowl, chill while covered for 2 hours.

Italian Sausage With Garlic Mash

Servings: 6
Cooking Time: 30 Min
Ingredients:
- 6 Italian sausages
- 4 large potatoes, peeled and cut into 1½-inch chunks
- 2 garlic cloves, smashed
- ⅓ cup butter, melted /44ml
- ¼ cup milk; at room temperature, or more as needed /62.5ml
- 1 ½ cups water /375ml
- 1 tbsp olive oil /15ml
- 1 tbsp chopped chives/15g
- salt and ground black pepper to taste

Directions:
1. Select Sear/Sauté, set to Medium High, and choose Start/Stop to preheat the pot and heat olive oil. Cook for 8-10 minutes, turning periodically until browned. Set aside. Wipe the pot with paper towels. Add in water and set the reversible rack over water. Place potatoes onto the reversible rack.
2. Seal the pressure lid, choose Pressure, set to High, and set the timer to 12 minutes. Press Start.
3. When ready, release the pressure quickly. Remove reversible rack from the pot. Drain water from the pot.

Return potatoes to pot. Add in salt, butter, pepper, garlic, and milk and use a hand masher to mash until no large lumps remain.
4. Using an immersion blender, blend potatoes on Low for 1 minute until fluffy and light. Avoid over-blending to ensure the potatoes do not become gluey!
5. Transfer the mash to a serving plate, top with sausages and scatter chopped chives over to serve.

Stuffed Manicotti

Servings: 4
Cooking Time: 50 Minutes
Ingredients:
- Nonstick cooking spray
- 8 manicotti shells, cooked & drained
- ½ onion, chopped
- 1 cloves garlic, chopped fine
- 1 cup mushrooms, chopped
- 16 oz. ricotta cheese, fat free
- ½ cup mozzarella cheese, grated
- 1 egg
- 1 cup spinach, chopped
- ¾ tsp Italian seasoning
- ¼ tsp pepper
- 1 cups light spaghetti sauce
- 1 tbsp. parmesan cheese, grated

Directions:
1. Spray the cooking pot and an 8x8-inch baking pan with cooking spray.
2. Set cooker to sauté on med-high heat. Add onion and garlic and cook until tender, about 3-4 minutes.
3. Add mushrooms and cook until browned. Turn off the heat.
4. In a large bowl, combine ricotta and mozzarella cheeses, egg, spinach, Italian seasoning, and pepper, mix well.
5. Add the mushroom mixture to the cheese mixture and stir to combine. Spoon into manicotti shells and lay in the prepared pan.
6. Pour the spaghetti sauce over the top and sprinkle with parmesan cheese. Cover with foil.
7. Place the rack in the cooking pot and add the manicotti. Add the tender-crisp lid and set to bake on 400°F (205°C). Bake 30-35 minutes or until heated through. Serve immediately.

Nutrition:
- InfoCalories 367,Total Fat 19g,Total Carbs 27g,Protein 24g,Sodium 308mg.

Garlic Bread Pizza

Servings:6
Cooking Time: 10 Minutes
Ingredients:
- 6 slices frozen garlic bread or Texas Toast
- ¾ cup tomato-basil sauce or your favorite tomato sauce
- 6 slices mozzarella cheese

Directions:
1. Insert Cook & Crisp Basket in pot. Close crisping lid. Select AIR CRISP, set temperature to 390°F (200°C), and set time to 5 minutes. Select START/STOP to begin preheating.
2. Once unit has preheated, place three of the garlic bread slices in the basket, and top with half the sauce and 3 slices of cheese. Close crisping lid.
3. Select AIR CRISP, set temperature to 375°F (190°C), and set time to 5 minutes. Select START/STOP to begin.
4. When cooking is complete, remove the pizzas from the basket. Repeat steps 2 and 3 with the remaining slices of garlic bread, sauce, and cheese.

Nutrition:
- InfoCalories: 192,Total Fat: 7g,Sodium: 548mg,Carbohydrates: 21g,Protein: 10g.

Roasted Cauliflower Salad

Servings:6
Cooking Time: 15 Minutes
Ingredients:
- 1 head cauliflower, cut into florets
- 1 can chickpeas, rinsed and drained
- 3 tablespoons, plus ¼ cup extra-virgin olive oil
- 1 tablespoon chili powder
- 2 teaspoons paprika
- 3 garlic cloves, minced
- 4 cups mixed baby greens
- 1 cucumber, sliced
- 3 tablespoons chopped fresh parsley
- Juice of 1 lemon
- 2 tablespoons honey
- 2 tablespoons Dijon mustard
- 2 tablespoons apple cider vinegar
- ⅓ cup crumbled feta cheese
- Sea salt
- Freshly ground black pepper

Directions:
1. Insert Cook & Crisp Basket in pot. Close crisping lid. Select AIR CRISP, set temperature to 390°F (200°C), and set the time to 5 minutes. Select START/STOP to begin preheating.
2. In a large bowl combine the cauliflower florets, chickpeas, 3 tablespoons of olive oil, chili powder, paprika, and garlic.
3. Once unit has preheated, open lid and add the cauliflower and chickpeas to the basket. Close lid.
4. Select AIR CRISP, set temperature to 390°F (200°C), and set time to 15 minutes. Select START/STOP to begin.
5. In another large bowl, combine the mixed greens, cucumber, and parsley.
6. In a small bowl, whisk together the lemon juice, honey, mustard, and vinegar.
7. When cooking is complete, carefully remove basket with cauliflower and chickpeas. Add them to the bowl of greens and toss well to combine. Top with feta cheese and dressing, season with salt and pepper, and serve.

Nutrition:
- InfoCalories: 291,Total Fat: 20g,Sodium: 226mg,Carbohydrates: 36g,Protein: 7g.

Creamy Golden Casserole

Servings: 6
Cooking Time: 40 Minutes
Ingredients:
- Nonstick cooking spray
- 2 lbs. summer squash, cut in 1-inch pieces
- ¾ cup sharp cheddar cheese, reduced fat, grated & divided
- ¼ cup light mayonnaise
- 2 eggs

- ¼ tsp salt
- ¼ tsp pepper

Directions:
1. Spray a 2-qt baking dish with cooking spray.
2. Add the squash to the cooking pot along with just enough water to cover. Set to saute on high heat and bring to a boil.
3. Reduce heat to medium and cook 8-10 minutes or until squash is tender. Drain.
4. Place the squash in a large bowl and add ½ cup cheese, mayonnaise, eggs, salt, and pepper and mix well. Spoon into prepared dish and sprinkle with remaining cheese.
5. Place the rack in the cooking pot and add the dish. Add the tender-crisp lid and set to bake on 375°F (190°C). Bake 30 minutes until heated through and top is golden brown. Serve.

Nutrition:
- InfoCalories 120,Total Fat 8g,Total Carbs 6g,Protein 7g,Sodium 303mg.

Roasted Squash And Rice With Crispy Tofu

Servings: 4
Cooking Time: 70 Min

Ingredients:
- 1 small butternut squash, peeled and diced
- 1 block extra-firm tofu, drained and cubed /450g
- 1 cup jasmine rice, cooked /130g
- ¾ cup water /188ml
- 1 tbsp coconut aminos /15g
- 2 tbsps melted butter; divided /30ml
- 2 tsp s arrowroot starch /10g
- 1 tsp salt /5g
- 1 tsp freshly ground black pepper /5g

Directions:
1. Pour the rice and water into the pot and mix with a spoon. Seal the pressure lid, choose Pressure, set to High and set the time to 2 minutes. Choose Start/Stop to boil the rice.
2. in a bowl, toss the butternut squash with 1 tbsp of melted butter and season with the salt and black pepper. Set aside.
3. In another bowl, mix the remaining butter with the coconut aminos, and toss the tofu in the mixture. Pour the arrowroot starch over the tofu and toss again to combine well.
4. When done cooking the rice, perform a quick pressure release, and carefully open the pressure lid. Put the reversible rack in the pot in the higher position and line with aluminum foil. Arrange the tofu and butternut squash on the rack.
5. Close the crisping lid. Choose Air Crisp, set the temperature to 400°F or 205°C, and set the time to 20 minutes. Choose Start/Stop to begin cooking.
6. After 10 minutes, use tongs to turn the butternut squash and tofu. When done cooking, check for your desired crispiness and serve the tofu and squash with the rice.

Creamy Spinach Soup

Servings: 6
Cooking Time: 20 Minutes

Ingredients:
- Nonstick cooking spray
- 1 tsp garlic, chopped fine
- ½ cup green onions, sliced thin
- 3 ½ cups vegetable broth, low sodium
- 20 oz. fresh spinach, chopped
- 3 tbsp. cornstarch
- 3 cups skim milk
- ½ tsp nutmeg
- 1/8 tsp salt
- ½ tsp pepper

Directions:
1. Spray the cooking pot with cooking spray. Set to sauté on med-high heat.
2. Add the garlic and green onions and cook 3-4 minutes, stirring frequently, until soft. Stir in broth and spinach.
3. Add the lid and set to pressure cook on high. Set the timer for 8 minutes. When the timer goes off, use natural release to remove the pressure.
4. Set back to sauté on medium heat.
5. In a small bowl, whisk together cornstarch and milk until smooth. Stir into soup until combined. Add remaining ingredients and cook, stirring constantly, 6-8 minutes until soup has thickened. Serve immediately.

Nutrition:
- InfoCalories 95,Total Fat 1g,Total Carbs 16g,Protein 7g,Sodium 559mg.

Italian Baked Zucchini

Servings: 6
Cooking Time: 45 Minutes

Ingredients:
- Nonstick cooking spray
- 2 tsp olive oil
- 2 lbs. zucchini, sliced ¼-inch thick
- ¼ cup onion, chopped
- 3 plum tomatoes, cut in ½- inch pieces
- 1 tbsp. parmesan cheese
- ½ cup Italian blend cheese, grated
- 1 tsp garlic powder
- 1 tsp Italian seasoning
- ¼ tsp pepper
- 1 tbsp. Italian bread crumbs

Directions:
1. Spray the cooking pot with cooking spray.
2. Add the oil to the cooking pot and set to sauté on med-high heat.
3. Add the zucchini and onion and cook, stirring occasionally, 5 minutes, until softened.
4. Stir in tomatoes, parmesan, Italian blend cheese, garlic powder, Italian seasonings, and pepper. Cook 3 minutes, stirring occasionally. Sprinkle bread crumbs over the top.
5. Add the tender-crisp lid and set to bake on 375°F (190°C). Bake 25-30 minutes until golden brown. Serve.

Nutrition:
- InfoCalories 91,Total Fat 4g,Total Carbs 8g,Protein 7g,Sodium 146mg.

Poultry

Chicken Cacciatore
Servings: 4
Cooking Time: 40 Min
Ingredients:
- 1 pound chicken drumsticks, boneless, skinless /450g
- ½ cup dry red wine /125ml
- ¾ cup chicken stock /188ml
- 1 cup black olives, pitted and sliced /130g
- 2 bay leaves
- 1 pinch red pepper flakes
- 1 can diced tomatoes /840g
- 1 carrot; chopped
- 1 red bell pepper; chopped
- 1 yellow bell pepper; chopped
- 1 onion; chopped
- 4 garlic cloves, thinly sliced
- 2 tsp olive oil /10ml
- 1 tsp dried basil /5g
- 1 tsp dried parsley /5g
- 2 tsp dried oregano /10g
- 1½ tsp freshly ground black pepper /7.5g
- 2 tsp salt /10g

Directions:
1. Warm oil on Sear/Sauté. Add pepper and salt to the chicken drumsticks. In batches, sear the chicken for 5-6 minutes until golden-brown. Set aside on a plate. Drain the cooker and remain with 1 tbsp of fat.
2. In the hot oil, sauté onion, garlic, and bell peppers for 4 minutes until softened; add red pepper flakes, basil, parsley, and oregano, and cook for 30 more seconds. Season with salt and pepper.
3. Stir in tomatoes, olives, chicken stock, red wine and bay leaves.
4. Return chicken to the pot. Seal the pressure lid, choose Pressure, set to High, and set the timer to 15 minutes. Press Start.
5. When ready, release the pressure quickly. Divide chicken between four serving bowls; top with tomato mixture before serving.

Korean Barbecued Satay
Servings: 4
Cooking Time: 4h 15 Min
Ingredients:
- 1 lb. boneless; skinless chicken tenders /450g
- ½ cup pineapple juice /125ml
- ½ cup soy sauce /125ml
- ⅓ cup sesame oil /84ml
- 4 scallions; chopped
- 1 pinch black pepper
- 4 cloves garlic; chopped
- 2 tsp sesame seeds, toasted /10g
- 1 tsp fresh ginger, grated /5g

Directions:
1. Skew each tender and trim any excess fat. Mix the other ingredients in one large bowl. Add the skewered chicken and place in the fridge for 4 to 24 hours.
2. Preheat the Foodi to 370 For 188°C. Using a paper towel, pat the chicken dry. Fry for 10 minutes on Air Crisp mode.

Sticky Drumsticks
Servings: 4
Cooking Time: 50 Min
Ingredients:
- 1 lb. drumsticks /450g
- 2 tbsp honey /30ml
- 2 tsp dijon mustard /10g
- Cooking spray
- Salt and pepper to taste

Directions:
1. Combine the honey, mustard, salt, and pepper in a large bowl. Add in the chicken and toss to coat. Cover and put in the fridge for 30 minutes.
2. Preheat your Foodi to 380 °F or 195°C. Grease the Foodi basket with cooking spray. Arrange the drumsticks on the basket. Cook for 20 minutes on Air Crisp mode. After 10 minutes, shake the drumsticks.

Lemon Turkey Risotto
Servings: 4
Cooking Time: 40 Min
Ingredients:
- 2 boneless turkey breasts; cut into strips
- 2 cups chicken broth /500ml
- 1 cup Arborio rice, rinsed /130g
- ¼ cup chopped fresh parsley, or to taste /32.5g
- 2 lemons, zested and juiced
- 1 onion; diced
- 8 lemon slices
- 2 garlic cloves; minced
- 1 tbsp dried oregano /15g
- 1½ tbsp olive oil /22.5ml
- ½ tsp sea salt /2.5g
- salt and freshly ground black pepper to taste

Directions:
1. In a ziplock back, mix turkey, oregano, sea salt, garlic, juice and zest of two lemons. Marinate for 10 minutes.
2. Warm oil on Sear/Sauté. Add onion and cook for 3 minutes until fragrant; add rice and chicken broth and season with pepper and salt.
3. Empty the ziplock having the chicken and marinade into the pot. Seal the pressure lid, choose Pressure, set to High, and set the timer to 12 minutes. Press Start. When ready, release the pressure quickly.
4. Divide the rice and turkey between 4 serving bowls; garnish with lemon slices and parsley.

Sweet Garlicky Chicken Wings
Servings: 4
Cooking Time: 20 Min
Ingredients:
- 16 chicken wings
- 4 garlic cloves; minced
- ¾ cup potato starch /98g
- ¼ cup butter /32.5g
- ¼ cup honey /62.5ml
- ½ tsp salt /2.5g

Directions:

Ninja Foodi Cookbook Guide

1. Rinse and pat dry the wings, and place them in a bowl. Add the starch to the bowl, and mix to coat the chicken.
2. Place the chicken in a baking dish that has been previously coated lightly with cooking oil. Close the crisping lid and cook for 5 minutes on Air Crisp mode at 370 °F or 185°C.
3. Meanwhile, whisk the rest of the ingredients together in a bowl. Pour the sauce over the wings and cook for another 10 minutes.

Refried Black Beans And Chicken Fajitas

Servings: 4
Cooking Time: 40 Min
Ingredients:
- 1 pound chicken breasts; sliced /450g
- 1 large can black beans /810g
- 1 yellow bell pepper; sliced
- 1 garlic clove, crushed
- 1 bacon slice, halved widthwise
- 1 red bell pepper; sliced
- 1 small onion; cut into 8 wedges
- 1 jalapeño pepper; sliced
- ¼ cup water /62.5ml
- 1 tbsp Mexican seasoning mix /15g
- 4 tbsp olive oil; divided /60ml
- 1 tsp salt /5g
- Corn tortillas to serve
- Avocado slices to serve
- Salsa to serve

Directions:
1. Pour the beans with liquid into the Foodi's inner pot. Stir in the garlic, bacon, water, and 2 tbsps of olive oil. Seal the pressure lid, choose Pressure; adjust to High and the cook time to 5 minutes. Press Start.
2. In a large bowl, mix the chicken, yellow and red bell peppers, jalapeño, and onion. Drizzle with the remaining oil, sprinkle with the salt and Mexican seasoning and toss to coat. Set aside.
3. When the beans are ready, do a quick pressure release, and carefully open the lid. Pour out the beans with liquid into a large bowl and cover with aluminum foil to keep warm; set aside.
4. Place the Crisping Basket into the inner pot. Close the crisping lid and select Air Crisp. Adjust the temperature to 375°F or 190°C and the time to 4 minutes. Press Start to preheat.
5. Uncover the beans. Remove and discard the bacon pieces and garlic clove. Fetch out about ¼ cup of the liquid and reserve it. Then, use a potato masher to break the beans into the remaining liquid until smooth while adding more liquid if needed. Cover the bowl again with aluminum foil.
6. When the pot has preheated, open the lid and add the vegetables and chicken to the basket. Close the crisping lid. Choose Air Crisp; adjust the temperature to 375°F or 190°C and the cook time to 10 minutes. Press Start to begin browning.
7. After 5 minutes, open the lid and use tongs to turn the vegetables and chicken. Continue cooking until the vegetables are slightly browned and the chicken tender. Wrap the chicken and beans in warm tortillas and garnish with the avocado and salsa to serve.

Mexican Style Green Chili Chicken

Servings: 4
Cooking Time: 40 Min
Ingredients:
- 1½ pounds boneless skinless chicken breasts /675g
- 12 ounces, baby plum tomatoes, halved /360g
- 2 jalapeño peppers, seeded and chopped
- 2 large serrano pepper seeded and cut into chunks
- 2 large garlic cloves; minced
- ½ lime, juiced
- Tortilla chips
- 1 small onion; sliced
- ¼ cup minced fresh cilantro /32.5g
- ¾ cup chicken stock /188ml
- ½ cup shredded Cheddar Cheese /65g
- 1 tbsp olive oil /15ml
- ½ tsp salt /2.5g
- ½ tsp ground cumin /2.5g
- 1 tsp Mexican seasoning mix /5g
- Cooking spray

Directions:
1. Choose Sear/Sauté on your Foodi and adjust to High. Press Start to preheat the inner pot. Heat the olive oil add the plum tomatoes; cook without turning, for 3 to 4 minutes.
2. Add the chicken stock while scraping the bottom of the pot to dissolve any browned bits. Stir in the cumin, Mexican seasoning, and salt. Add the chicken, jalapeños, serrano pepper, garlic, onion, and half the cilantro.
3. Seal the pressure lid, choose pressure; adjust the pressure to High and the cook time to 10 minutes. Press Start.
4. Meanwhile, grease the reversible rack with cooking spray and fix the rack in the upper position of the pot. Cut out a circle of aluminum foil to fit the rack and place on the rack.
5. Lay on a single layer of tortilla chips, sprinkle with half of the Cheddar cheese and repeat with another layer of chips and cheese. Set aside.
6. After cooking, perform a natural pressure release for 5 minutes. Take out the chicken from the pot and set aside. Then, with an immersion blender, purée the vegetables into the sauce.
7. Shred the chicken with two forks and return the pieces to the sauce. Add the remaining cilantro and the lime juice. Taste and adjust the seasoning and carefully transfer the rack of chips to the pot.
8. Close the crisping lid and Choose Air Crisp; adjust the temperature to 375°F or 190°C and the time to 5 minutes; press Start. When done cooking, open the lid. Carefully take out the rack and pour the chips into a platter. Serve the chili in bowls with the chips on the side.

Sesame Crusted Chicken

Servings: 6
Cooking Time: 10 Minutes
Ingredients:
- Nonstick cooking spray
- 1 egg
- 2 tbsp. water
- ½ cup Italian-seasoned bread crumbs
- 2 tbsp. sesame seeds
- 1 tsp thyme
- 1 tsp garlic powder
- ¼ tsp salt

- ¼ tsp pepper
- 4 chicken breasts, boneless & skinless

Directions:
1. Spray the fryer basket with cooking spray and place it in the cooking pot.
2. In a shallow dish, whisk egg and water until combined.
3. In another shallow dish, combine remaining ingredients, mix well.
4. Place chicken between 2 sheets of plastic wrap and pound out to ¼-inch thick.
5. Dip chicken first in the egg then coat with bread crumb mixture. Place in the fryer basket.
6. Add the tender-crisp lid and set to air fry on 375°F (190°C). Cook chicken 10 minutes, turning over halfway through cooking time, or until chicken is no longer pink. Serve.

Nutrition:
- InfoCalories 155,Total Fat 5g,Total Carbs 7g,Protein 20g,Sodium 210mg.

Chicken Meatballs Primavera

Servings: 4
Cooking Time: 30 Min

Ingredients:
- 1 lb. ground chicken /450g
- ½ lb. chopped asparagus /225g
- 1 cup chopped tomatoes /130g
- 1 cup chicken broth /250ml
- 1 red bell pepper, seeded and sliced
- 2 cups chopped green beans /260g
- 1 egg, cracked into a bowl
- 2 tbsp chopped basil + extra to garnish /30g
- 1 tbsp olive oil + ½ tbsp olive oil /22.5ml
- 6 tsp flour /30g
- 1 ½ tsp Italian Seasoning /7.5g
- Salt and black pepper to taste

Directions:
1. In a mixing bowl, add the chicken, egg, flour, salt, pepper, 2 tbsps of basil, 1 tbsp of olive oil, and Italian seasoning. Mix them well with hands and make 16 large balls out of the mixture. Set the meatballs aside.
2. Select Sear/Sauté mode. Heat half tsp of olive oil, and add peppers, green beans, and asparagus. Cook for 3 minutes, stirring frequently.
3. After 3 minutes, use a spoon the veggies onto a plate and set aside. Pour the remaining oil in the pot to heat and then fry the meatballs in it in batches. Fry them for 2 minutes on each side to brown them lightly.
4. After, put all the meatballs back into the pot as well as the vegetables. Also, pour the chicken broth over it.
5. Close the lid, secure the pressure valve, and select Pressure mode on High pressure for 10 minutes. Press Start/Stop. Do a quick pressure release. Close the crisping lid and select Air Crisp. Cook for 5 minutes at 400 °F or 205°C, until nice and crispy.
6. Dish the meatballs with sauce into a serving bowl and garnish it with basil. Serve with over cooked pasta.

Country Chicken Casserole

Servings: 6
Cooking Time: 50 Minutes

Ingredients:
- 1 tbsp. olive oil
- ½ cup onion, chopped
- 1 cup mushrooms, sliced
- 1 ½ cups brown rice, cooked
- 2 cups broccoli, steamed & chopped
- 10 ½ oz. cream of chicken soup, low fat
- ½ cup sour cream, fat free
- 1 ¼ cup cheddar cheese, reduced fat, grated & divided
- 2 tbsp. Dijon mustard
- 1 tsp garlic powder
- ½ tsp pepper
- 2 cups chicken, cooked & chopped

Directions:
1. Add oil to the cooking pot and set to sauté on medium heat.
2. Add the onion and mushrooms and cook 3-5 minutes until they start to soften.
3. Stir in rice and turn off the sauté function. Place broccoli in an even layer over the rice mixture.
4. In a medium bowl, combine soup, sour cream, 1 cup cheese, mustard, garlic powder, and pepper and mix well. Stir in chicken and spoon over the top of the broccoli.
5. Add the tender-crisp lid and set to bake on 350°F (175°C). Bake 35 minutes.
6. Sprinkle the remaining cheese over the top and bake another 5-10 minutes until cheese is melted and bubbly. Serve.

Nutrition:
- InfoCalories 309,Total Fat 15g,Total Carbs 22g,Protein 22g,Sodium 452mg.

Cheesy Chicken And Broccoli Casserole

Servings:6
Cooking Time: 30 Minutes

Ingredients:
- 4 boneless, skinless chicken breasts
- 2 cups chicken stock
- 1 cup whole milk
- 1 cans condensed Cheddar cheese soup
- 1 teaspoon paprika
- 2 cups shredded Cheddar cheese
- Kosher salt
- Freshly ground black pepper
- 2 cups crushed buttered crackers

Directions:
1. Place the chicken and stock in the pot. Assemble pressure lid, making sure the pressure release valve is in the SEAL position.
2. Select PRESSURE and set to HI. Set timer to 20 minutes. Select START/STOP to begin.
3. When pressure cooking is complete, quick release the pressure by turning the pressure release valve to the VENT position. Carefully remove lid when unit has finished releasing pressure.
4. Using silicone-tipped utensils, shred the chicken inside the pot.
5. Add the milk, condensed soup, paprika, and cheese. Stir to combine with the chicken. Season with salt and pepper. Top with the crushed crackers. Close crisping lid.
6. Select AIR CRISP, set temperature to 360°F (180°C), and set time to 10 minutes. Select START/STOP to begin.
7. When cooking is complete, open lid and let cool before serving.

Nutrition:
- InfoCalories: 449,Total Fat: 23g,Sodium: 925mg,Carbohydrates: 18g,Protein: 42g.

Tuscan Chicken & Pasta

Servings: 8
Cooking Time: 2 ½ Hours
Ingredients:
- 2½ cups chicken broth, low sodium
- 1 tbsp. Italian seasoning
- ½ tsp salt
- ½ cup mushrooms, sliced
- ¼ tsp crushed red pepper flakes
- 1½ lbs. chicken thighs, boneless, skinless & cut in 1-inch pieces
- ½ lb. macaroni
- ½ cup sun-dried tomatoes with herbs, chopped
- 8 oz. cream cheese, cubed
- 1 cup parmesan cheese
- 1 ½ cups fresh baby spinach

Directions:
1. Spray the cooking pot with cooking spray.
2. Add the broth, Italian seasoning, mushrooms, salt, and pepper flakes to the pot and stir to mix.
3. Stir in chicken. Add the lid and set to slow cook on high. Cook 1 ½ - 2 hours or until chicken is cooked through.
4. Add the pasta and tomatoes and stir to mix. Recover and cook another 25-30 minutes or until pasta is tender, stirring occasionally.
5. Add cream cheese and parmesan and stir until cheeses melt. Stir in spinach and recover. Cook another 5-10 minutes until spinach is wilted and tender. Stir well and serve hot.

Nutrition:
- InfoCalories 438,Total Fat 20g,Total Carbs 27g,Protein 35g,Sodium 788mg.

Shredded Chicken With Lentils And Rice

Servings: 4
Cooking Time: 45 Min
Ingredients:
- 4 boneless; skinless chicken thighs
- 1 garlic clove; minced
- 1 small yellow onion; chopped
- 1 cup white rice /130g
- ½ cup dried lentils/65g
- 3 cups chicken broth; divided /750ml
- 1 tsp olive oil /5ml
- Chopped fresh parsley for garnish
- Salt and ground black pepper to taste

Directions:
1. Set your Foodi to Sear/Sauté, set to Medium High, and choose Start/Stop to preheat the pot. Warm oil. Add in onion and garlic and cook for 3 minutes until soft; add in broth, rice, lentils, and chicken.
2. Season with pepper and salt. Seal the pressure lid, choose Pressure, set to High, and set the timer to 15 minutes. Press Start.
3. Once ready, do a quick release. Remove and shred the chicken in a large bowl. Set the lentils and rice into serving plates, top with shredded chicken and parsley and serve.

Sour Cream & Cheese Chicken

Servings: 8
Cooking Time: 25 Minutes
Ingredients:
- Nonstick cooking spray
- 1 cup sour cream
- 2 tsp garlic powder
- 1 tsp seasoned salt
- ½ tsp pepper
- 1 ½ cups parmesan cheese, divided
- 3 lbs. chicken breasts, boneless

Directions:
1. Spray the cooking pot with cooking spray.
2. In a medium bowl, combine sour cream, garlic powder, seasoned salt, pepper, and 1 cup parmesan cheese, mix well.
3. Place the chicken in the cooking pot. Spread the sour cream mixture over the top and sprinkle with remaining parmesan cheese.
4. Add the tender-crisp lid and set to bake on 375°F (190°C). Bake chicken 25-30 minutes until cooked through.
5. Set cooker to broil and cook another 2-3 minutes until top is lightly browned. Serve immediately.

Nutrition:
- InfoCalories 377,Total Fat 21g,Total Carbs 3g,Protein 41g,Sodium 737mg.

Mexican Chicken Soup

Servings: 4
Cooking Time: 20 Minutes
Ingredients:
- 2 cups chicken, shredded
- 4 tablespoons olive oil
- ½ cup cilantro, chopped
- 8 cups chicken broth
- 1/3 cup salsa
- 1 teaspoon onion powder
- ½ cup scallions, chopped
- 4 ounces green chillies, chopped
- ½ teaspoon habanero, minced
- 1 cup celery root, chopped
- 1 teaspoon cumin
- 1 teaspoon garlic powder
- Black pepper and salt to taste

Directions:
1. Add all ingredients to Ninja Foodi.
2. Stir and lock lid, cook on "HIGH" pressure for 10 minutes.
3. Release pressure naturally over 10 minutes.
4. Serve and enjoy.

Nutrition:
- InfoCalories: 204; Fat: 14g; Carbohydrates: 4g; Protein: 14g

Chipotle Raspberry Chicken

Servings: 8
Cooking Time: 6 Hours
Ingredients:
- Nonstick cooking spray
- 2 lbs. chicken breasts, boneless & skinless
- 1 cup raspberry preserves, sugar free
- 2 tbsp. chipotle in adobo sauce
- 2 tbsp. fresh lime juice
- ½ tsp cumin

Directions:
1. Spray the cooking pot with cooking spray and add the chicken.

2. In a medium bowl, combine remaining ingredients. Pour over chicken.
3. Add the lid and set to slow cook on low. Cook 6 hours or until chicken is tender. Stir well before serving.
Nutrition:
- InfoCalories 168,Total Fat 4g,Total Carbs 8g,Protein 26g,Sodium 144mg.

Turkey And Brown Rice Salad With Peanuts

Servings: 4
Cooking Time: 60 Min
Ingredients:
- 1 pound turkey tenderloins /450g
- 3 celery stalks, thinly sliced
- 1 apple, cored and cubed
- 1 cup brown rice /130g
- ½ cup peanuts, toasted /65g
- 4 cups water /1000ml
- A pinch of sugar
- 3 tbsp apple cider vinegar /45ml
- ⅛ tsp freshly ground black pepper /0.625g
- ¼ tsp celery seeds /1.25g
- 2¼ tsp salt /11.25g
- 3 tsp peanut oil; divided /15ml

Directions:
1. Pour the water into the inner pot. Stir in the brown rice and 1 tsp or 5g of salt. Lock the pressure lid into the Seal position. Choose Pressure; adjust the pressure to High and the cook time to 10 minutes. Press Start.
2. Season the turkey on both sides with salt; set aside. After cooking the brown rice, perform a natural pressure release for 10 minutes. Carefully open the lid and spoon the rice into a large bowl to cool completely.
3. Put the turkey in the Crisping Basket and brush with 2 tsp s of peanut oil. Fix in the basket. Close the crisping lid and Choose Bake/Roast; adjust the temperature to 375°F or 190°C and the cook time to 12 minutes; press Start.
4. Pour the remaining peanut oil and the vinegar into a jar with a tight-fitting lid. Add the black pepper, celery seeds, salt, and sugar.
5. Close the jar and shake until the ingredients properly combined. When the turkey is ready, transfer to a plate to cool for several minutes. Cut it into bite-size chunks and add to the rice along with the peanuts, celery, and apple.
6. Pour half the dressing over the salad and toss gently to coat, adding more dressing as desired. Proceed to serve the salad.

Buttermilk Fried Chicken

Servings: 4
Cooking Time: 30 Minutes
Ingredients:
- 1½ pounds boneless, skinless chicken breasts
- 1 to 2 cups buttermilk
- 2 large eggs
- ¾ cup all-purpose flour
- ¾ cup potato starch
- ½ teaspoon granulated garlic, divided
- 1 teaspoon salt, divided
- 2 teaspoons freshly ground black pepper, divided
- 1 cup bread crumbs
- ½ cup panko bread crumbs
- Olive oil or cooking spray

Directions:
1. In a large bowl, combine the chicken breasts and buttermilk, turning the chicken to coat. Cover the bowl with plastic wrap and refrigerate the chicken to soak at least 4 hours or overnight.
2. In a medium shallow bowl, whisk the eggs. In a second shallow bowl, stir together the flour, potato starch, ¼ teaspoon of granulated garlic, ½ teaspoon of salt, and 1 teaspoon of pepper. In a third shallow bowl, stir together the bread crumbs, panko, remaining ¼ teaspoon of granulated garlic, remaining ½ teaspoon of salt, and remaining 1 teaspoon of pepper.
3. Working one piece at a time, remove the chicken from the buttermilk, letting the excess drip into the bowl. Dredge the chicken in the flour mixture, coating well on both sides. Then dip the chicken in the eggs, coating both sides. Finally, dip the chicken in the bread crumb mixture, coating both sides and pressing the crumbs onto the chicken. Spritz both sides of the coated chicken pieces with olive oil.
4. Place the Cook & Crisp Basket into the unit.
5. Select AIR CRISP, set the temperature to 400°F (205°C), and set the time to 30 minutes. Select START/STOP to begin and allow to preheat for 5 minutes.
6. Spritz both sides of the coated chicken pieces with olive oil. Working in batches as needed, place the chicken breasts in the Cook & Crisp Basket, ensuring the chicken pieces do not touch each other.
7. After 12 minutes, turn the chicken with a spatula so you don't tear the breading. Close the crisping lid and continue to cook, checking the chicken for an internal temperature of 165°F (75°C).
8. When cooking is complete, transfer the chicken to a wire rack to cool.
Nutrition:
- InfoCalories: 574,Total Fat: 7g,Sodium: 995mg,Carbohydrates: 67g,Protein: 51g.

Healthy Chicken Stew

Servings: 4
Cooking Time: 4 Hours
Ingredients:
- 1 large potato, peeled & chopped
- 2 carrots, peeled & sliced
- ½ tsp salt
- ¼ tsp pepper
- 2 cloves garlic, chopped fine
- 3 cups chicken broth, low sodium
- 2 bay leaves
- 2 chicken breasts, boneless, skinless & cut in pieces
- ½ tsp thyme
- ¼ tsp basil
- 1 tsp paprika
- 2 tbsp. cornstarch
- ½ cup water
- 1 cup green peas

Directions:
1. Add the potatoes, carrots, salt, pepper, garlic, broth, bay leaves, chicken, thyme, basil, and paprika to the cooking pot, stir to mix.
2. Add the lid and set to slow cook on high. Cook 4 hours or until vegetables and chicken are tender.
3. In a small bowl, whisk together cornstarch and water until smooth. Stir into the cooking pot along with the peas.
4. Recover and cook another 15 minutes. Stir well before serving.
Nutrition:
- InfoCalories 187,Total Fat 2g,Total Carbs 25g,Protein 17g,Sodium 1038mg.

Turkey Enchilada Casserole

Servings: 6
Cooking Time: 70 Min
Ingredients:
- 1 pound boneless; skinless turkey breasts /450g
- 2 cups shredded Monterey Jack cheese; divided /260g
- 2 cups enchilada sauce /500ml
- 1 yellow onion; diced
- 2 garlic cloves; minced
- 1 can pinto beans, drained and rinsed /450g
- 1 bag frozen corn /480g
- 8 tortillas, each cut into 8 pieces
- 1 tbsp butter /15g
- ¼ tsp salt /1.25g
- ¼ tsp freshly ground black pepper /1.25g

Directions:
1. Choose Sear/Sauté on the pot and set to Medium High. Choose Start/Stop to preheat the pot. Melt the butter and cook the onion for 3 minutes, stirring occasionally. Stir in the garlic and cook until fragrant, about 1 minute more.
2. Put the turkey and enchilada sauce in the pot, and season with salt and black pepper. Stir to combine. Seal the pressure lid, choose Pressure, set to High, and set the time to 15 minutes. Choose Start/Stop.
3. When done cooking, perform a quick pressure release and carefully open the lid. Shred the turkey with two long forks while being careful not to burn your hands. Mix in the pinto beans, tortilla pieces, corn, and half of the cheese to the pot. Sprinkle the remaining cheese evenly on top of the casserole.
4. Close the crisping lid. Choose Broil and set the time to 5 minutes. Press Start/Stop to begin broiling. When ready, allow the casserole to sit for 5 minutes before serving.

Roasted Chicken With Potato Mash

Servings: 4
Cooking Time: 70 Min
Ingredients:
- 2 bone-in chicken breasts
- ¾ cup chicken stock /188ml
- 3 medium Yukon Gold potatoes; scrubbed
- 3 tbsp melted butter /45ml
- 2 tbsp warm heavy cream /30ml
- 2½ tsp salt /12.5g
- 4 tsp Cajun seasoning /20g

Directions:
1. Pat the chicken dry with a paper towel and carefully slide your hands underneath the skin to slightly separate the meat from the skin.
2. Then in a small bowl, combine the salt and Cajun seasoning, and rub half of the mixture under the skin and cavity of the chicken.
3. Pour the chicken stock into the inner pot of the Foodi. Fix the reversible rack in a lower position of the pot and lay the chicken, on the side in the center of the rack. Also, arrange the potatoes around the chicken.
4. Seal the pressure lid, choose pressure; adjust the pressure to High and the cook time to 13 minutes. Press Start to begin cooking the chicken. Mix the remaining spice mixture with 2 tbsps or 30ml of the melted butter, and set aside.
5. When done pressure cooking, perform a natural pressure release for 10 minutes. Remove the potatoes and chicken onto a cutting board. Pour the cooking juices into a bowl and return the rack with chicken only to the pot. Baste the outer side of the chicken with half of the spice-butter mixture.
6. Close the crisping lid and choose Air Crisp; adjust the temperature to 360°F (180°C) and the cook time to 16 minutes. Press Start. After 8 minutes, open the lid and flip the chicken over. Baste this side with the remaining butter mixture and close the lid to continue cooking.
7. With a potato masher, smoothly puree the potatoes, and add the remaining salt, melted butter, heavy cream, and 2 tbsps of the reserved cooking juice; stir to combine. Taste and adjust the seasoning with salt and pepper and cover the bowl with aluminum foil to keep warm.
8. After cooking, transfer the chicken to a cutting board, leaving the rack in the pot.
9. Pour the remaining cooking sauce into the pot, choose Sear/Sauté and adjust to Medium-High. Place the bowl of potatoes on the rack to keep warm as the sauce reduces. Press Start and boil the sauce for 2 to 3 minutes or until reduced by about half.
10. Meanwhile, slice the chicken and lay the pieces on a platter. Remove the mashed potato from the pot and remove the rack. Spoon the sauce over the chicken slices and serve with the creamy potatoes.

Shredded Chicken And Wild Rice

Servings: 6
Cooking Time: 45 Min
Ingredients:
- 6 chicken thighs, skinless
- 3 cups chicken broth; divided /750ml
- 1 ½ cups wild rice /195g
- 1 cup pumpkin, peeled and cubed /130g
- 2 celery stalks; diced
- 2 onions; diced
- 2 garlic cloves, crushed
- 2 tbsp olive oil /30ml
- 1/8 tsp smoked paprika /0.625g
- ½ tsp ground white pepper /2.5g
- ½ tsp onion powder /2.5g
- 1 tsp Cajun seasoning /5g
- 1 tsp salt /5g
- ½ tsp ground red pepper /2.5g

Directions:
1. Season the chicken with salt, onion powder, Cajun seasoning, ground white pepper, ground red pepper, and smoked paprika. Warm oil on Sear/Sauté.
2. Stir in celery and pumpkin and cook for 5 minutes until tender; set the vegetables on a plate. In batches, sear chicken in oil for 3 minutes each side until golden brown; set on a plate.
3. In the Foodi, add 1/4 cup or 62.5ml chicken stock to deglaze the pan, scrape away any browned bits from the bottom; add garlic and onion and cook for 2 minutes until fragrant.
4. Take back the celery and pumpkin to Foodi; add the wild rice and remaining chicken stock. Place the chicken over the rice mixture.
5. Seal the pressure lid, choose Pressure, set to High, and set the timer to 10 minutes. Press Start. When ready, release the pressure quickly. Place rice and chicken pieces in serving plates and serve.

Ninja Foodi Cookbook Guide

Chicken With Black Beans

Servings: 4
Cooking Time: 25 Min
Ingredients:
- 4 boneless; skinless chicken drumsticks
- 2 green onions, thinly sliced
- 3 garlic cloves, grated
- 2 cups canned black beans/260g
- ½ cup soy sauce /125ml
- ½ cup chicken broth /125ml
- 1 piece fresh ginger, grated
- 1 tbsp sriracha /15g
- 1 tbsp sesame oil /15ml
- 1 tbsp cornstarch /15g
- 1 tbsp water /15ml
- 2 tbsp toasted sesame seeds; divided /30g
- 3 tbsp honey /45ml
- 2 tbsp tomato paste/30ml

Directions:
1. In your Foodi, mix the soy sauce, honey, ginger, tomato paste, chicken broth, sriracha, and garlic. Stir well until smooth; toss in the chicken to coat.
2. Seal the pressure lid, choose Pressure, set to High, and set the timer to 3 minutes. Press Start. Release the pressure immediately.
3. Open the lid and Press Sear/Sauté. In a small bowl, mix water and cornstarch until no lumps remain; stir into the sauce and cook for 5 minutes until thickened.
4. Stir sesame oil and 1½ tbsp or 22.5g sesame seeds through the chicken mixture; garnish with extra sesame seeds and green onions. Serve with black beans.

Coq Au Vin

Servings: 4
Cooking Time: 60 Min
Ingredients:
- 4 chicken leg quarters, skin on
- 4 serrano ham slices; cut into thirds
- 1¼ cups dry red wine /312.5ml
- ⅓ cup chicken stock /84ml
- ½ cup sautéed mushrooms /65g
- ¾ cup shallots; sliced /98g
- ¼ cup brown onion slices /32.5g
- 1 tbsp olive oil /15ml
- 1½ tsp tomato puree/7.5ml
- ½ tsp brown sugar /2.5g
- 1½ tsp salt /7.5g
- Black pepper to taste

Dircctions:
1. Season the chicken on both sides with 1 tsp of salt and set aside on a wire rack. On the Foodi, choose Sear/Sauté and adjust to Medium. Press Start to preheat the inner pot.
2. Heat the olive oil and place the ham in the pot in a single layer and cook for 3 to 4 minutes or until browned. Remove the ham to a plate and set aside.
3. Add the chicken quarters to the pot. Cook for 5 minutes or until the skin is golden brown. Turn the chicken over and cook further for 2 minutes; remove to a plate.
4. Carefully pour out almost all the fat leaving about a tbsp to cover the bottom of the pot. Then, stir in the sliced onion and cook until the onion begins to brown.
5. Add ½ cup of red wine, stir, and scrape the bottom of the pan to let off any browned bits. Then, boil the mixture until the wine reduces by about 1/3, about 2 minutes.
6. Pour the remaining red wine, chicken stock, tomato puree, brown sugar, and a few grinds of black pepper into the pot. Boil the sauce for 1 minute, stirring to make sure the tomato paste is properly mixed. Add the chicken pieces with skin- side up, to the pot.
7. Put the pressure lid in place and lock to seal. Choose Pressure; adjust the pressure to High and the cook time to 12 minutes. Press Start to continue cooking.
8. After cooking, perform a natural pressure release for 10 minutes. Remove the chicken from the pot. Pour the sauce into a bowl and allow sitting until the fat rises to the top and starts firming up. Use a spoon to fetch off the fat on top of the sauce.
9. Pour the sauce back into the pot and stir in the mushrooms and pearl onions. Place the chicken on the sauce with skin side up. Close the crisping lid and select Broil. Adjust the cook time to 7 minutes; press Start.
10. When done cooking, open the lid and transfer the chicken to a serving platter. Spoon the sauce with mushrooms and pearl onions all around the chicken and crumble the reserved ham on top.

Buttermilk Chicken Thighs

Servings: 6
Cooking Time: 4 Hours 40 Min
Ingredients:
- 1 ½ lb. chicken thighs /675g
- 2 cups buttermilk /500ml
- 2 cups flour /260g
- 1 tbsp paprika /15g
- 1 tbsp baking powder /15g
- 2 tsp black pepper /10g
- 1 tsp cayenne pepper /5g
- 3 tsp salt divided /15g

Directions:
1. Rinse and pat dry the chicken thighs. Place the chicken thighs in a bowl. Add cayenne pepper, 2 tsp or 10g salt, black pepper, and buttermilk, and stir to coat well.
2. Refrigerate for 4 hours. Preheat the Foodi to 350 °F or 175°C. In another bowl, mix the flour, paprika, 1 tsp or 5g salt, and baking powder.
3. Dredge half of the chicken thighs, one at a time, in the flour, and then place on a lined dish. Close the crisping lid and cook for 18 minutes on Air Crisp mode, flipping once halfway through. Repeat with the other batch.

Chicken With Prunes

Servings: 6
Cooking Time: 55 Min
Ingredients:
- 1 whole chicken, 3 lb /1350g
- ¼ cup packed brown sugar /32.5g
- ½ cup pitted prunes /65g
- 2 bay leaves
- 3 minced cloves of garlic
- 2 tbsp olive oil /30ml
- 2 tbsp capers /30g
- 1 tbsp dried oregano /15g
- 1 tbsp chopped fresh parsley /15g
- 2 tbsp red wine vinegar /30ml
- Salt and black pepper to taste

Directions:
1. In a big and deep bowl, mix the prunes, olives, capers, garlic, olive oil, bay leaves, oregano, vinegar, salt, and pepper.

Ninja Foodi Cookbook Guide

2. Spread the mixture on the bottom of a baking tray, and place the chicken.
3. Preheat the Foodi to 360° °F or 180°C. Sprinkle a little bit of brown sugar on top of the chicken, close the crisping lid and cook for 45-55 minutes on Air Crisp mode. When ready, garnish with fresh parsley.

Whole Chicken With Lemon And Onion Stuffing

Servings: 6
Cooking Time: 55 Min
Ingredients:
- 4 lb. whole chicken /1800g
- 1 yellow onion, peeled and quartered
- 1 lemon, quartered
- 2 cloves garlic, peeled
- 1 ¼ cups chicken broth /312.5ml
- 1 tbsp herbes de Provence Seasoning /15g
- 1 tbsp olive oil /15ml
- 1 tsp garlic powder /5g
- Salt and black pepper to season

Directions:
1. Put the chicken on a clean flat surface and pat dry using paper towels. Sprinkle the top and cavity of the chicken with salt, black pepper, Herbes de Provence, and garlic powder.
2. Stuff the onion, lemon quarters, and garlic cloves into the cavity. In the Foodi, fit the reversible rack. Pour the broth in and place the chicken on the rack. Seal the lid, and select Pressure mode on High for 25 minutes.
3. Press Start/Stop to start cooking. Once ready, do a natural pressure release for about 10 minutes, then a quick pressure release to let the remaining steam out, and press Stop.
4. Close the crisping lid and broil the chicken for 5 minutes on Broil mode, to ensure that it attains a golden brown color on each side.
5. Dish the chicken on a bed of steamed mixed veggies. Right here, the choice is yours to whip up some good veggies together as your appetite tells you.

Simple Chicken Parmesan

Servings:4
Cooking Time: 20 Minutes
Ingredients:
- 1 cup all-purpose flour
- 1 teaspoon sea salt
- 2 eggs, beaten
- 2 tablespoons water
- 1 cup seasoned bread crumbs
- ½ cup grated Parmesan cheese
- 4 chicken cutlets
- 2 tablespoons extra-virgin olive oil
- ¼ cup marinara sauce
- 1 cup shredded mozzarella cheese

Directions:
1. Place the flour and salt in a shallow bowl and stir. In another shallow bowl, add the eggs and water, whisking to combine. Place the bread crumbs and Parmesan cheese in a third shallow bowl.
2. Dredge each piece of chicken in the flour. Tap off any excess, then coat the chicken in the egg wash. Transfer the chicken to the breadcrumb mixture and evenly coat. Repeat until all the chicken is coated.
3. Place Reversible Rack in pot, making sure it is in the higher position. Place the chicken on the rack and brush lightly with the oil. Close crisping lid.

4. Select AIR CRISP, set temperature to 325°F (160°C), and set time to 15 minutes. Select START/STOP to begin.
5. After 15 minutes, open lid and spread the marinara sauce on top of the chicken. Top with the mozzarella. Close crisping lid.
6. Select BROIL and set time to 5 minutes. Select START/STOP to begin.
7. When the cheese is fully melted, cooking is complete. Serve.

Nutrition:
- InfoCalories: 589,Total Fat: 23g,Sodium: 1215mg,Carbohydrates: 38g,Protein: 54g.

Taco Stuffed Avocados

Servings: 4
Cooking Time: 15 Minutes
Ingredients:
- 2 ripe avocados, halved, peeled & pitted
- 1 cup chicken, cooked & shredded
- ½ cup fresh salsa, drained
- 1 green onion, sliced thin
- ½ tsp cumin
- 1 tbsp. cilantro, chopped
- 1/8 cup cheddar cheese, reduced fat, grated

Directions:
1. Place the rack in the cooking pot and top with a sheet of foil.
2. Place the avocados, cut side down, on the foil and add the tender-crisp lid. Set to bake on 400°F (205°C). Cook the avocados 10 minutes, then set aside to cool slightly.
3. In a medium bowl, combine chicken, salsa, green onion, cumin, and cilantro, mix well. Spoon into centers of avocado. Sprinkle with cheese.
4. Use the foil to place the avocados back on the rack. Add the tender-crisp lid again and set to broil. Cook 2-3 minutes until cheese is melted and just starting to brown. Serve.

Nutrition:
- InfoCalories 248,Total Fat 18g,Total Carbs 11g,Protein 13g,Sodium 285mg.

Crunchy Chicken Schnitzels

Servings: 4
Cooking Time: 25 Min
Ingredients:
- 4 chicken breasts, boneless
- 2 eggs, beaten
- 4 slices cold butter
- 4 slices lemon
- 1 cup flour /130g
- 1 cup breadcrumbs /130g
- 2 tbsp fresh parsley; chopped 30g
- Cooking spray
- Salt and pepper to taste

Directions:
1. Combine the breadcrumbs with the parsley in a dish and set aside. Season the chicken with salt and pepper. Coat in flour; shake off any excess. Dip the coated chicken into the beaten egg followed by breadcrumbs. Spray the schnitzels with cooking spray.
2. Put them into the Foodi basket, close the crisping lid and cook for 10 minutes at 380 °F or 195°C. After 5 minutes, turn the schnitzels over. Arrange the schnitzels on a serving platter and place the butter and lemon slices over to serve.

Creamy Tuscan Chicken Pasta

Servings: 8
Cooking Time: 6 Minutes
Ingredients:
- 32 ounces chicken stock
- 1 jar oil-packed sun-dried tomatoes, drained
- 2 teaspoons Italian seasoning
- 3 garlic cloves, minced
- 1 pound chicken breast, cubed
- 1 box penne pasta
- 4 cups spinach
- 1 package cream cheese, cubed
- 1 cup shredded Parmesan cheese
- Kosher salt
- Freshly ground black pepper

Directions:
1. Place the chicken stock, sun-dried tomatoes, Italian seasoning, garlic, chicken breast, and pasta and stir. Assemble pressure lid, making sure the pressure release valve is in the SEAL position.
2. Select PRESSURE and set to HI. Set time to 6 minutes. Select START/STOP to begin.
3. When pressure cooking is complete, quick release the pressure by turning the pressure release valve to the VENT position. Carefully remove lid when unit has finished releasing pressure.
4. Add the spinach and stir, allowing it to wilt with the residual heat. Add the cream cheese, Parmesan cheese, salt and pepper and stir until melted. Serve.

Nutrition:
- InfoCalories: 429, Total Fat: 21g, Sodium: 567mg, Carbohydrates: 32g, Protein: 29g.

Chicken With Mushroom Sauce

Servings: 10
Cooking Time: 6 Hours
Ingredients:
- 8 oz. tomato sauce
- 1 cup mushrooms, sliced
- ½ cup dry white wine
- 1 onion, chopped
- 1 clove garlic, chopped fine
- ¼ tsp salt
- ¼ tsp pepper
- 3 lbs. chicken pieces, skinless
- 2 tbsp. water
- 1 tbsp. flour

Directions:
1. Add the tomato sauce, mushrooms, wine, onion, garlic, salt and pepper to the cooking pot, stir to mix.
2. Add the chicken and turn to coat well
3. Add the lid and set to slow cook on low heat. Cook 6 hours or until chicken is cooked through and tender. Transfer chicken to a serving plate.
4. In a small bowl, whisk together water and flour until smooth. Stir into the sauce and cook 10-15 minutes, stirring frequently, until sauce thickens. Serve chicken topped with sauce.

Nutrition:
- InfoCalories 176, Total Fat 4g, Total Carbs 4g, Protein 28g, Sodium 164mg.

Pulled Chicken And Peach Salsa

Servings: 4
Cooking Time: 40 Min
Ingredients:
- 4 boneless; skinless chicken thighs
- 15 ounces canned peach chunks /450g
- 2 cloves garlic; minced
- 14 ounces canned diced tomatoes /420g
- ½ tsp cumin /2.5g
- ½ tsp salt /2.5g
- Cheddar shredded cheese
- Fresh chopped mint leaves

Directions:
1. Strain canned peach chunks. Reserve the juice and set aside. In your Foodi, add chicken, tomatoes, cumin, garlic, peach juice, and salt.
2. Seal the pressure lid, choose Pressure, set to High, and set the timer to 15 minutes. Press Start. When ready, do a quick pressure release.
3. Shred chicken with the use of two forks. Transfer to a serving plate. Add peach chunks to the cooking juices and mix until well combined.
4. Pour the peach salsa over the chicken, top with chopped mint leaves and shredded cheese. Serve immediately.

Red Chili Chicken

Servings: 6
Cooking Time: 1 Hour
Ingredients:
- 1 tbsp. olive oil
- 1 ¼ cup Mexican red chili sauce
- 2 tbsp. cider vinegar
- ½ tsp cloves
- ½ tsp allspice
- 1 tsp cinnamon
- ¼ tsp cumin
- ¼ tsp pepper
- ¼ tsp oregano
- 1 tsp garlic, chopped fine
- 3 lbs. chicken thighs
- 1 tsp salt

Directions:
1. Add oil to the cooking pot and set to sauté on medium heat.
2. Add the chili sauce, vinegar, cloves, allspice, cinnamon, cumin, pepper, oregano, and garlic. Bring to a simmer and cook 5 minutes. Turn off heat and let cool.
3. Sprinkle chicken with salt and place in a large Ziploc bag. Add the sauce and turn to coat. Refrigerate at least 1 hour or overnight is best.
4. Place the chicken, skin side up, in the cooking pot. Add the tender-crisp lid and set to roast on 350°F (175°C). Cook 34-50 minutes or until cooked through and juices run clear. Serve garnished with cilantro.

Nutrition:
- InfoCalories 179, Total Fat 13g, Total Carbs 2g, Protein 14g, Sodium 83mg.

Creamy Turkey And Mushroom Ragu

Servings: 4
Cooking Time: 40 Minutes
Ingredients:
- 2 tablespoons unsalted butter
- 1 pound ground turkey
- 8 ounces cremini mushrooms, sliced
- 1 can condensed cream of celery soup
- 4 cups chicken stock
- 1 package egg noodles
- 16 ounces frozen peas
- 1 cup sour cream
- ¾ cup grated Parmesan cheese
- Kosher salt
- Freshly ground black pepper

Directions:
1. Select SEAR/SAUTÉ and set to MED. Press START/STOP to begin. Let preheat for 3 minutes.
2. Add the butter, ground turkey, and mushrooms. Using a silicone-tipped utensil, break up the turkey as it browns, about 10 minutes.
3. Add the condensed soup and stock. Whisk well to combine. Bring to a simmer for 15 minutes.
4. Add the egg noodles and peas and stir well. Cook until the noodles are tender and cooked through, 8 to 10 minutes.
5. Select START/STOP to stop cooking. Stir in sour cream and Parmesan cheese until melted and incorporated. Season with salt and pepper. Serve immediately.

Nutrition:
- InfoCalories: 854, Total Fat: 39g, Sodium: 1714mg, Carbohydrates: 79g, Protein: 48g.

Buffalo Chicken And Navy Bean Chili

Servings: 6
Cooking Time: 45 Min
Ingredients:
- 1 ½ pounds chicken sausage; sliced /675g
- 1 can diced tomatoes with green chilies /420g
- 2 cans navy beans, drained and rinsed /420g
- 1 can crushed tomatoes /840g
- ¾ cup Buffalo wing sauce /188ml
- 1 shallot; diced
- ½ cup fennel; chopped /65g
- ¼ cup minced garlic /32.5g
- 1 tbsp olive oil /15ml
- 1 tbsp smoked paprika /15ml
- 2 tsp chili powder /10g
- 2 tsp ground cumin /10g
- ½ tsp salt /2.5g
- ½ tsp ground white pepper /2.5g

Directions:
1. Warm oil on Sear/Sauté. Add the sausages and brown for 5 minutes, turning frequently. Set aside on a plate.
2. In the same fat, sauté onion, roasted red peppers, fennel, and garlic for 4 minutes until soft; season with paprika, cumin, pepper, salt, and chili powder.
3. Stir in crushed tomatoes; diced tomatoes with green chilies, buffalo sauce, and navy beans. Return the sausages to the pot.
4. Seal the pressure lid, choose Pressure, set to High, and set the timer to 30 minutes. Press Start. When ready, do a quick pressure release. Spoon chili into bowls and serve warm.

Chicken Chickpea Chili

Servings: 4
Cooking Time: 25 Min
Ingredients:
- 1 pound boneless; skinless chicken breast; cubed /450g
- 2 cans chickpeas, drained and rinsed /435g
- 1 jalapeño pepper; diced
- 1 lime; cut into six wedges
- 3 large serrano peppers; diced *chilli green*
- 1 onion; diced
- ½ cup chopped fresh cilantro /65g *Coriander*
- ½ cup shredded Monterey Jack cheese /65g
- 2 ½ cups water; divided /675ml
- 1 tbsp olive oil /15ml
- 2 tbsp chili powder /30g
- 1 tsp ground cumin /5g
- 1 tsp minced fresh garlic /5g
- 1 tsp salt /5g

Directions:
1. Warm oil on Sear/Sauté. Add in onion, serrano peppers, and jalapeno pepper and cook for 5 minutes until tender; add salt, cumin and garlic for seasoning.
2. Stir chicken with vegetable mixture; cook for 3 to 6 minutes until no longer pink; add 2 cups or 500ml water and chickpeas.
3. Seal the pressure lid, choose Pressure, set to High, and set the timer to 5 minutes. Press Start. Release pressure naturally for 5 minutes. Press Start. Stir chili powder with remaining ½ cup or 125ml water; mix in chili.
4. Press Sear/Sauté. Boil the chili as you stir and cook until slightly thickened. Divide chili into plates; garnish with cheese and cilantro. Over the chili, squeeze a lime wedge.

Hainanese Chicken

Servings: 4
Cooking Time: 4 Hours
Ingredients:
- 1 ounce's ginger, peeled
- 6 garlic cloves, crushed
- 6 bundles cilantro/basil leaves
- 1 teaspoon salt
- 1 tablespoon sesame oil
- 3 1 and ½ pounds each chicken meat, ready to cook
- For Dip
- 2 tablespoons ginger, minced
- 1 teaspoon garlic, minced
- 1 tablespoon chicken stock
- 1 teaspoon sesame oil
- ½ teaspoon erythritol
- Salt to taste

Directions:
1. Add chicken, garlic, ginger, leaves, and salt to your Ninja Food.
2. Add enough water to fully submerge chicken; Lock and secure the Ninja Foodi's lid cooks on SLOW COOK mode on LOW for 4 hours.
3. Release pressure naturally.
4. Take chicken out of the pot and chill for 10 minutes.

Ninja Foodi Cookbook Guide

5. Take a suitable and add all the dipping ingredients and blend well in a food processor.
6. Take chicken out of ice bath and drain, chop into serving pieces.
7. Set onto a serving platter.
8. Brush chicken with sesame oil.
9. Serve with ginger dip.
10. Enjoy.

Nutrition:
- InfoCalories: 535; Fat: 45g; Carbohydrates: 5g; Protein: 28g

Butternut Turkey Stew

Servings: 6
Cooking Time: 4 Hours
Ingredients:
- 1 tbsp. olive oil
- 1 onion, chopped
- 2 carrots, chopped
- 3 cloves garlic, chopped
- 1 butternut squash, peeled & chopped
- 4 cups turkey, cooked & chopped
- 7 cups chicken broth, low sodium
- ½ tsp salt
- ½ tsp pepper
- 1 cup green peas, frozen

Directions:
1. Add oil to the cooking pot and set to sauté on med-high.
2. Add the onions and cook 3-5 minutes until translucent.
3. Set cooker to slow cook on high. Add remaining ingredients, except the peas and stir to mix.
4. Add the lid and cook 4 hours, stirring occasionally. Add the peas in the last 30 minutes of cooking time. Ladle into bowls and serve.

Nutrition:
- InfoCalories 235, Total Fat 8g, Total Carbs 17g, Protein 25g, Sodium 992mg.

Butter Chicken

Servings: 6
Cooking Time: 30 Min
Ingredients:
- 2 pounds boneless; skinless chicken legs /900g
- 3 Roma tomatoes, pureed in a blender
- 1 can coconut milk, refrigerated overnight /435ml
- 1 large onion; minced
- ½ cup chopped fresh cilantro; divided /65g
- 2 tbsp Indian curry paste /30ml
- 2 tbsp dried fenugreek /30g
- 1 tbsp Kashmiri red chili powder /15g
- 2 tbsp butter /30g
- 1 tbsp grated fresh ginger /15g
- 1 tbsp minced fresh garlic /15g
- 1 tsp salt /5g
- 2 tsp sugar /10g
- ½ tsp ground turmeric /2.5g
- 1 tsp garam masala /5g
- Salt to taste

Directions:
1. Set your Foodi to Sear/Sauté, set to Medium High, and choose Start/Stop to preheat the pot and melt butter. Add in 1 tsp salt and onion. Cook for 2 to 3 minutes until fragrant. Stir in ginger, turmeric, garlic, and red chili powder to coat; cook for 2 more minutes.
2. Place water and coconut cream into separate bowls. Stir the water from the coconut milk can, pureed tomatoes, and chicken with the onion mixture. Seal the pressure lid, choose Pressure, set to High, and set the timer to 8 minutes. Press Start. When ready, release the pressure quickly.
3. Stir sugar, coconut cream, fenugreek, curry paste, half the cilantro, and garam masala through the chicken mixture; apply salt for seasoning. Simmer the mixture and cook for 10 minutes until the sauce thickens, on Sear/Sauté. Garnish with the rest of the cilantro before serving.

Chicken Thighs With Cabbage

Servings: 4
Cooking Time: 35 Min
Ingredients:
- 1 pound green cabbage, shredded /450g
- 4 slices pancetta; diced
- 4 chicken thighs, boneless skinless
- 1 cup chicken broth /250ml
- 1 tbsp Dijon mustard /15g
- 1 tbsp lard /15g
- Fresh parsley; chopped
- salt and ground black pepper to taste

Directions:
1. Warm lard on Sear/Sauté. Fry pancetta for 5 minutes until crisp. Set aside. Season chicken with pepper and salt. Sear in Foodi for 2 minutes each side until browned. In a bowl, mix mustard and chicken broth.
2. In your Foodi, add pancetta and chicken broth mixture. Seal the pressure lid, choose Pressure, set to High, and set the timer to 6 minutes. Press Start. When ready, release the pressure quickly.
3. Open the lid, mix in green cabbage, seal again, and cook on High Pressure for 2 minutes. When ready, release the pressure quickly. Serve with sprinkled parsley.

Thyme Chicken With Veggies

Servings: 4
Cooking Time: 40 Min
Ingredients:
- 4 skin-on, bone-in chicken legs
- ½ cup dry white wine /125ml
- 1¼ cups chicken stock /312.5ml
- 1 cup carrots, thinly sliced /130g
- 1 cup parsnip, thinly sliced /130g
- 4 slices lemon
- 4 cloves garlic; minced
- 3 tomatoes, thinly sliced
- 2 tbsp olive oil /30ml
- 1 tbsp honey /15ml
- 1 tsp fresh chopped thyme /5g
- salt and freshly ground black pepper to taste
- Fresh thyme; chopped for garnish

Directions:
1. Season the chicken with pepper and salt. Warm oil on Sear/Sauté. Arrange chicken legs into the hot oil; cook for 3 to 5 minutes each side until browned. Place in a bowl and set aside. Cook thyme and garlic in the chicken fat for 1 minute until soft and lightly golden.

2. Add wine into the pot to deglaze, scrape the pot's bottom to get rid of any brown bits of food. Simmer the wine for 2 to 3 minutes until slightly reduced in volume.
3. Add stock, carrots, parsnips, tomatoes, pepper and salt into the pot.
4. Lay reversible rack onto veggies. Into the Foodi's steamer basket, arrange chicken legs. Set the steamer basket onto the reversible rack. Drizzle the chicken with honey then top with lemon slices.
5. Seal the pressure lid, choose Pressure, set to High, and set the timer to 12 minutes. Press Start. Release pressure naturally for 10 minutes. Place the chicken onto a bowl. Drain the veggies and place them around the chicken. Garnish with fresh thyme leaves before serving.

Lemon, Barley & Turkey Soup

Servings: 6
Cooking Time: 4 Hours
Ingredients:
- 3 tbsp. extra virgin olive oil
- 1 onion, chopped fine
- 3 cloves garlic, chopped fine
- 1 tsp turmeric
- ½ tsp cumin
- ½ tsp ginger
- ½ tsp salt
- ½ tsp pepper
- 6 cups chicken broth, low sodium
- 6-8 strips of lemon peel, pith removed
- 1 cup barley
- 2 cups turkey, cooked & chopped
- 2 tbsp. lemon juice
- ¼ cup fresh parsley, chopped
- ¼ cup cilantro, chopped

Directions:
1. Add the oil to the cooking pot and set to saute on med-heat.
2. Add the onion and cook 2-3 minutes until translucent. Stir in the garlic and cook 1 minute more.
3. Add turmeric, cumin, ginger, and salt, stir to mix. Pour in the broth, zest, and barley. Add the lid and set to slow cook on low. Cook 3-3 ½ hours until barley is tender.
4. When the barley is cooked, add the turkey, lemon juice, parsley, cilantro, salt, and pepper and cook 30 minutes or until heated through. Discard the lemon peel before serving.

Nutrition:
- InfoCalories 94,Total Fat 4g,Total Carbs 9g,Protein 6g,Sodium 156mg.

Chicken And Sweet Potato Corn Chowder

Servings: 8
Cooking Time: 40 Min
Ingredients:
- 4 boneless; skinless chicken breast; diced
- 19 ounces corn kernels, frozen /570g
- 1 sweet potato, peeled and cubed
- 4 ounces canned diced green chiles, drained /120g
- 3 garlic cloves; minced
- 2 cups cheddar cheese, shredded /260g
- 2 cups creme fraiche /500ml
- 1 cup chicken stock /250ml
- Cilantro leaves; chopped
- 2 tsp chili powder /10g
- 1 tsp ground cumin /5g
- Salt and black pepper to taste

Directions:
1. Mix chicken, corn, chili powder, cumin, chicken stock, sweet potato, green chiles, and garlic in the pot of the Foodi. Seal the pressure lid, choose Pressure, set to High, and set the timer to 10 minutes. Press Start.
2. When ready, release the pressure quickly. Set the chicken to a cutting board and use two forks to shred it. Return to pot and stir well into the liquid.
3. Stir in cheese and creme fraiche; season with pepper and salt. Cook for 2 to 3 minutes until cheese is melted. Place chowder into plates and top with cilantro.

Moo Shu Chicken

Servings: 4
Cooking Time: 20 Minutes
Ingredients:
- 1 tbsp. sesame oil
- 1 cup mushrooms, sliced
- 2 cups cabbage, shredded
- ½ cup green onion, sliced thin
- 3 cups chicken, cooked & shredded
- 2 eggs, lightly beaten
- ¼ cup hoisin sauce
- 2 tbsp. tamari
- 2 tsp sriracha sauce

Directions:
1. Add the oil to the cooking pot and set to sauté on med-high heat.
2. Add the mushrooms and cook 5-6 minutes, stirring frequently, until mushrooms have browned and liquid has evaporated.
3. Add cabbage and green onion, cook, stirring, 2 minutes.
4. Stir in chicken and cook 3-5 minutes until heated through.
5. Add the eggs and cook, stirring to scramble, until eggs are cooked.
6. Stir in remaining ingredients. Reduce heat and simmer until heated through. Serve immediately.

Nutrition:
- InfoCalories 378,Total Fat 25g,Total Carbs 15g,Protein 23g,Sodium 1067mg.

Greek Chicken

Servings: 6
Cooking Time: 45 Min
Ingredients:
- 1 whole chicken; cut in pieces /1350g
- ½ cup olive oil /125ml
- 3 garlic cloves; minced
- Juice from 1 lemon
- ½ cup white wine /125ml
- 1 tbsp chopped fresh oregano /15g
- 1 tbsp fresh thyme /15g
- 1 tbsp fresh rosemary /15g
- Salt and black pepper, to taste

Directions:
1. In a large bowl, combine the garlic, rosemary, thyme, olive oil, lemon juice, oregano, salt, and pepper. Mix all ingredients very well and spread the mixture into the Foodi basket.
2. Stir in the chicken. Sprinkle with wine and cook for 45 minutes on Air Crisp mode at 380 °F or 195°C.

Honey Chicken & Veggies

Servings: 6
Cooking Time: 6 Hours
Ingredients:
- ½ cup honey
- 1/3 cup balsamic vinegar
- 3 tbsp. tomato paste
- ½ tsp salt
- ½ tsp pepper
- 3 cloves garlic, chopped fine
- 1 tsp ginger
- ¼ tsp red pepper flakes
- 6 chicken thighs
- 2 cups baby carrots
- 2 cups baby red potatoes, quartered
- 1 tbsp. fresh parsley, chopped

Directions:
1. In a small bowl, whisk together honey, vinegar, tomato paste, salt, pepper, garlic, ginger, and pepper flakes until combined.
2. Add chicken, carrots, and potatoes to the cooking pot.
3. Pour honey mixture over the top, reserving ½ cup. Toss gently to mix.
4. Add the lid and set to slow cook on low. Cook 6-8 hours until vegetables are tender and chicken is cooked through.
5. Pour remaining glaze over chicken and vegetables and serve garnished with parsley.

Nutrition:
- InfoCalories 299, Total Fat 13g, Total Carbs 34g, Protein 14g, Sodium 320mg.

Chicken With Roasted Red Pepper Sauce

Servings: 4
Cooking Time: 23 Min
Ingredients:
- 4 chicken breasts; skinless and boneless
- ¼ cup roasted red peppers; chopped /32.5g
- ½ cup chicken broth /125ml
- ½ cup heavy cream /125ml
- 1 tbsp basil pesto /15g
- 1 tbsp cornstarch /15g
- ⅓ tsp Italian Seasoning /1.67g
- ⅓ tsp minced garlic /1.67g
- Salt and black pepper to taste

Directions:
1. In the inner pot of the Foodi, add the chicken at the bottom. Pour the chicken broth and add Italian seasoning, garlic, salt, and pepper.
2. Close the pressure lid, secure the pressure valve, and select Pressure mode on High for 15 minutes. Press Start/Stop.
3. Once the timer has ended, do a natural pressure release for 5 minutes and open the lid. Use a spoon to remove the chicken onto a plate. Scoop out any fat or unwanted chunks from the sauce.
4. In a small bowl, add the cream, cornstarch, red peppers, and pesto. Mix them with a spoon. Pour the creamy mixture into the pot and close the crisping lid.
5. Select Broil mode and cook for 4 minutes. Serve the chicken with sauce over on a bed of cooked quinoa.

Skinny Chicken & Dumplings

Servings: 6
Cooking Time: 4 Hours 30 Minutes
Ingredients:
- 6 cups chicken broth, low sodium
- 2 chicken breast, boneless & skinless
- ½ cup peas, frozen
- ½ cup carrots, chopped fine
- 1 onion, chopped fine
- ½ cup celery, chopped fine
- 3 cloves garlic, chopped fine
- 2 tsp thyme
- 2 tsp basil
- 1 tsp sage
- 1 cup whole wheat flour
- 1 tsp baking powder
- ½ tsp garlic powder
- ½ tsp onion powder
- 3 tbsp. butter, cubed
- 1/3 cup skim milk

Directions:
1. Add the broth, chicken, peas, carrots, onion, celery, garlic, thyme, basil, and sage in the cooking pot, stir to mix.
2. Add the lid and set to slow cook on high. Cook 4 hours, stirring occasionally.
3. In a large bowl, flour, baking powder, garlic powder, and onion powder. Cut in butter with a pastry blender until mixture resembles fine crumbs.
4. Slowly add the milk until a thick, sticky batter forms.
5. Transfer the chicken to a cutting board and shred. Return it to the pot. Drop the dumpling batter by tablespoons into the pot. Recover and cook 20-30 minutes or until dumplings are cooked. Serve immediately.

Nutrition:
- InfoCalories 297, Total Fat 10g, Total Carbs 23g, Protein 20g, Sodium 194mg.

Spicy Onion Crusted Chicken Tenders

Servings: 6
Cooking Time: 10 Minutes
Ingredients:
- Nonstick cooking spray
- ½ cup hot pepper sauce
- 2 cups French-fried onions, crushed
- 1 ½ lbs. chicken tenders

Directions:
1. Spray fryer basket with cooking spray.
2. Pour the hot sauce in a shallow dish.
3. In a separate shallow dish, place the crushed onions.
4. Dip each piece of chicken in the hot sauce then coat with onions. Place in a single layer in the fryer basket, these will need to be cooked in batches.
5. Add the tender-crisp lid and to air fry on 400°F (205°C). Cook chicken 10 minutes, until golden brown and cooked through, turning over halfway through cooking tine. Serve immediately.

Nutrition:
- InfoCalories 154, Total Fat 3g, Total Carbs 6g, Protein 24g, Sodium 541mg.

Ninja Foodi Cookbook Guide

Beef, Pork & Lamb

Pork Tenderloin With Warm Balsamic And Apple Chutney

Servings: 4
Cooking Time: 23 Minutes
Ingredients:
- 1 pound pork tenderloin
- 2½ tablespoons minced rosemary, divided
- 2½ tablespoons minced thyme, divided
- Kosher salt
- Freshly ground black pepper
- 2 tablespoons extra-virgin olive oil
- 1 small white onion
- 1 tablespoon minced garlic
- ¾ cup apple juice
- 2 apples, cut into ½-inch cubes
- 2½ tablespoons balsamic vinegar
- 1 tablespoon honey
- 2½ teaspoons cornstarch
- 3 tablespoons unsalted butter, cubed

Directions:
1. Select SEAR/SAUTÉ and set to HI. Select START/STOP to begin. Let preheat for 5 minutes.
2. Season the pork with 1 tablespoon of rosemary, 1 tablespoon of thyme, salt, and pepper.
3. Once unit is preheated, add the olive oil. Once hot, add the pork and sear for 3 minutes on each side. Once seared, place the pork on a plate and set aside.
4. Add the onion, garlic, and apple juice. Stir, scraping the bottom of the pot to remove any brown bits. Add apples and vinegar and stir. Return the pork to the pot, nestling it in the apple mixture. Assemble pressure lid, making sure the pressure release valve is in the SEAL position.
5. Select PRESSURE and set to HI. Set time to 7 minutes. Select START/STOP to begin.
6. When pressure cooking is complete, allow pressure to naturally release for 14 minutes. After 14 minutes, quick release the pressure by turning the pressure release valve to the VENT position. Carefully remove lid when unit has finished releasing pressure.
7. Remove the pork from the pot, place it on a plate, and cover with aluminum foil.
8. Slightly mash the apples with a potato masher. Stir the honey into the mixture.
9. Remove ¼ cup of cooking liquid from the pot and mix it with the cornstarch until smooth. Pour this mixture into the pot and stir until thickened. Add the butter, 1 tablespoon of rosemary, and 1 tablespoon of thyme and stir until the butter is melted.
10. Slice the pork and serve it with the chutney. Garish with the remaining ½ tablespoon of rosemary and ½ tablespoon of thyme.

Nutrition:
- InfoCalories: 406, Total Fat: 20g, Sodium: 107mg, Carbohydrates: 33g, Protein: 24g.

Caribbean Ropa Vieja

Servings: 6
Cooking Time: 1 Hr 10 Min
Ingredients:
- 2 pounds beef skirt steak /900g
- ¼ cup cheddar cheese, shredded /32.5g
- 1 cup tomato sauce /250ml
- 3½ cups beef stock /875ml
- 1 cup dry red wine /250ml
- ¼ cup minced garlic /32.5g
- ¼ cup olive oil /62.5ml
- 1 green bell pepper, thinly sliced
- 1 red bell pepper, thinly sliced
- 2 bay leaves
- 1 red onion, halved and thinly sliced
- 1 tbsp vinegar /15ml
- 1 tsp dried oregano /5g
- 1 tsp ground cumin 5g
- Salt and ground black pepper to taste

Directions:
1. Season the skirt steak with pepper and salt. Add water into Foodi; mix in bay leaves and flank steak. Seal the pressure lid, choose Pressure, set to High, and set the timer to 35 minutes. Press Start. When ready, release the pressure quickly.
2. Remove skirt steak to a cutting board and allow to sit for about 5 minutes. Press Start. When cooled, shred the beef using two forks. Drain the pressure cooker, and reserve the bay leaves and 1 cup liquid.
3. Warm the oil on Sear/Sauté. Add onion, red bell pepper, cumin, garlic, green bell pepper, and oregano and continue cooking for 5 minutes until vegetables are softened.
4. Stir in reserved liquid, tomato sauce, bay leaves and red wine. Return shredded beef to the pot with vinegar; season with pepper and salt.
5. Seal the pressure lid, choose Pressure, set to High, and set the timer to 15 minutes. Press Start. Release pressure naturally for 10 minutes, then turn steam vent valve to Venting to release the remaining pressure quickly. Serve with shredded cheese.

Asian Beef

Servings: 6
Cooking Time: 15 Minutes
Ingredients:
- 1/4 cup soy sauce
- 1/2 cup beef broth
- 1 tablespoon sesame oil
- 1/4 cup brown erythritol, packed
- 4 cloves garlic, minced
- 1 teaspoon hot sauce
- 1 tablespoon rice wine vinegar
- 1 tablespoon ginger, grated
- 1/2 teaspoon onion powder
- 1/2 teaspoon pepper
- 3 lb. boneless beef chuck roast, cubed
- 3 tablespoons corn starch dissolved in 1 teaspoon water

Directions:
1. Mix all the seasonings in a suitable bowl except the chuck roast and corn starch.
2. Pour the mixture into the Ninja Foodi. Stir in the beef. Seal the pot.
3. Select pressure. Cook at "HIGH" pressure for 15 minutes.
4. Do a quick pressure release. Stir in the corn starch.
5. Select sauté setting to thicken the sauce.

Nutrition:
- InfoCalories: 482; Fat: 16.6g; Carbohydrate: 8.4g; Protein: 70.1g

Braised Lamb Shanks

Servings: 4
Cooking Time: 4 Hours 15 Minutes
Ingredients:
- 2 bone-in lamb shanks, 2 to 2½ pounds each
- Kosher salt
- Freshly ground black pepper
- 2 tablespoons canola oil
- 2 Yukon gold potatoes, cut into 1-inch pieces
- 2 carrots, cut into 2-inch pieces
- 2 parsnips, peeled and cut into 2-inch pieces
- 1 bag frozen pearl onions
- 1 bottle red wine
- 1 cup chicken stock
- 1 tablespoon chopped fresh rosemary

Directions:
1. Select SEAR/SAUTÉ and set to HI. Select START/STOP to begin. Let preheat for 5 minutes.
2. Season the lamb shanks with salt and pepper.
3. Add the oil and lamb. Cook for 5 minutes on one side, then turn and cook for an additional 5 minutes. Remove the lamb and set aside.
4. Add the potatoes, carrots, parsnips, and pearl onions. Cook for 5 minutes, stirring occasionally.
5. Stir in the red wine, chicken stock, and rosemary. Add the lamb back to the pot and press down on the shanks to ensure they are mostly submerged in liquid. Assemble pressure lid, making sure the pressure release valve is in the VENT position.
6. Select SLOW COOK and set to HI. Set time to 4 hours. Select START/STOP to begin.
7. When cooking is complete, remove lid and serve.

Nutrition:
- InfoCalories: 791, Total Fat: 34g, Sodium: 591mg, Carbohydrates: 47g, Protein: 51g.

Beef Stir Fry

Servings: 4
Cooking Time: 11 Minutes
Ingredients:
- 1 lb. beef sirloin, sliced into strips
- 1 tablespoon vegetable oil
- 1-1/2 lb. broccoli florets
- 1 red bell pepper, sliced into strips
- 1 yellow pepper, sliced into strips
- 1 green bell pepper, sliced into strips
- 1/2 cup onion, sliced into strips
- Marinade:
- 1/4 cup of hoisin sauce
- 1 teaspoon sesame oil
- 2 teaspoons garlic, minced
- 1 teaspoon of ground ginger
- 1 tablespoon soy sauce
- 1/4 cup of water

Directions:
1. Put all the marinade ingredients in a suitable. Divide it in half.
2. Soak the beef in the marinade for 20 minutes. Toss the vegetables in the other half.
3. Place the vegetables in the Ninja Foodi basket. Seal the crisping lid.
4. Select air crisp. Cook at 200 °F (95°C) for 5 minutes.
5. Remove the vegetables and set them aside. Put the meat on the basket.
6. Seal and cook at 360 °F (180°C) or 6 minutes.

Nutrition:
- InfoCalories: 390; Fat: 13g; Carbohydrate: 28.9g; Protein: 41.3g

Short Ribs With Egg Noodles

Servings: 4
Cooking Time: 65 Min
Ingredients:
- 4 pounds bone-in short ribs /1800g
- 1 garlic clove; minced
- 1½ cups panko bread crumbs /195g
- Low-sodium beef broth
- 6 ounces egg noodles /180g
- 3 tbsp melted unsalted butter /45ml
- 2 tbsp prepared horseradish /30g
- 6 tbsp Dijon mustard /90g
- 2½ tsp salt /12.5g
- ½ tsp freshly ground black pepper /2.5g

Directions:
1. Season the short ribs on all sides with 1½ tsp s or 7.5g of salt. Pour 1 cup 250ml of broth into the inner pot. Put the reversible rack in the lower position in the pot, and place the short ribs on top. Seal the pressure lid, choose Pressure; adjust the pressure to High and the time to 25 minutes; press Start. After cooking, perform a natural pressure release for 5 minutes, then a quick pressure release, and carefully open the lid. Remove the rack and short ribs.
2. Pour the cooking liquid into a measuring cup to get 2 cups. If lesser than 2 cups, add more broth and season with salt and pepper.
3. Add the egg noodles and the remaining salt. Stir and submerge the noodles as much as possible. Seal the pressure lid, choose Pressure; adjust the pressure to High and the cook time to 4 minutes; press Start.
4. In a bowl, combine the horseradish, Dijon mustard, garlic, and black pepper. Brush the sauce on all sides of the short ribs and reserve any extra sauce.
5. In a bowl, mix the butter and breadcrumbs. Coat the ribs with the crumbs. Put the ribs back on the rack. After cooking, do a quick pressure release, and carefully open the lid. Stir the noodles, which may not be quite done but will continue cooking.
6. Return the rack and beef to the pot in the upper position.
7. Close the crisping lid and Choose Bake/Roast; adjust the temperature to 400°F or 205°C and the cook time to 15 minutes. Press Start. After 8 minutes, open the lid and turn the ribs over. Close the lid and continue cooking. Serve the beef and noodles, with the extra sauce on the side, if desired.

Beef And Garbanzo Bean Chili

Servings: 10
Cooking Time: 45 Min
Ingredients:
- 1 pound garbanzo beans; soaked overnight, rinsed /900g
- 2 ½ pounds ground beef /1150g
- 1 can tomato puree /180ml
- 1 small jalapeño with seeds; minced
- 6 garlic cloves; minced
- 2 onions, finely chopped

- 2 ½ cups beef broth /625ml
- ¼ cup chili powder /32.5g
- 2 tbsp ground cumin /30g
- 1 tbsp olive oil /15ml
- 1 tsp garlic powder /5g
- ¼ tsp cayenne pepper /1.25g
- 1 tsp dried oregano /5g
- 2 tsp salt /10g
- 1 tsp smoked paprika /5g

Directions:
1. Add the garbanzo beans to the Foodi and pour in cold water to cover 1 inch. Seal the pressure lid, choose Pressure, set to High, and set the timer to 20 minutes. Press Start. When ready, release the pressure quickly.
2. Drain beans and rinse with cold water. Set aside. Wipe clean the Foodi and set to Sear/Sauté, set to Medium High, and choose Start/Stop to preheat the pot. Press Start. Warm olive oil, add in onion, and cook for 3 minutes until soft.
3. Add jalapeño, ground beef, and minced garlic, and stir-fry for 5 minutes until everything is cooked through. Stir in chili powder, kosher salt, garlic powder, paprika, cumin, oregano, and cayenne pepper, and cook until soft, about 30 seconds. Pour beef broth, garbanzo beans, and tomato paste into the pot.
4. Seal the pressure lid, choose Pressure, set to High, and set the timer to 20 minutes; press Start. When ready, release pressure naturally for about 10 minutes. Open the lid, press Sear/Sauté, and cook as you stir until desired consistency is attained. Spoon chili into bowls and serve.

Beef Lasagna

Servings: 4
Cooking Time: 10-15 Minutes
Ingredients:
- 2 small onions
- 2 garlic cloves, minced
- 1-pound ground beef
- 1 large egg
- 1 and 1/2 cups ricotta cheese
- 1/2 cup parmesan cheese
- 1 jar 25 ounces0 marinara sauce
- 8 ounces mozzarella cheese, sliced

Directions:
1. Select "Sauté" mode on your Ninja Foodi and stir in beef, brown the beef.
2. Add onion and garlic.
3. Add parmesan, ricotta, egg in a small dish and keep it on the side.
4. Stir in sauce to browned meat, reserve half for later.
5. Sprinkle mozzarella and half of ricotta cheese into the browned meat.
6. Top with remaining meat sauce.
7. For the final layer, add more mozzarella cheese and the remaining ricotta.
8. Stir well.
9. Cover with a foil transfer to Ninja Foodi.
10. Lock and secure the Ninja Foodi's lid, then cook on "HIGH" pressure for 8-10 minutes.
11. Quick-release pressure.
12. Drizzle parmesan cheese on top.
13. Enjoy.

Nutrition:
- InfoCalories: 365; Fats: 25g; Carbohydrates: 6g; Protein: 25g

Carne Guisada

Servings: 4
Cooking Time: 45 Minutes
Ingredients:
- 3 pounds beef stew
- 3 tablespoon seasoned salt
- 1 tablespoon oregano chilli powder
- 1 tablespoon cumin
- 1 pinch crushed red pepper
- 2 tablespoons olive oil
- 1/2 medium lime, juiced
- 1 cup beef bone broth
- 3 ounces tomato paste
- 1 large onion, sliced

Directions:
1. Trim the beef stew to taste into small bite-sized portions.
2. Toss the beef stew pieces with dry seasoning.
3. Select "Sauté" mode on your Ninja Foodi and stir in oil; allow the oil to heat up.
4. Add seasoned beef pieces and brown them.
5. Combine the browned beef pieces with the rest of the ingredients.
6. Lock the Ninja foodi's lid and cook on "HIGH" pressure for 3 minutes.
7. Release the pressure naturally.
8. Enjoy.

Nutrition:
- InfoProtein: 33g; Carbohydrates: 11g; Fats: 12g; Calories: 274

Crusted Pork Chops

Servings: 6
Cooking Time: 12 Minutes
Ingredients:
- Cooking spray
- 6 pork chops
- Black pepper and salt to taste
- 1/2 cup bread crumbs
- 2 tablespoons Parmesan cheese, grated
- 1/4 cup cornflakes, crushed
- 1-1/4 teaspoon sweet paprika
- 1/2 teaspoon onion powder
- 1/2 teaspoon garlic powder
- 1/4 teaspoon chilli powder
- 1 egg, beaten

Directions:
1. Season the pork chops liberally with black pepper and salt.
2. In a suitable, mix the rest of the ingredients except the egg.
3. Beat the egg in a suitable. Dip the pork chops in the egg.
4. Coat the pork with the breading. Place the pork on the Ninja Foodi basket.
5. Set it to air crisp and close the crisping lid.
6. Cook at 400 °F (205°C) for about 12 minutes, flipping halfway through.

Nutrition:
- InfoCalories: 310; Fat: 21.3g; Carbohydrate: 8.2g; rotein: 20.3g

Ninja Foodi Cookbook Guide

Chinese Bbq Ribs

Servings: 6
Cooking Time: 8 Hours
Ingredients:
- 4 tbsp. hoisin sauce
- 4 tbsp. oyster sauce
- 2 tbsp. soy sauce, low sodium
- 2 tbsp. rice wine
- 2 lbs. pork ribs, cut in 6 pieces
- Nonstick cooking spray
- 2-inch piece fresh ginger, grated
- 3 green onions, sliced
- 2 tbsp. honey

Directions:
1. In a large bowl, whisk together hoisin sauce, oyster sauce, soy sauce, and rice wine. Add the ribs and turn to coat. Cover and refrigerate overnight.
2. Spray the cooking pot with cooking spray.
3. Add the ribs and marinade. Top with ginger and green onions. Add the lid and set to slow cook on low. Cook 6-8 hours or until ribs are tender.
4. Transfer ribs to a serving plate. Spray the rack with the cooking spray and place in the pot. Lay the ribs, in a single layer, on the rack and brush with honey.
5. Add the tender-crisp lid and set to broil. Cook 3-4 minutes to caramelize the ribs. Serve.

Nutrition:
- InfoCalories 135,Total Fat 4g,Total Carbs 6g,Protein 17g,Sodium 419mg.

Smoky Horseradish Spare Ribs

Servings: 4
Cooking Time: 55 Min
Ingredients:
- 1 spare rack ribs
- 1 cup smoky horseradish sauce /250ml
- 1 tsp salt /5g

Directions:
1. Season all sides of the rack with salt and cut into 3 pieces. Cut the rack into 3 pieces. Pour 1 cup of water into the Foodi's inner pot. Fix the reversible rack in the pot in the lower position and put the ribs on top, bone-side down.
2. Seal the pressure lid, choose Pressure; adjust the pressure to High and the cook time to 18 minutes. Press Start. After cooking, perform a quick pressure release and carefully open the lid.
3. Take out the rack with ribs and pour out the water from the pot. Return the inner pot to the base. Set the reversible rack and ribs in the pot in the lower position. Close the crisping lid and Choose Air Crisp; adjust the temperature to 400°F or 205°C and the cook time to 20 minutes. Press Start.
4. After 10 minutes, open the lid and turn the ribs. Lightly baste the bony side of the ribs with the smoky horseradish sauce and close the lid to cook further. After 4 minutes, open the lid and turn the ribs again. Baste the meat side with the remaining sauce and close the lid to cook until the ribs are done.

Peppercorn Meatloaf

Servings: 8
Cooking Time: 35 Min
Ingredients:
- 4 lb. ground beef /1800g
- 10 whole peppercorns, for garnishing
- 1 onion; diced
- 1 cup breadcrumbs /130g
- 1 tbsp parsley /15g
- 1 tbsp Worcestershire sauce /15ml
- 3 tbsp ketchup /45ml
- 1 tbsp basil /15g
- 1 tbsp oregano /15g
- ½ tsp salt /2.5g
- 1 tsp ground peppercorns /5g

Directions:
1. Place the beef in a large bowl. Add all of the ingredients except the whole peppercorns and the breadcrumbs. Mix with your hand until well combined. Stir in the breadcrumbs.
2. Put the meatloaf on a lined baking dish. Insert in the Foodi, close the crisping lid and cook for 25 minutes on Air Crisp mode at 350 °F or 175°C.
3. Garnish the meatloaf with the whole peppercorns and let cool slightly before serving.

Caribbean Pork Pot

Servings: 6
Cooking Time: 15 Minutes
Ingredients:
- 1 tbsp. olive oil
- 1 ½ lb. pork tenderloin, cut in ¾-inch cubes
- 20 oz. chunked pineapple in juice, drained with liquid reserved
- 8 oz. water chestnuts, drained & sliced
- 1 cup fresh broccoli florets
- 1 red bell pepper, cut in ¾-inch strips
- 2 tbsp. soy sauce, low sodium
- 1 tbsp. vinegar
- 1 tbsp. ketchup
- 2 tbsp. cornstarch
- 2 tbsp. sugar

Directions:
1. Add the oil to the cooking pot and set to sauté on med-high heat.
2. Add the pork and cook 4-5 minutes until no longer pink, stirring frequently.
3. Add the pineapple, water chestnuts, broccoli, and bell pepper and cook, stirring frequently, 6-8 minutes or until vegetables are tender-crisp.
4. In a small bowl, whisk together reserved pineapple juice, soy sauce, vinegar, ketchup, cornstarch, and sugar until smooth. Stir into pork mixture and cook 4 minutes until sauce has thickened. Serve immediately.

Nutrition:
- InfoCalories 266,Total Fat 6g,Total Carbs 41g,Protein 26g,Sodium 263mg.

Lone Star Chili

Servings: 8
Cooking Time: 8 Hours
Ingredients:
- 2 tbsp. flour
- 2 lbs. lean beef chuck, cubed
- 1 tbsp. olive oil
- 1 onion, chopped fine
- 2 jalapeño peppers, chopped
- 4 cloves garlic, chopped fine
- 1 tbsp. cumin

Ninja Foodi Cookbook Guide

- 4 oz. green chilies, drained & chopped
- 3 tbsp. Ancho chili powder
- 1 tsp crushed red pepper flakes
- 1 tsp oregano
- 3 cups beef broth, fat-free & low-sodium
- 28 oz. tomatoes, diced, undrained
- ¼ cup Greek yogurt, fat free
- 3 tbsp. green onions, chopped

Directions:
1. Place the flour in a large Ziploc bag. Add the beef and toss to coat.
2. Add the oil to the cooking pot and set to sauté on med-high.
3. Add the beef and cook, stirring occasionally, until browned on all sides. Add the onions and jalapenos and cook until soft. Stir in the garlic and cook 1 minute more.
4. Stir in remaining ingredients, except yogurt and green onions, mix well. Add the lid and set to slow cook on low. Cook 7-8 hours until chili is thick and beef is tender.
5. Ladle into bowls and top with a dollop of yogurt and green onions. Serve.

Nutrition:
- InfoCalories 267, Total Fat 9g, Total Carbs 8g, Protein 36g, Sodium 317mg.

Picadillo Dish

Servings: 4
Cooking Time: 15-20 Minutes
Ingredients:
- 1/2-pound lean ground beef
- 2 garlic cloves, minced
- 1/2 large onion, chopped
- 1 teaspoon salt
- 1 tomato, chopped
- 1/2 red bell pepper, chopped
- 1 tablespoon cilantro, chopped
- 1/2 can 4 ounces tomato sauce
- 1 teaspoon ground cumin
- 1-2 bay leaves
- 2 tablespoons green olives, capers
- 2 tablespoons brine
- 3 tablespoons water

Directions:
1. Select "Sauté" mode on your Ninja Foodi and stir in meat, salt, and pepper, slightly brown.
2. Add garlic, tomato, onion, cilantro and Sauté for 1 minute.
3. Add olives, brine, leaf, cumin, and mix.
4. Pour in sauce, water, and stir. Lock and secure the Ninja Foodi's lid, then cook on "HIGH" pressure for 15 minutes.
5. Quick-release pressure.

Nutrition:
- InfoCalories: 207; Fats: 8g; Carbohydrates: 4g; Protein: 25g

Garlicky Pork Chops

Servings: 2
Cooking Time: 10 Minutes
Ingredients:
- 1 tablespoon coconut butter
- 1 tablespoon coconut oil
- 2 teaspoons cloves garlic, grated
- 2 teaspoons parsley, chopped
- Black pepper and salt to taste
- 4 pork chops, sliced into strips

Directions:
1. Combine all the ingredients except the pork strips. Mix well.
2. Marinate the pork in the mixture for 1 hour. Put the pork on the Ninja Foodi basket.
3. Set it inside the pot. Seal with the crisping lid. Choose air crisp function.
4. Cook at 400 °F (205°C)or 10 minutes.

Nutrition:
- InfoCalories: 388; Fat: 23.3g; Carbohydrate: 0.5g; Protein: 18.1g

Beef And Bacon Chili

Servings: 6
Cooking Time: 1 Hr
Ingredients:
- 2 pounds stewing beef, trimmed /900g
- 29 ounces canned whole tomatoes /870g
- 15 ounces canned kidney beans, drained and rinsed /450g
- 4 ounces smoked bacon; cut into strips /120g
- 1 chipotle in adobo sauce, finely chopped
- 1 onion; diced
- 2 bell peppers; diced
- 3 garlic cloves; minced
- 2 cups beef broth /500ml
- 1 tbsp ground cumin/15g
- 2 tsp olive oil; divided /10ml
- 1 tsp chili powder /5g
- ½ tsp cayenne pepper /2.5g
- 4 tsp salt; divided /20g
- 1 tsp freshly ground black pepper; divided /5g

Directions:
1. Set on Sear/Sauté, set to Medium High, and choose Start/Stop to preheat the pot and fry the bacon until crispy, about 5 minutes. Set aside.
2. Rub the beef with ½ tsp or 5g black pepper and 1 tsp or 5g salt. In the bacon fat, brown beef for 5-6 minutes; transfer to a plate.
3. Warm the oil. Add in garlic, peppers and onion and cook for 3 to 4 minutes until soft. Stir in cumin, cayenne pepper, the extra pepper and salt; chopped chipotle, and chili powder and cook for 30 seconds until soft.
4. Return beef and bacon to the pot with vegetables and spices; add in tomatoes and broth.
5. Seal the pressure lid, choose Pressure, set to High, and set the timer to 45 minutes. Press Start. When ready, release the pressure quickly. Stir in beans. Let simmer on Keep Warm for 10 minutes until flavors combine.

Mexican Pork Stir Fry

Servings: 4
Cooking Time: 15 Minutes
Ingredients:
- 12 oz. pork tenderloin
- 4 slices hickory bacon, chopped
- 1 chipotle chili, chopped
- 1 tbsp. olive oil
- 1 tsp cumin
- 1 tsp oregano
- 2 cloves garlic, chopped

- 1 red bell pepper, cut in strips
- 1 onion, halved & sliced thin
- 3 cups lettuce, chopped

Directions:
1. Slice tenderloin in half lengthwise, and then cut crosswise thinly. Toss pork, bacon and chipotle pieces together in small bowl; set aside.
2. Add oil, cumin, oregano, and garlic to the cooking pot. Set to sauté on med-high heat.
3. Add bell pepper and onion and cook, stirring frequently, 3-4 minutes until tender-crisp. Transfer to a bowl.
4. Add pork mixture to the pot and cook, stirring frequently, 3-4 minutes until bacon is crisp and pork is no longer pink.
5. Return vegetables to the pot and cook until heated through. Serve over a bed of lettuce.

Nutrition:
- InfoCalories 322,Total Fat 18g,Total Carbs 5g,Protein 34g,Sodium 192mg.

Honey Short Ribs With Rosemary Potatoes

Servings: 4
Cooking Time: 105 Min

Ingredients:
- 4 bone-in beef short ribs, silver skin
- 2 potatoes, peeled and cut into 1-inch pieces
- ½ cup beef broth /125ml
- 3 garlic cloves; minced
- 1 onion; chopped
- 2 tbsp olive oil /30ml
- 2 tbsp honey /30ml
- 2 tbsp minced fresh rosemary /30ml
- 1 tsp salt /5g
- 1 tsp black pepper /5g

Directions:
1. Choose Sear/Sauté on the pot and set to High. Choose Start/Stop to preheat the pot. Season the short ribs on all sides with ½ tsp or 2.5g of salt and ½ tsp or 2.5g of pepper. Heat 1 tbsp of olive oil and brown the ribs on all sides, about 10 minutes total. Stir in the onion, honey, broth, 1 tbsp of rosemary, and garlic.
2. Seal the pressure lid, choose Pressure, set to High, and set the time to 40 minutes. Choose Start/Stop to begin. In a large bowl, toss the potatoes with the remaining oil, rosemary, salt, and black pepper.
3. When the ribs are ready, perform a quick pressure release and carefully open the lid.
4. Fix the reversible rack in the higher position of the pot, which is over the ribs. Put the potatoes on the rack. Close the crisping lid. Choose Bake/Roast, set the temperature to 350°F or 175°C, and set the time to 15 minutes. Choose Start/Stop to begin roasting.
5. Once the potatoes are tender and roasted, use tongs to pick the potatoes and the short ribs into a plate; set aside. Choose Sear/Sauté and set to High. Simmer the sauce for 5 minutes and spoon the sauce into a bowl.
6. Allow sitting for 2 minutes and scoop off the fat that forms on top. Serve the ribs with the potatoes and sauce.

Lamb Chops And Potato Mash

Servings: 8
Cooking Time: 40 Min

Ingredients:
- 5 potatoes, peeled and chopped
- 4 cilantro leaves, for garnish
- 8 lamb cutlets
- 1 green onion; chopped
- ⅓ cup milk /88ml
- 1 cup beef stock /250ml
- 3 sprigs rosemary leaves; chopped
- 3 tbsp butter, softened /45g
- 1 tbsp olive oil /15ml
- 1 tbsp tomato puree /15ml
- salt to taste

Directions:
1. Rub rosemary leaves and salt to the lamb chops. Warm oil and 2 tbsp or 30g of butter on Sear/Sauté. Add in the lamb chops and cook for 1 minute for each side until browned; set aside on a plate.
2. In the pot, mix tomato puree and green onion; cook for 2-3 minutes. Add beef stock into the pot to deglaze, scrape the bottom to get rid of any browned bits of food.
3. Return lamb cutlets alongside any accumulated juices to the pot. Set a reversible rack on lamb cutlets. Place steamer basket on the reversible rack. Arrange potatoes in the steamer basket.
4. Seal the pressure lid, choose Pressure, set to High, and set the timer to 4 minutes. Press Start.
5. When ready, release the pressure quickly. Remove trivet and steamer basket from pot. In a high speed blender, add potatoes, milk, salt, and remaining tbsp butter. Blend well until you obtain a smooth consistency.
6. Divide the potato mash between serving dishes. Lay lamb chops on the mash. Drizzle with cooking liquid obtained from pressure cooker; apply cilantro sprigs for garnish.

Braised Short Ribs With Creamy Sauce

Servings: 6
Cooking Time: 1 Hr 55 Min

Ingredients:
- 3 pounds beef short ribs /1350g
- 1 can diced tomatoes /435g
- 1 celery stalk; chopped
- 3 garlic cloves; chopped
- 1 onion; chopped
- 1 large carrot; chopped
- 2 cups beef broth /500ml
- ½ cup cheese cream /65g
- ½ cup dry red wine /125ml
- ¼ cup red wine vinegar /62.5ml
- 2 bay leaves
- 2 tbsp olive oil /30ml
- 2 tbsp chopped parsley /30g
- ¼ tsp red pepper flakes /1.25g
- 2 tsp salt; divided /10g
- 1½ tsp freshly ground black pepper; divided /7.5g

Directions:
1. Season your short ribs with 1 tsp black pepper and 1 tsp salt. Warm olive oil on Sear/Sauté. Add in short ribs and sear for 3 minutes each side until browned. Set aside on a bowl.
2. Drain everything only to be left with 1 tbsp of the remaining fat from the pot. Set on Sear/Sauté, and stir-fry

garlic, carrot, onion, and celery in the hot fat for 4 to 6 minutes until fragrant.
3. Stir in broth, wine, red pepper flakes, vinegar, tomatoes, bay leaves, and remaining pepper and salt; turn the Foodi to Sear/Sauté on Low and bring the mixture to a boil.
4. With the bone-side up, lay short ribs into the braising liquid. Seal the pressure lid, choose Pressure, set to High, and set the timer to 40 minutes. Press Start.
5. When ready, release the pressure quickly. Set the short ribs on a plate. Get rid of bay leaves. Skim and get rid of the fat from the surface of braising liquid.
6. Using an immersion blender, blend the liquid for 1 minute; add cream cheese, pepper and salt and blitz until smooth Arrange the ribs onto a serving plate, pour the sauce over and top with parsley.

Meatballs With Spaghetti Sauce

Servings: 6
Cooking Time: 20 Min
Ingredients:
- 2 lb. ground beef /900g
- 1 cup grated Parmesan cheese /130g
- 4 cups spaghetti sauce /1000ml
- 1 cup breadcrumbs /130g
- 1 cup water /250ml
- 2 cloves garlic; minced
- 2 eggs, cracked into a bowl
- 1 onion, finely chopped
- 3 tbsp milk /45ml
- 1 tbsp olive oil /15ml
- 1 tsp dried oregano /5g
- Salt and pepper, to taste

Directions:
1. In a bowl, add beef, onion, breadcrumbs, parmesan, eggs, garlic, milk, salt, oregano, and pepper. Mix well with hands and shape bite-size balls.
2. Open the pot, and add the spaghetti sauce, water and the meatballs. Close the lid, secure the pressure valve, and select Steam mode on High pressure for 6 minutes. Press Start/Stop.
3. Once the timer is done, do a natural pressure release for 5 minutes, then do a quick pressure release to let out any extra steam, and open the lid. Dish the meatball sauce over cooked pasta and serve.

Healthier Meatloaf

Servings: 4
Cooking Time: 6 Hours
Ingredients:
- Nonstick cooking spray
- 1 lb. lean ground pork
- 1 cup oats
- 8 oz. tomato sauce, divided
- 1 onion, chopped fine
- ½ cup zucchini, grated & excess liquid squeezed out
- 1 clove garlic, chopped fine
- 1 egg, lightly beaten
- 1 tsp salt
- 1/8 tsp pepper
- ½ tsp Italian seasoning

Directions:
1. Spray the cooking pot with cooking spray.
2. In a large bowl, combine pork, oats, half the tomato sauce, onion, zucchini, garlic, egg, salt, pepper, and Italian seasoning, mix well.
3. Fold a large sheet of foil in half, then in half again. Place along the bottom up two sides of the cooking pot.
4. Add the pork mixture and form into a loaf shape. Spoon remaining tomato sauce over the top.
5. Add the lid and set to slow cook on low. Cook 6 hours or until meatloaf is cooked through.
6. Use the foil sling to remove the meatloaf from the cooking pot. Let rest 5 minutes before slicing and serving.

Nutrition:
- InfoCalories 335,Total Fat 7g,Total Carbs 36g,Protein 33g,Sodium 947mg.

Crispy Pork Chops

Servings: 4
Cooking Time: 20 Minutes
Ingredients:
- 3 oz. pork rinds, crushed
- 1 tsp salt
- 1 tsp smoked paprika
- ½ tsp garlic powder
- ½ tsp onion powder
- 2 eggs
- Nonstick cooking spray
- 4 pork chops, boneless

Directions:
1. In a shallow bowl, combine pork rinds and seasonings.
2. In a separate shallow bowl, add eggs and beat lightly.
3. Spray the fryer basket with cooking spray.
4. Dip the chops first in the egg then coat with pork rind mixture. Place in the basket.
5. Add the tender-crisp lid and set to air fry on 400°F (205°C). Cook 1-inch chops 12 minutes, and 2-inch thick chops 20 minutes, turning chops over halfway through cooking time. Serve immediately.

Nutrition:
- InfoCalories 277,Total Fat 15g,Total Carbs 1g,Protein 32g,Sodium 680mg.

Adobo Steak

Servings: 4
Cooking Time: 25 Minutes
Ingredients:
- 2 cups of water
- 8 steaks, cubed, 28 ounces pack
- Pepper to taste
- 1 and 3/4 teaspoons adobo seasoning
- 1 can 8 ounces tomato sauce
- 1/3 cup green pitted olives
- 2 tablespoons brine
- 1 small red pepper
- 1/2 a medium onion, sliced

Directions:
1. Chop peppers, onions into ¼ inch strips.
2. Prepare beef by seasoning with adobo and pepper.
3. Add into Ninja Foodi.
4. Stir in remaining ingredients and Lock lid, cook on "HIGH" pressure for 25 minutes.
5. Release pressure naturally.
6. Serve and enjoy.

Nutrition:
- InfoCalories: 154; Fat: 5g; Carbohydrates: 3g; Protein: 23g

Chunky Pork Meatloaf With Mashed Potatoes

Servings: 4
Cooking Time: 55 Min
Ingredients:
- 2 pounds potatoes; cut into large chunks /900g
- 12 ounces pork meatloaf /360g
- 2 garlic cloves; minced
- 2 large eggs
- 12 individual saltine crackers, crushed
- 1¾ cups full cream milk; divided /438ml
- 1 cup chopped white onion /130g
- ½ cup heavy cream /125ml
- ¼ cup barbecue sauce /62.5ml
- 1 tbsp olive oil /15ml
- 3 tbsp chopped fresh cilantro /45g
- 3 tbsp unsalted butter /45g
- ¼ tsp dried rosemary /1.25g
- 1 tsp yellow mustard /5g
- 1 tsp Worcestershire sauce /5ml
- 2 tsp salt /10g
- ½ tsp black pepper /2.5g

Directions:
1. Select Sear/Sauté and adjust to Medium. Press Start to preheat the pot for 5 minutes. Heat the olive oil until shimmering and sauté the onion and garlic in the oil. Cook for about 2 minutes until the onion softens. Transfer the onion and garlic to a plate and set aside.
2. In a bowl, crumble the meatloaf mix into small pieces. Sprinkle with 1 tsp of salt, the pepper, cilantro, and thyme. Add the sautéed onion and garlic. Sprinkle the crushed saltine crackers over the meat and seasonings.
3. In a small bowl, beat ¼ cup of milk, the eggs, mustard, and Worcestershire sauce. Pour the mixture on the layered cracker crumbs and gently mix the ingredients in the bowl with your hands. Shape the meat mixture into an 8-inch round.
4. Cover the reversible rack with aluminum foil and carefully lift the meatloaf into the rack. Pour the remaining 1½ cups of milk and the heavy cream into the inner pot. Add the potatoes, butter, and remaining salt. Place the rack with meatloaf over the potatoes in the upper position in the pot.
5. Seal the pressure lid, choose Pressure; adjust the pressure to High and the cook time to 25 minutes; press Start. After cooking, perform a quick pressure release, and carefully open the pressure lid. Brush the meatloaf with the barbecue sauce.
6. Close the crisping lid; choose Broil and adjust the cook time to 7 minutes. Press Start to begin grilling. When the top has browned, remove the rack, and transfer the meatloaf to a serving platter. Mash the potatoes in the pot. Slice the meatloaf and serve with the mashed potatoes.

Italian Pot Roast

Servings: 8
Cooking Time: 8 Hours
Ingredients:
- 1 tsp salt
- ½ tsp pepper
- 1 tsp garlic powder
- 1 tsp onion powder
- 2 tsp Italian seasoning
- 6 oz. tomato paste
- 2 lb. beef sirloin roast
- 1 onion, sliced thin
- 1 green bell pepper, sliced thin
- 1 banana pepper, sliced thin
- ½ cup beef broth, low sodium

Directions:
1. In a small bowl, combine salt, pepper, garlic powder, onion powder, Italian seasoning, and tomato paste, mix well.
2. Coat the roast, on all sides, with spice mixture and place in the cooking pot. Place the onions and peppers on top of the roast and pour in the broth.
3. Add the lid and set to slow cook on low. Cook 7-8 hours or until beef is tender.
4. You can slice the beef and serve topped with the onions and peppers. Or, you can shred the beef and use it to make sandwiches.

Nutrition:
- InfoCalories 270,Total Fat 16g,Total Carbs 6g,Protein 24g,Sodium 392mg.

Ground Beef Stuffed Empanadas

Servings: 2
Cooking Time: 60 Min
Ingredients:
- ¼ pound ground beef /112.5g
- 2 small tomatoes; chopped
- 8 square gyoza wrappers
- 1 egg, beaten
- 1 garlic clove; minced
- ½ white onion; chopped
- 6 green olives, pitted and chopped
- 1 tbsp olive oil /15ml
- ¼ tsp cumin powder /1.25g
- ¼ tsp paprika /1.25g
- ⅛ tsp cinnamon powder /0.625g

Directions:
1. Choose Sear/Sauté on the pot and set to Medium High. Choose Start/Stop to preheat the pot. Put the oil, garlic, onion, and beef in the preheated pot and cook for 5 minutes, stirring occasionally, until the fragrant and the beef is no longer pink.
2. Stir in the olives, cumin, paprika, and cinnamon and cook for an additional 3 minutes. Add the tomatoes and cook for 1 more minute.
3. Spoon the beef mixture into a plate and allow cooling for a few minutes.
4. Meanwhile, put the Crisping Basket in the pot. Close the crisping lid; choose Air Crisp, set the temperature to 400°F or 205°C, and the time to 5 minutes. Press Start.
5. Lay the gyoza wrappers on a flat surface. Place 1 to 2 tbsps of the beef mixture in the middle of each wrapper. Brush the edges of the wrapper with egg and fold in half to form a triangle. Pinch the edges together to seal.
6. Place 4 empanadas in a single layer in the preheated Basket. Close the crisping lid. Choose Air Crisp, set the temperature to 400°F or 205°C, and set the time to 7 minutes. Choose Start/Stop to begin frying.
7. Once the timer is done, remove the empanadas from the basket and transfer to a plate. Repeat with the remaining empanadas.

Pot Roast With Biscuits

Servings: 6
Cooking Time: 75 Min
Ingredients:
- 1 chuck roast /1350g
- 1 pound small butternut squash; diced /450g
- 1 small red onion, peeled and quartered
- 2 carrots, peeled and cut into 1-inch pieces
- 6 refrigerated biscuits
- 1 bay leaf
- ⅔ cup dry red wine /176ml
- ⅔ cup beef broth /176ml
- ¾ cup frozen pearl onions /98g
- 2 tbsp olive oil /30ml
- 1½ tsp salt /7.5g
- 1 tsp dried oregano leaves /5g
- ¼ tsp black pepper /1.25g

Directions:
1. On the Foodi, choose Sear/Sauté and adjust to Medium-High. Press Start to preheat the pot. Heat the olive oil until shimmering. Season the beef on both sides with salt and add to the pot. Cook, undisturbed, for 3 minutes or until deeply browned. Flip the roast over and brown the other side for 3 minutes. Transfer the beef to a wire rack.
2. Pour the oil out of the pot and add the wine to the pot. Stir with a wooden spoon, scraping the bottom of the pot to let off any browned bits. Bring to a boil and cook for 1 to 2 minutes or until the wine has reduced by half.
3. Mix in the beef broth, oregano, bay leaf, black pepper, and red onion. Stir to combine and add the beef with its juices. Seal the pressure lid and choose Pressure; adjust the pressure to High and the cook time to 35 minutes. Press Start to begin cooking.
4. After cooking, perform a quick pressure release. Carefully open the pressure lid.
5. Add the butternut squash, carrots, and pearl onions to the pot. Lock the pressure lid into place, set to Seal position and Choose Pressure; adjust the pressure to High and the cook time to 2 minutes. Press Start to cook the vegetables.
6. After cooking, perform a quick pressure release, and open the lid. Transfer the beef to a cutting board and cover with aluminum foil.
7. Put the reversible rack in the upper position of the pot and cover with a circular piece of aluminum foil. Put the biscuits on the rack and put the rack in the pot.
8. Close the crisping lid and Choose Bake/Roast; adjust the temperature to 300°F and the cook time to 15 minutes. Press Start. After 8 minutes, open the lid and carefully flip the biscuits over. After baking, remove the rack and biscuits. Allow the biscuits to cool for a few minutes before serving.
9. While the biscuits cook, remove the foil from the beef and cut it against the grain into slices. Remove and discard the bay leaf and transfer the beef to a serving platter. Spoon the vegetables and the sauce over the beef. Serve with the biscuits.

Bolognese Pizza

Servings: 4
Cooking Time: 70 Min
Ingredients:
- ½ lb. ground pork, meat cooked and crumbled /225g
- 1 cup shredded mozzarella cheese /130g
- ½ cup canned crushed tomatoes /65g
- 1 yellow bell pepper; sliced; divided
- 4 pizza crusts
- 1 tbsp chopped fresh basil, for garnish /15g
- 1 tsp red chili flakes; divided /5g
- Cooking spray

Directions:
1. Place the reversible rack in the pot. Close the crisping lid; choose Air Crisp, set the temperature to 400°F or 205°C, and the time to 5 minutes.
2. Grease one side of a pizza crust with cooking spray and lay on the preheated rack, oiled side up. Close the crisping lid. Choose Air Crisp, set the temperature to 400°F (205°C), and set the time to 4 minutes. Choose Start/Stop to begin baking.
3. Remove the crust from the rack and flip so the crispy side is down. Top the crust with 2 tbsps of crushed tomatoes, a quarter of bell pepper, 2 ounces or 60g of ground pork, ¼ cup or 32.5g of mozzarella cheese, and ¼ tbsp or 1.25g of red chili flakes.
4. Close the crisping lid. Choose Broil and set the time to 3 minutes. Choose Start/Stop to continue baking. When done baking and crispy as desired, remove the pizza from the rack. Repeat with the remaining pizza crusts and ingredients. Top each pizza with some basil and serve.

Cuban Pork

Servings: 8
Cooking Time: 2 Hr 30 Min
Ingredients:
- 3 pounds pork shoulder /1350g
- ¼ cup lime juice /62.5ml
- ½ cup orange juice /125ml
- ¼ cup canola oil /62.5ml
- ¼ cup chopped fresh cilantro /32.5g
- 8 cloves garlic; minced
- 1 tbsp fresh oregano /15g
- 1 tbsp ground cumin /15g
- 1 tsp red pepper flakes /5g
- 2 tsp ground black pepper /10g
- 1 tsp salt /5g

Directions:
1. In a bowl, mix orange juice, olive oil, cumin, salt, pepper, oregano, lime juice, and garlic; add into a large plastic bag alongside the pork. Seal and massage the bag to ensure the marinade covers the pork completely.
2. Place in the refrigerator for an hour to overnight. In the Foodi, set your removed pork from bag. Add the marinade on top. Seal the pressure lid, choose Pressure, set to High, and set the timer to 50 minutes. Press Start.
3. Release pressure naturally for 15 minutes. Transfer the pork to a cutting board; use a fork to break into smaller pieces.
4. Skim and get rid of the fat from liquid in the cooker. Serve the liquid with pork and sprinkle with cilantro.

Hamburger & Macaroni Skillet

Servings: 4
Cooking Time: 20 Minutes
Ingredients:
- 1 tbsp. olive oil
- 1 lb. lean ground beef
- 1 onion, chopped
- ½ tsp seasoned salt
- 1/8 tsp red pepper flakes

Ninja Foodi Cookbook Guide

- ½ tsp celery seed
- 28 oz. tomatoes, diced, undrained
- 2 tbsp. Worcestershire sauce
- 2 cups macaroni, cooked & drained, reserve ½ cup pasta water
- 1/4 cup chopped fresh parsley

Directions:
1. Add the oil to the cooking pot and set to sauté on med-high heat.
2. Add the ground beef and cook, breaking up slightly with a spatula, until meat is no longer pink.
3. Add the onions and cook another 4-6 minutes until they are soft. Stir in seasonings, tomatoes, and Worcestershire. Simmer 5 minutes.
4. Add the macaroni and parsley, if the mixture is too dry, stir in the reserved water from the pasta. Cook, stirring occasionally, 5 minutes until heated through. Salt and pepper to taste and serve.

Nutrition:
- InfoCalories 156,Total Fat 9g,Total Carbs 12g,Protein 6g,Sodium 235mg.

Cheesy Ham & Potato Casserole

Servings: 6
Cooking Time: 35 Minutes
Ingredients:
- 1 tbsp. butter
- 1 sweet potato, peeled & chopped
- 1 cup onion, chopped
- 2 cloves garlic, chopped fine
- 8 oz. cream cheese, low fat
- 14 ½ oz. chicken broth, low sodium
- ½ cup sour cream, low fat
- ½ tsp thyme, crushed
- ¼ tsp pepper
- 32 oz. hash brown potatoes, thawed
- 1 ½ cups white cheddar cheese, low fat, grated
- 1 cup ham, chopped
- 1 cup grape tomatoes, sliced
- 2 green onions, sliced

Directions:
1. Add butter to the cooking pot and set to sauté on medium heat. Once the butter has melted, add sweet potato, onion, and garlic and cook 5-8 minutes or until potato is tender.
2. Stir in cream cheese until melted. Add broth, sour cream, thyme, and pepper and mix well.
3. Add hash browns, cheese, and ham and mix until combined. Lay the sliced tomatoes evenly over the top.
4. Add the tender-crisp lid and set to bake on 375°F (190°C). Bake 30-35 minutes until hot and bubbly and top is lightly browned. Let rest 5 minutes, then serve garnished with green onions.

Nutrition:
- InfoCalories 369,Total Fat 13g,Total Carbs 41g,Protein 21g,Sodium 1541mg.

Beef Broccoli

Servings: 6
Cooking Time: 16 Minutes
Ingredients:
- 1-1/2 lb. beef chuck roast boneless, trimmed and sliced
- Black pepper and salt to taste
- 2 teaspoons olive oil
- 1 onion, chopped
- 4 cloves garlic, minced
- 3/4 cup beef broth
- 1/2 cup soy sauce
- 1/3 cup erythritol
- 2 tablespoons sesame oil
- 1 lb. broccoli florets
- 3 tablespoons water
- 3 tablespoons corn starch

Directions:
1. Season the beef strips with black pepper and salt.
2. Stir in the olive oil to the Ninja Foodi. Switch it to sauté.
3. Add the onion and saute for 1 minute. Stir in the garlic and cook for 30 seconds.
4. Stir in the beef and cook in batches until brown on both sides.
5. Deglaze the pot with broth and soy sauce.
6. Stir in the erythritol and sesame oil. Cover the pot.
7. Set it to pressure. Cook at "HIGH" pressure for 12 minutes.
8. Release the pressure naturally. Stir in the broccoli. Seal the pot.
9. Cook at "HIGH" pressure for 3 minutes. Release the pressure quickly.
10. Mix corn starch with water and add to the pot.
11. Simmer until the sauce has thickened.
12. Serve warm.

Nutrition:
- InfoCalories: 563; Fat: 38.1g; Carbohydrate: 10.7g; Protein: 34.1g

Sticky Baby Back Ribs

Servings: 8
Cooking Time: 30 Minutes
Ingredients:
- 1 tsp onion powder
- 1 tsp garlic powder
- 1 tbsp. chili powder
- 1 tbsp. brown sugar
- 1 tsp pepper
- 1 tsp smoked paprika
- 1 tsp salt
- 1 cup water
- 4 lbs. baby back ribs, bone-in
- 1 cup barbecue sauce, no sugar added

Directions:
1. In a small bowl, combine the onion powder, garlic powder, chili powder, brown sugar, paprika, pepper, and salt. Mix well. Coat all sides of the ribs with the seasoning mixture, lightly rubbing the mixture into the ribs. Wrap the ribs in plastic wrap and refrigerate for 2 hours or overnight.
2. Add the trivet to the cooking pot. Pour in the water. Place the ribs in the cooking pot in a circle, standing up.
3. Add the lid and set to pressure cook on high. Set the timer for 23 minutes. When the timer goes off let sit for 5 minutes. Then use manual release to remove the pressure.
4. Transfer ribs to serving plates, brush with barbecue sauce and serve.

Nutrition:
- InfoCalories 587,Total Fat 26g,Total Carbs 17g,Protein 67g,Sodium 894mg.

Jamaican Pork

Servings: 4
Cooking Time: 25 Minutes
Ingredients:
- 1 tbsp. butter
- 1 tsp curry powder
- 2 bananas, sliced ½-inch thick
- 1 lb. pork tenderloin, cubed
- ½ tsp salt
- ½ cup pineapple juice, unsweetened
- ¼ cup onion, chopped fine
- ¼ cup coconut flakes, unsweetened

Directions:
1. Add butter to the cooking pot and set to sauté on medium heat.
2. Once the butter has melted, stir in curry powder until foamy.
3. Add bananas and cook until golden brown, about 3-5 minutes. Transfer to a plate.
4. Add pork and cook until golden brown, about 6-8 minutes. Season with salt.
5. Stir in pineapple juice and onion. Cover, reduce heat, and simmer 10 minutes until pork is tender.
6. Stir in coconut and bananas and toss gently to combine. Serve over cooked rice.

Nutrition:
- InfoCalories 247,Total Fat 7g,Total Carbs 21g,Protein 25g,Sodium 100mg.

Italian Sausage And Cannellini Stew

Servings: 6
Cooking Time: 45 Min
Ingredients:
- 1 pound Italian sausages, halved /450g
- 2 cups vegetable stock /500ml
- 3 cups fresh spinach /390g
- 1 cup Cannellini Beans; soaked and rinsed /130g
- 1 carrot; chopped
- 1 onion; chopped
- 1 celery stalk; chopped
- 1 sprig fresh rosemary
- 1 bay leaf
- 1 sprig fresh sage
- 1 tbsp olive oil /15ml
- 1 tsp salt /5g

Directions:
1. Warm oil on Sear/Sauté. Add in sausage pieces and sear for 5 minutes until browned; set aside on a plate. To the pot, add celery, onion, bay leaf, sage, carrot, and rosemary; cook for 3 minutes to soften slightly.
2. Stir in vegetable stock and beans. Arrange seared sausage pieces on top of the beans. Seal the pressure lid, choose Pressure, set to High, and set the timer to 10 minutes. Press Start. Release pressure naturally for 20 minutes,
3. Once ready, do a quick release. Get rid of bay leaf, rosemary and sage. Mix spinach into the mixture to serve.

Flank Steak With Bell Pepper Salsa

Servings: 6
Cooking Time: 30 Minutes
Ingredients:
- 2 tbsp. soy sauce, low sodium
- 4 tbsp. apple cider vinegar, divided
- 5 cloves garlic, chopped fine, divided
- 4 tbsp. olive oil, divided
- ¼ tsp pepper
- 2 lb. flank steak
- 1 green bell pepper, chopped fine
- 4 green onions, sliced thin
- 2 tbsp. fresh basil, chopped
- ¼ tsp red pepper flakes
- Salt & pepper to taste

Directions:
1. In a large bowl, combine soy sauce, 2 tablespoons vinegar, 4 cloves of garlic, 2 tablespoons oil, and pepper, mix well. Place the steak in the bowl and turn to coat. Let sit 20 minutes.
2. In a medium bowl, combine bell pepper, green onions, 1 clove garlic, basil, pepper flakes, remaining vinegar and oil, mix well. Salt and pepper to taste. Cover until ready to use.
3. Spray the rack with cooking spray and place in the cooking pot.
4. Lay the steak on the rack. Add the tender-crisp lid and set to broil. Cook steak 3-4 minutes per side, for rare, 5-6 minutes per side for medium rare, or to desired doneness.
5. Transfer meat to a cutting board and tent with foil. Let rest 10-15 minutes before slicing.
6. Slice against the grain and top with salsa to serve.

Nutrition:
- InfoCalories 161,Total Fat 10g,Total Carbs 2g,Protein 15g,Sodium 312mg.

Simple Beef & Shallot Curry

Servings: 4
Cooking Time: 40 Minutes
Ingredients:
- 1 lb. beef stew meat
- ¼ tsp salt
- 1/8 tsp turmeric
- 2 tbsp. olive oil
- 2 tbsp. shallots, sliced
- 1 tbsp. fresh ginger, grated
- 1 tbsp. garlic, chopped fine
- 3 cups water
- 2 tsp fish sauce
- 8 shallots, peeled & left whole
- ½ tsp chili powder

Directions:
1. In a large bowl, combine beef, salt, and turmeric, use your fingers to massage the seasonings into the meat. Cover and refrigerate 1 hour.
2. Add the oil to the cooking pot and set to sauté on med-high.
3. Add the sliced shallot and cook until golden brown, 6-8 minutes. Transfer to a bowl.
4. Add the garlic and ginger to the pot and cook 1 minute or until fragrant.
5. Add the beef and cook until no pink shows, about 5-6 minutes. Stir in the water and fish sauce until combined.
6. Add the lid and set to pressure cook on high. Set the timer for 20 minutes. When the timer goes off, use manual release to remove the pressure.
7. Set back to sauté on med-high and add the fried shallots, whole shallots, and chili powder. Cook, stirring frequently, until shallots are soft and sauce has thickened, about 10 minutes. Serve.

Nutrition:
- InfoCalories 70,Total Fat 9g,Total Carbs 4g,Protein 7g,Sodium 130mg.

Italian Pasta Potpie

Servings: 8
Cooking Time: 55 Minutes
Ingredients:
- 5 cups, plus 1 teaspoon water, divided
- 1 box rigatoni pasta
- 4 fresh Italian sausage links
- 1 bag frozen cooked meatballs
- 16 ounces whole milk ricotta
- 1 jar marinara sauce
- 2 cups shredded mozzarella cheese
- 1 refrigerated store-bought pie crust, room temperature
- 1 large egg

Directions:
1. Pour 5 cups of water and the rigatoni in the pot. Assemble pressure lid, making sure the pressure release valve is in the SEAL position.
2. Select PRESSURE and set to LO. Set time to 0 minutes. Select START/STOP to begin.
3. When pressure cooking is complete, quick release the pressure by turning the pressure release valve to the VENT position. Carefully remove lid when unit has finished releasing pressure.
4. Drain the pasta and set it aside, keeping warm. Wipe out pot and return it to base. Insert Cook & Crisp Basket into pot. Close crisping lid.
5. Select AIR CRISP, set temperature to 390°F (200°C), and set time to 15 minutes. Select START/STOP to begin. Let preheat for 5 minutes.
6. Open lid and place the sausages in the basket. Close lid and cook for 10 minutes.
7. When cooking is complete, remove sausages to a cutting board. Add the meatballs to the basket. Close crisping lid.
8. Select AIR CRISP, set temperature to 390°F (200°C), and set time to 10 minutes. Select START/STOP to begin.
9. Slice sausages into very thin rounds.
10. When cooking is complete, transfer the meatballs to the cutting board and slice them in half.
11. In the pot, in this order, add a layer of ricotta, marinara sauce, sausage, mozzarella cheese, pasta, marinara sauce, meatballs, mozzarella cheese, pasta, ricotta, and marinara sauce. Place the pie crust on top of the filling.
12. In a small bowl, whisk together the egg and remaining 1 teaspoon of water. Brush this on top of the pie crust. With a knife, slice a couple of small holes in the middle of crust to vent it. Close crisping lid.
13. Select BAKE/ROAST, set temperature to 350°F (175°C), and set time to 30 minutes. Select START/STOP to begin.
14. When cooking is complete, open lid. Let sit for 10 minutes before serving.

Nutrition:
- InfoCalories: 821, Total Fat: 41g, Sodium: 1414mg, Carbohydrates: 67g, Protein: 40g.

Braised Short Ribs With Mushrooms

Servings: 4
Cooking Time: 1 Hr
Ingredients:
- 2 pounds beef short ribs /900g
- 1 small onion; sliced
- 1 bell pepper; diced
- 4 garlic cloves, smashed
- ⅓ cup beef broth /88ml
- 1 cup beer /250ml
- 1 cup crimini mushrooms; sliced /130g
- 1 tbsp olive oil /15ml
- 1 tbsp soy sauce /15ml
- 1 tsp smoked paprika /5g
- ½ tsp dried oregano /2.5g
- ½ tsp cayenne pepper /2.5g
- salt and ground black pepper to taste

Directions:
1. In a small bowl, combine pepper, paprika, cayenne pepper, salt, and oregano. Rub the seasoning mixture on all sides of the short ribs.
2. Warm oil on Sear/Sauté. Add mushrooms and cook until browned, about 6-8 minutes; set aside. Add short ribs to the Foodi, and cook for 3 minutes for each side until browned; set aside on a plate.
3. Throw in garlic and onion to the oil and stir-fry for 2 minutes until fragrant. Add in beer to deglaze, scrape the pot's bottom to get rid of any browned bits of food; bring to a simmer and cook for 2 minutes until reduced slightly.
4. Stir in soy sauce, bell pepper and beef broth. Dip short ribs into the liquid in a single layer. Seal the pressure lid, choose Pressure, set to High, and set the timer to 40 minutes. Press Start. Release pressure naturally for about 10 minutes. Divide the ribs with the sauce into bowls and top with fried mushrooms.

Sausage & Roasted Red Pepper Linguine

Servings: 4
Cooking Time: 15 Minutes
Ingredients:
- 1 tbsp. extra virgin olive oil
- ¾ lb. Italian sausage
- 3 cloves garlic, chopped fine
- 1 cup roasted red bell peppers, chopped
- 1 tbsp. capers
- ½ cup black olives, pitted & halved
- 3 tomatoes, seeded & chopped
- ¼ cup fresh basil, chopped
- 1 lb. linguine, cooked & drained

Directions:
1. Add the oil to the cooking pot and set to sauté on medium heat.
2. Add sausage and break it up while it's cooking. When it starts to brown add the garlic and cook 1 minute more.
3. Stir in the peppers, capers, and olives and cook stirring 2 minutes.
4. Increase heat to high and add tomatoes and basil, cook 2 minutes more.
5. Add the pasta to the sausage mixture and toss to combine. Serve.

Nutrition:
- InfoCalories 203, Total Fat 9g, Total Carbs 23g, Protein 7g, Sodium 200mg.

Cheddar Cheeseburgers

Servings: 4
Cooking Time: 20 Min
Ingredients:
- 1 lb. ground beef /900g
- 1 packet dry onion soup mix /30g
- 4 burger buns
- 4 tomato slices
- 4 Cheddar cheese slices
- 4 small leaves lettuce
- 1 cup water /250ml
- Mayonnaise
- Ketchup
- Mustard

Directions:
1. In a bowl, add beef and onion mix, and mix well with hands. Shape in 4 patties and wrap each in foil paper. Pour the water into the inner steel insert of Foodi, and fit in the steamer rack. Place the wrapped patties on the trivet, close the lid, and secure the pressure valve, and cook on 10 minutes on Pressure mode on High pressure.
2. Once the timer has stopped, do a natural pressure release for 5 minutes, then a quick pressure release to let out the remaining steam.
3. Use a set of tongs to remove the wrapped beef onto a flat surface and carefully unwrap the patties.
4. To assemble the burgers:
5. In each half of the buns, put a lettuce leaf, then a beef patty, a slice of cheese, and a slice of tomato. Top it with the other halves of buns. Serve with some ketchup, mayonnaise, and mustard.

Crispy Korean-style Ribs

Servings: 4
Cooking Time: 25 Minutes
Ingredients:
- ½ cup soy sauce
- 2 tablespoons rice vinegar
- 2 tablespoons sesame oil
- 1 tablespoon cayenne pepper
- 8 garlic cloves, minced
- 1 tablespoon grated fresh ginger
- 1 small onion, minced
- 1 rack baby back ribs, cut into quarters
- ½ cup water
- ¼ cup honey
- Sesame seeds, for garnish

Directions:
1. In a mixing bowl, combine the soy sauce, rice vinegar, sesame oil, cayenne pepper, garlic, ginger, and onion. Pour the mixture over the ribs, cover, and let marinate in the refrigerator for 30 minutes.
2. Place the ribs in the Cook & Crisp Basket, reserving the remaining marinade. Pour the water in the pot and place basket in pot. Assemble pressure lid, making sure the pressure release valve is in the SEAL position.
3. Select PRESURE and set to HI. Set time to 10 minutes. Select START/STOP to begin.
4. When pressure cooking is complete, quick release the pressure by turning the pressure release valve to the VENT position. Carefully remove lid when pressure has finished releasing.
5. Pour the remaining marinade over the ribs. Close lid.
6. Select AIR CRISP, set temperature to 400°F (205°C), and set time to 15 minutes. Select START/STOP to begin.
7. After 10 minutes, open lid and liberally brush the ribs with the honey. Close lid and continue cooking.
8. When cooking is complete, open lid and remove the ribs. Cut them into individual ribs. Sprinkle with the sesame seeds and serve.

Nutrition:
- InfoCalories: 1133, Total Fat: 88g, Sodium: 2055mg, Carbohydrates: 25g, Protein: 57g.

Pork Pie

Servings: 8
Cooking Time: 45 Minutes
Ingredients:
- 2 tablespoons extra-virgin olive oil
- 1 pound ground pork
- 1 yellow onion, diced
- 1 can black beans, drained
- 1 cup frozen corn kernels
- 1 can green chiles
- 2 tablespoons chili powder
- 1 box cornbread mix
- 1½ cups milk
- 1 cup shredded Cheddar cheese

Directions:
1. Select SEAR/SAUTÉ and set temperature to MED. Select START/STOP to begin. Let preheat for 3 minutes.
2. Add the olive oil, pork, and onion. Brown the pork, stirring frequently to break the meat into smaller pieces, until cooked through, about 5 minutes.
3. Add the beans, corn, chiles, and chili powder and stir. Simmer, stirring frequently, about 10 minutes.
4. In a medium bowl, combine the cornbread mix, milk, and cheese. Pour it over simmering mixture in an even layer. Close crisping lid.
5. Select BAKE/ROAST, set temperature to 360°F (180°C), and set time for 25 minutes. Select START/STOP to begin.
6. After 20 minutes, use wooden toothpick to check if cornbread is done. If the toothpick inserted into the cornbread does not come out clean, close lid and cook for the remaining 5 minutes.
7. When cooking is complete, open lid. Let cool for 10 minutes before slicing and serving.

Nutrition:
- InfoCalories: 491, Total Fat: 24g, Sodium: 667mg, Carbohydrates: 47g, Protein: 24g.

Pork Tenderloin With Ginger And Garlic

Servings: 4
Cooking Time: 23 Min
Ingredients:
- 2 lb. pork tenderloin /900g
- ½ cup water + 2 tbsp water /155ml
- ½ cup soy sauce /125ml
- ¼ cup sugar /32.5g
- 2 cloves garlic; minced
- 3 tbsp grated ginger /45g
- 2 tbsp sesame oil /30ml
- 2 tsp cornstarch /10g
- Chopped scallions to garnish

- Sesame seeds to garnish

Directions:
1. In the Foodi's inner pot, add soy sauce, sugar, half cup of water, ginger, garlic, and sesame oil. Use a spoon to stir them. Then, add the pork. Close the lid, secure the pressure valve, and select Pressure mode on High pressure for 12 minutes. Press Start/Stop.
2. Once the timer has ended, do a quick pressure release, and open the pot. Remove the pork and set aside.
3. In a bowl, mix the cornstarch with the remaining water until smooth and pour it into the pot. Bring back the pork. Close the crisping lid and press Broil.
4. Cook for 5 minutes, until the sauce has thickened. Stir the sauce frequently, every 1-2 minutes, to avoid burning. Once the sauce is ready, serve the pork with a side endive salad or steamed veggies. Spoon the sauce all over it.

Taco Meatballs

Servings: 4
Cooking Time: 11 Minutes
Ingredients:
- 2 cups ground beef
- 1 egg, beaten
- 1 teaspoon taco seasoning
- 1 tablespoon sugar-free marinara sauce
- 1 teaspoon garlic, minced
- 1/2 teaspoon salt

Directions:
1. Take a suitable mixing bowl and place all the ingredients into the bowl.
2. Stir in all the ingredients into the bowl. Mix together all the ingredients by using a spoon or fingertips. Then make the small size meatballs and put them in a layer in the air fryer rack.
3. Lower the air fryer lid.
4. Cook the meatballs for 11 minutes at 350 °F (175°C).
5. Serve immediately and enjoy.

Nutrition:
- InfoCalories: 205; Fat: 12.2g; Carbohydrates: 2.2g; Protein: 19.4g

Sticky Barbeque Baby Back Ribs

Servings: 4
Cooking Time: 35 Min
Ingredients:
- 1 rack baby back ribs; cut into quarters /1350g
- 1 cup beer /250ml
- 1 cup barbecue sauce /250ml
- 3 tbsp brown sugar /45g
- 1½ tbsp smoked paprika /22.5g
- 1 tbsp salt /15g
- 1 tbsp black pepper /15g
- 2 tsp garlic powder /10g

Directions:
1. In a bowl, mix the paprika, brown sugar, garlic, salt, and black pepper. Season all sides of the ribs with the rub. Pour the beer into the pot, put the ribs in the Crisping Basket, and place the basket in the pot. Seal the pressure lid, choose Pressure, set to High, and set the time to 10 minutes. Choose Start/Stop.
2. When done cooking, perform a quick pressure release, and carefully the open the lid. Close the crisping lid. Choose Air Crisp, set the temperature to 400°F or 205°C, and the time to 15 minutes. Choose Start/Stop to begin crisping.
3. After 10 minutes, open the lid, and brush the ribs with the barbecue sauce. Close the lid to cook further for 5 minutes.

Corned Beef

Servings: 4
Cooking Time: 60 Minutes
Ingredients:
- 4 pounds beef brisket
- 2 garlic cloves, peeled and minced
- 2 yellow onions, peeled and sliced
- 11 ounces celery, sliced
- 1 tablespoon dried dill
- 3 bay leaves
- 4 cinnamon sticks, cut into halves
- Black pepper and salt to taste
- 17 ounces of water

Directions:
1. Take a suitable and stir in beef, add water and cover, let it soak for 2-3 hours.
2. Drain and transfer to the Ninja Foodi.
3. Stir in celery, onions, garlic, bay leaves, dill, cinnamon, dill, salt, pepper and the rest of the water to the Ninja Foodi.
4. Stir and combine it well.
5. Lock and secure the Ninja Foodi's lid, then cook on "HIGH" pressure for 50 minutes.
6. Release pressure naturally over 10 minutes.
7. Transfer meat to cutting board and slice, divide amongst plates and pour the cooking liquid alongside veggies over the servings.
8. Enjoy.

Nutrition:
- InfoCalories: 289; Fat: 21g; Carbohydrates: 14g; Protein: 9g

Spiced Lamb Meatballs

Servings: 8
Cooking Time: 29 Minutes
Ingredients:
- 2 pounds ground lamb
- ¼ cup bread crumbs
- 2 large eggs, beaten
- 3 garlic cloves, minced
- 2 teaspoons ground cumin
- 1 teaspoon smoked paprika
- ½ teaspoon cinnamon
- ½ teaspoon chili flakes
- ¼ cup minced onion
- ¼ cup chopped parsley
- Kosher salt
- Freshly ground black pepper
- Cooking spray

Directions:
1. In a large bowl, add the lamb, bread crumbs, eggs, garlic, cumin, paprika, cinnamon, chili flakes, onion, parsley, salt, and pepper. Using your hands, mix together until combined and sticky.
2. Using a ¼ cup measuring cup, measure out the mixture and roll into meatballs by hand.
3. Insert Cook & Crisp Basket into pot. Close crisping lid. Select AIR CRISP, set temperature to 390°F (200°C), and

set time to 29 minutes. Select START/STOP to begin. Let preheat for 5 minutes.
4. Open lid and place half the meatballs into the basket. Spray them with the cooking spray. Close lid and cook for 12 minutes.
5. Open lid and place the cooked meatballs in a bowl. Add the remaining meatballs to the basket and coat them with the cooking spray. Close lid and cook for the remaining 12 minutes.
6. When cooking is complete, open lid and serve.
Nutrition:
- InfoCalories: 329,Total Fat: 16g,Sodium: 129mg,Carbohydrates: 4g,Protein: 21g.

Steak And Chips

Servings: 4
Cooking Time: 50 Min
Ingredients:
- 4 potatoes; cut into wedges
- 4 rib eye steaks
- 1 tbsp olive oil /15ml
- 1 tsp sweet paprika /5g
- 1 tsp salt; divided /5g
- 1 tsp ground black pepper /5g
- Cooking spray

Directions:
1. Put the Crisping Basket in the pot. Close the crisping lid. Choose Air Crisp, set the temperature to 390°F or 200°C, and set the time to 5 minutes. Press Start. Meanwhile, rub all over with olive oil. Put the potatoes in the preheated Crisping Basket and season with ½ tsp or 2.5g of salt and ½ tsp or 2.5g of black pepper and sweet paprika.
2. Close the crisping lid. Choose Air Crisp, set the temperature to 400°F or 205°C, and set the time to 35 minutes. Choose Start/Stop to begin baking.
3. Season the steak on both sides with the remaining salt and black pepper. When done cooking, remove potatoes to a plate.
4. Grease the Crisping Basket with cooking spray and put the steaks in the basket.
5. Close the crisping lid. Choose Air Crisp, set the temperature to 400°F or 205°C, and set the time to 8 minutes. Choose Start/Stop to begin grilling.
6. When ready, check the steaks for your preferred doneness and cook for a few more minutes if needed. Take out the steaks from the basket and rest for 5 minutes. Serve the steaks with the potato wedges and the steak sauce.

Pesto Pork Chops & Asparagus

Servings: 4
Cooking Time: 20 Minutes
Ingredients:
- Nonstick cooking spray
- 4 pork chops, bone-in, 1-inch thick
- 1 tsp salt, divided
- 1 tsp pepper, divided
- 1 bunch asparagus, trimmed
- 1 cup cherry tomatoes
- 3 tbsp. extra-virgin olive oil, divided
- ¼ cup pesto
- ¼ cup fresh basil, chopped

Directions:
1. Spray the rack with cooking spray and place it in the cooking pot.
2. Rub chops with 2 tablespoons oil and sprinkle with ½ teaspoon salt and pepper on both sides. Cover and let sit 20 minutes.
3. Place chops on the rack and add the tender-crisp lid. Set to broil. Cook chops 6-8 minutes per side or until they reach desired doneness. Remove to serving plate.
4. Place the asparagus and tomatoes in a large bowl and add remaining oil, salt, and pepper, toss to coat. Place the vegetables on the rack and broil 6-8 minutes until asparagus is tender-crisp and tomatoes start to char, turning vegetables every couple of minutes.
5. Place pork chops and vegetables on serving plates, drizzle with pesto and sprinkle with basil. Serve immediately.
Nutrition:
- InfoCalories 332,Total Fat 24g,Total Carbs 4g,Protein 25g,Sodium 647mg.

Stuffed Cabbage Rolls

Servings: 6
Cooking Time: 5 Hours
Ingredients:
- 12 cabbage leaves
- 3 ¼ tsp salt, divided
- 15 oz. tomato sauce
- 2 tbsp. honey
- 1 tsp paprika
- ½ tsp thyme
- 2 tbsp. lemon juice
- 2 tbsp. ketchup
- 1 tsp Worcestershire sauce
- 1 ¼ tsp pepper
- 1 cup long grain brown rice, cooked
- 1 egg, beaten
- ¼ cup milk
- ¼ cup onion, chopped fine
- 1 clove garlic, chopped fine
- 1 lb. lean ground beef

Directions:
1. Fill a large pot with water and add 2 teaspoons salt. Bring to a boil on high heat. Add cabbage leaves and boil 2 minutes. Transfer leaves to a plate and let cool.
2. In a medium bowl, whisk together tomato sauce, honey, spices, lemon juice, ketchup, Worcestershire, remaining salt, and pepper until smooth.
3. In a separate bowl, combine rice, egg, milk, onion, garlic, and beef. Stir in ¼ of the sauce and mix well.
4. Spoon ¼ cup of beef mixture into the center of each cabbage leaf. Roll up, tucking in the ends. Place in the cooking pot. Pour remaining sauce over the rolls.
5. Add the lid and set to slow cook in high. Cook 4-5 hours until cabbage is tender and filling is cooked through. Serve.
Nutrition:
- InfoCalories 282,Total Fat 10g,Total Carbs 25g,Protein 24g,Sodium 1732mg.

Beef Bourguignon(1)

Servings: 4
Cooking Time: 30 Minutes
Ingredients:
- 1-pound stewing steak
- 1/2-pound bacon

- 5 medium carrots, diced
- 1 large red onion, peeled and sliced
- 2 garlic cloves, minced
- 2 teaspoons salt
- 2 tablespoons fresh thyme
- 2 tablespoons fresh parsley, chopped
- 2 teaspoons ground pepper
- 1/2 cup beef broth
- 1 tablespoon olive oil
- 1 tablespoon sugar-free maple syrup

Directions:
1. Select "Sauté" mode on your Ninja Foodi and stir in 1 tablespoon of oil, allow the oil to heat up.
2. Pat your beef dry and season it well.
3. Stir in beef into the Ninja Foodi in batches and Sauté them until nicely browned up.
4. Slice up the cooked bacon into strips and add the strips to the pot.
5. Add onions as well and brown them.
6. Stir in the rest of the listed ingredients and lock up the lid.
7. Cook for 30 minutes on "HIGH" pressure.
8. Allow the pressure to release naturally over 10 minutes. Enjoy.

Nutrition:
- InfoCalories: 416; Fats: 18g; Carbohydrates: 12g; Protein:27g

Crunchy Cashew Lamb Rack

Servings: 4
Cooking Time: 30 Min
Ingredients:
- 1 ½ lb. rack of lamb /675g
- 3 oz. chopped cashews /90g
- 1 garlic clove; minced
- 1 egg, beaten
- 1 tbsp chopped rosemary /15g
- 1 tbsp olive oil /15ml
- 1 tbsp breadcrumbs /15g
- Salt and pepper, to taste

Directions:
1. Combine the olive oil with the garlic and brush this mixture onto the lamb. Combine the rosemary, cashews, and breadcrumbs, in a small bowl. Brush the egg over the lambs, and then coat it with the cashew mixture.
2. Place the lamb in the Foodi, close the crisping lid and cook for 25 minutes on Air Crisp at 320 °F or 160°C. Then increase to 390 °F or 200°C, and cook for 5 more minutes. Cover with a foil and let sit for a couple of minutes before serving.

Thai Roasted Beef

Servings: 2
Cooking Time: 4 Hours 20 Min
Ingredients:
- 1 lb. ground beef /450g
- Thumb-sized piece of ginger; chopped
- 3 chilies, deseeded and chopped
- 4 garlic cloves; chopped
- Juice of 1 lime
- 2 tbsp oil /30ml
- 2 tbsp fish sauce/30ml
- 2 tbsp soy sauce /30ml
- 2 tbsp mirin /30ml
- 2 tbsp coriander; chopped /30g
- 2 tbsp basil; chopped /30g
- ½ tsp salt /2.5g
- ½ tsp pepper /2.5g
- 1 tsp brown sugar

Directions:
1. Place all ingredients, except beef, salt, and pepper, in a blender; pulse until smooth. Season the beef with salt and pepper. Place the meat and Thai mixture in a zipper bag. Shake well to combine and let marinate in the fridge for about 4 hours.
2. Place the beef in the Foodi basket and cook for about 12 minutes, or a little more for well done, on Air Crisp mode at 350 °F or 175°C. Let sit for 5 minutes before serving.

Ropa Vieja

Servings:6
Cooking Time: 1 Hour, 25 Minutes
Ingredients:
- 2 tablespoons canola oil, divided
- 1 red bell pepper, thinly sliced
- 1 yellow bell pepper, thinly sliced
- 1 green bell pepper, thinly sliced
- 1 large onion, thinly sliced
- 4 garlic cloves, minced
- Kosher salt
- Freshly ground black pepper
- 2½ pounds chuck roast, cut in half
- 1 cup beef stock
- 2 bay leaves
- ½ cup dry white wine
- 1 tablespoon white vinegar
- 1 can crushed tomatoes
- 1 can tomato paste
- 2 teaspoons dried oregano
- 1½ teaspoons ground cumin
- 1 teaspoon paprika
- ⅛ teaspoon ground allspice
- 1 cup green olives with pimentos
- Cilantro, for garnish
- Lime wedges, for garnish

Directions:
1. Select SEAR/SAUTÉ and set to HI. Select START/STOP to begin. Let preheat for 5 minutes.
2. Add 1 tablespoon of oil, the bell peppers, onions, and garlic, and season with salt and pepper. Cook, stirring occasionally, for about 5 minutes, or until vegetables have softened and are fragrant.
3. Liberally season the chuck with salt and pepper.
4. When the vegetables are cooked, remove and set aside.
5. Add the remaining 1 tablespoon of oil and meat. Sear the roast on both sides so that a dark crust forms, about 5 minutes per side.
6. Add the beef stock and bay leaves. Scrape the bottom of the pot with a rubber or wooden spoon to release any browned bits stuck to it. Assemble pressure lid, making sure the pressure release valve is in the SEAL position.
7. Select PRESSURE and set to HI. Set time to 40 minutes. Select START/STOP to begin.
8. When pressure cooking is complete, quick release the pressure by turning the pressure release valve to the VENT

position. Carefully remove lid when unit has finished releasing pressure.
9. Carefully shred the beef in the pot using two forks.
10. Select SEAR/SAUTÉ and set to MED. Select START/STOP to begin. Add the vegetables, wine, vinegar, crushed tomatoes, tomato paste, oregano, cumin, paprika, and allspice and stir with a rubber or wooden spoon, being sure to scrape the bottom of the pot. Simmer, stirring occasionally, for about 25 minutes or until sauce has reduced and thickened.
11. Add the olives and continue cooking for 2 minutes. Serve, garnished with cilantro and lime wedges.
Nutrition:
- InfoCalories: 479,Total Fat: 23g,Sodium: 624mg,Carbohydrates: 21g,Protein: 44g.

Beef Brisket & Carrots

Servings: 10
Cooking Time: 8 Hours 15 Minutes
Ingredients:
- 4 -5 lb. beef brisket,
- 1 ½ tsp salt
- 3 onions, sliced
- 6 cloves garlic, chopped fine
- 1 sprig thyme
- 1 sprig rosemary
- 4 bay leaves
- 2 cups beef broth, low sodium
- 3 carrots, peeled & sliced ½-inch thick
- 1 tbsp. mustard

Directions:
1. Use a sharp knife and score the fat side of the brisket in parallel lines, being careful to only slice through the fat, not the meat. Repeat to create a cross-hatch pattern. Sprinkle with salt and let sit 30 minutes.
2. Set the cooker to sear on med-high and lay brisket, fat side down, in the pot. Cook 5-8 minutes to render the fat. Turn the brisket over and brown the other side. Transfer to a plate.
3. Add the onions and season with salt. Cook, stirring frequently, until onions are browned, about 5-8 minutes. Add the garlic and cook 1 minute more.
4. Stir in remaining ingredients. Add the brisket back to the pot, pushing it down to cover as much as possible by the broth.
5. Add the lid and set to slow cook on low. Cook 8-9 hours or until brisket is tender. Transfer brisket to cutting board and tent with foil. Let rest 10-15 minutes. Slice across the grain to serve with carrots, onions and some of the cooking liquid.

Nutrition:
- InfoCalories 143,Total Fat 10g,Total Carbs 2g,Protein 10g,Sodium 833mg.

Beef And Cherry Tagine

Servings: 4
Cooking Time: 1 Hr 20 Min
Ingredients:
- 1 ½ pounds stewing beef, trimmed /675g
- 1 onion; chopped
- 1-star anise
- ¼ cup toasted almonds, slivered /32.5g
- 1 cup dried cherries, halved /130g
- 1 cup water /250ml
- 1 tbsp honey /15ml
- 2 tbsp olive oil /30ml
- ¼ tsp ground allspice /1.25g
- 1 tsp ground cinnamon /5g
- ½ tsp paprika /2.5g
- ½ tsp turmeric /2.5g
- ½ tsp salt /2.5g
- ¼ tsp ground ginger /1.25g

Directions:
1. Set your Foodi to Sear/Sauté, set to Medium High, and choose Start/Stop to preheat the pot. Warm olive oil. Add in onions and cook for 3 minutes until fragrant. Mix in beef and cook for 2 minutes each side until browned.
2. Stir in anise, cinnamon, turmeric, allspice, salt, paprika, and ginger; cook for 2 minutes until aromatic.
3. Add in honey and water. Seal the pressure lid, choose Pressure, set to High, and set the timer to 50 minutes. Press Start.
4. Meanwhile, in a bowl, soak dried cherries in hot water until softened. Once ready, release pressure naturally for 15 minutes. Drain cherries and stir into the tagine. Top with toasted almonds before serving.

Herbed Lamb Chops

Servings: 4
Cooking Time: 30 Min
Ingredients:
- 4 lamb chops
- 1 garlic clove, peeled
- ½ tbsp oregano /2.5g
- 1 tbsp plus /5g
- ½ tbsp thyme /2.5g
- 2 tsp olive oil /10ml
- ½ tsp salt /2.5g
- ¼ tsp black pepper /1.25g

Directions:
1. Coat the garlic clove with 1 tsp of olive oil and cook in the Foodi for 10 minutes on Air Crisp mode. Meanwhile, mix the herbs and seasonings with the remaining olive oil.
2. Using a towel, squeeze the hot roasted garlic clove into the herb mixture and stir to combine. Coat the lamb chops with the mixture well, and place in the Foodi.
3. Close the crisping lid and cook for about 8 to 12 minutes on Air Crisp mode at 390 °F or 200°C, until crispy on the outside.

Tex Mex Beef Stew

Servings: 10
Cooking Time: 25 Minutes
Ingredients:
- 2 tsp cumin
- 1 tsp salt
- 1 tsp garlic powder
- 2 tbsp. coconut oil
- 1 lb. lean ground beef
- 1 lb. beef chuck, boneless & cut in 1-inch cubes
- 2 cups sweet onions, chopped
- 1 yellow bell pepper, seeded & chopped
- 1 orange bell pepper, seeded & chopped
- 1 sweet potato, peeled & chopped
- 2 28 oz. cans tomatoes, crushed
- 1 cup beef broth, low sodium
- 3 chipotle peppers in adobo sauce, chopped

- ¼ cup cilantro, chopped, divided

Directions:
1. In a small bowl, combine cumin, salt, and garlic powder.
2. Add oil to the cooking pot and set to sauté on med-high heat.
3. Add the ground beef and half the spice mixture. Cook until beef is no longer pink. Use a slotted spoon to transfer beef to a bowl.
4. Add beef chuck and remaining spice mixture and cook until meat is browned on all sides.
5. Add the ground beef back to the pot. Add remaining ingredients, except cilantro, and stir to mix.
6. Add the lid and set to pressure cook on high. Set timer for 12 minutes. When the timer goes off, use manual release to remove the pressure. Stir in 2 tablespoons cilantro. Ladle into bowls and garnish with remaining cilantro. Serve.

Nutrition:
- InfoCalories 261,Total Fat 11g,Total Carbs 18g,Protein 24g,Sodium 461mg.

Korean Cabbage Cups

Servings: 4
Cooking Time: 15 Minutes
Ingredients:
- 1 lb. lean ground beef
- 1 onion, chopped
- 4 cloves garlic, chopped fine
- 2 tsp fresh ginger, grated
- 1 tbsp. sesame oil
- 3 tbsp. soy sauce, low sodium
- 1 tsp red chili paste
- 2 tbsp. rice wine vinegar
- 8 large cabbage leaves
- ¼ cup green onion, chopped
- ¼ cup cilantro, chopped

Directions:
1. Add the beef to the cooking pot and set to sauté on med-high heat. Cook, breaking up with a spatula, until no longer pink, about 5 minutes. Drain off fat.
2. Add onion, garlic, ginger, and sesame oil and cook until onion becomes translucent, about 3-5 minutes.
3. Stir in the soy sauce, chili paste, and vinegar and bring to a simmer. Simmer, stirring occasionally, about 3 minutes.
4. Lay the cabbage leaves on serving plates, two to a plate. Spoon 2-3 tablespoons of beef mixture on each leaf and top with green onion and cilantro. Serve hot.

Nutrition:
- InfoCalories 268,Total Fat 15g,Total Carbs 8g,Protein 25g,Sodium 473mg.

Beef In Basil Sauce

Servings: 4
Cooking Time: 15 Minutes
Ingredients:
- 2 tbsp. olive oil
- 2 shallots, sliced thin
- 7 cloves garlic sliced
- 1 tbsp. fresh ginger, peeled & grated
- 1/2 red bell pepper, sliced thin
- 1 lb. lean ground beef
- 2 tsp brown sugar
- 2 tbsp. fish sauce
- 6 tbsp. soy sauce, low sodium
- 3 tsp oyster sauce
- 2 tbsp. Asian garlic chili paste
- ½ cup beef broth, low sodium
- ¼ cup water
- 1 tsp cornstarch
- 1 cup basil leaves, chopped
- Cooked Jasmine rice for serving

Directions:
1. Add the oil to the cooking pot and set to sauté on med-high heat.
2. Add the shallots, garlic, ginger, and bell peppers to the pot and cook, stirring frequently, 3 minutes. Use a slotted spoon to transfer mixture to a bowl.
3. Increase heat to high and add the ground beef, cook, breaking it up with a spoon until beef is no longer pink.
4. In a small bowl, whisk together brown sugar, fish sauce, soy sauce, oyster sauce, cornstarch, broth, and water until smooth.
5. Add the pepper mixture back to the pot and pour the sauce over. Cook, stirring, 2 minutes until sauce has thickened.
6. Stir in basil and cook until wilted, about 2 minutes. Serve over hot rice.

Nutrition:
- InfoCalories 359,Total Fat 20g,Total Carbs 10g,Protein 34g,Sodium 1785mg.

Pork Chops With Gravy

Servings: 5
Cooking Time: 10 Minutes
Ingredients:
- 5 pork chops
- 1 tablespoon olive oil
- 1 teaspoon salt
- 1/2 teaspoon pepper
- 1/2 teaspoon garlic powder
- 2 cups beef broth
- 1 packet ranch dressing mix
- 10-1/2 oz. cream of chicken soup
- 1 packet brown gravy mix
- 2 tablespoons corn starch
- 2 tablespoons water

Directions:
1. Season both sides of the pat dried pork chops with salt, pepper and garlic powder.
2. Pour the olive oil into the Ninja Foodi. Set it to sauté.
3. Brown the pork chops on both sides. Remove and set aside.
4. Pour the beef broth to deglaze the pot.
5. Stir in the rest of the ingredients except the corn starch. Seal the pot.
6. Set it to pressure. Cook at "HIGH" pressure for 8 minutes. Release the pressure naturally.
7. Remove the pork chops. Turn the pot to sauté. Stir in the corn starch.
8. Simmer to thicken. Pour the gravy over the pork chops.

Nutrition:
- InfoCalories: 357; Fat: 26.8g; Carbohydrate 6g; Protein: 21.6g

Soups & Stews

Chicken Tomatillo Stew

Servings: 4
Cooking Time: 46 Minutes
Ingredients:
- 3 medium onions, quartered
- 3 garlic cloves, whole
- 2 poblano peppers, seeded and quartered
- ½ pound tomatillos
- 2 small jalapeño peppers, seeded and quartered (optional)
- 2 tablespoons canola oil, divided
- Kosher salt
- Freshly ground black pepper
- 2½ pounds boneless, skinless chicken thighs
- 1 cup chicken stock
- 1 teaspoon cumin
- 1 tablespoon oregano
- 1 tablespoon all-purpose flour
- 1 cup water

Directions:
1. Place Cook & Crisp Basket in pot and close crisping lid. Select AIR CRISP and set to HIGH. Set time to 25 minutes. Select START/STOP to begin. Let preheat for 5 minutes.
2. Place the onions, garlic, poblano peppers, tomatillos, jalapeños, 1 tablespoon of canola oil, salt, and pepper in a medium-sized bowl and mix until vegetables are evenly coated.
3. Once unit has preheated, open lid and place the vegetables in the basket. Close lid and cook for 20 minutes.
4. After 10 minutes, open lid, then lift basket and shake the vegetables or toss them with silicone-tipped tongs. Lower basket back into pot and close lid to continue cooking.
5. When cooking is complete, remove basket and vegetables and set aside.
6. Select SEAR/SAUTÉ and set to HI. Select START/STOP to begin. Let preheat for 5 minutes.
7. Season the chicken thighs with salt and pepper.
8. After 5 minutes, add the remaining 1 tablespoon of oil and chicken. Sear the chicken, about 3 minutes on each side.
9. Add the chicken stock, cumin, and oregano. Scrape the pot with a rubber or wooden spoon to release any pieces that are sticking to the bottom. Assemble pressure lid, making sure the pressure release valve is in the SEAL position.
10. Select PRESSURE and set to HI. Set time to 10 minutes. Select START/STOP to begin.
11. Remove the vegetables from the basket and roughly chop.
12. In a small bowl, add the flour and water and stir.
13. When pressure cooking is complete, quick release the pressure by turning the pressure release valve to the VENT position. Carefully remove lid when unit has finished releasing pressure.
14. Remove the chicken and shred it using two forks.
15. Select SEAR/SAUTÉ and set to MED. Select START/STOP to begin. Return the chicken and vegetables and stir with a rubber or wooden spoon, being sure to scrape the bottom of the pot. Slowly stir in the flour mixture. Bring to a simmer and cook for 10 minutes, or until the broth becomes clear and has thickened.
16. When cooking is complete, serve as is or garnish with sour cream, lime, cilantro, and a flour tortilla for dipping.

Nutrition:
- InfoCalories: 487, Total Fat: 20g, Sodium: 382mg, Carbohydrates: 19g, Protein: 59g.

Chickpea, Spinach, And Sweet Potato Stew

Servings: 6
Cooking Time: 23 Minutes
Ingredients:
- 1 tablespoon extra-virgin olive oil
- 1 yellow onion, diced
- 4 garlic cloves, minced
- 4 sweet potatoes, peeled and diced
- 4 cups vegetable broth
- 1 can fire-roasted diced tomatoes, undrained
- 2 cans chickpeas, drained
- 1½ teaspoons ground cumin
- 1 teaspoon ground coriander
- ½ teaspoon paprika
- ½ teaspoon sea salt
- ½ teaspoon freshly ground black pepper
- 4 cups baby spinach

Directions:
1. Select SEAR/SAUTÉ and set to MD:HI. Select START/STOP to begin. Allow the pot to preheat for 5 minutes.
2. Combine the oil, onion, and garlic in the pot. Cook, stirring occasionally, for 5 minutes.
3. Add the sweet potatoes, vegetable broth, tomatoes, chickpeas, cumin, coriander, paprika, salt, and black pepper to the pot. Assemble the pressure lid, making sure the pressure release valve is in the SEAL position.
4. Select PRESSURE and set to HI. Set the time to 8 minutes, then select START/STOP to begin.
5. When pressure cooking is complete, quick release the pressure by moving the pressure release valve to the VENT position. Carefully remove the lid when the unit has finished releasing pressure.
6. Add the spinach to the pot and stir until wilted. Serve.

Nutrition:
- InfoCalories: 220, Total Fat: 4g, Sodium: 593mg, Carbohydrates: 42g, Protein: 7g.

Roasted Tomato And Seafood Stew

Servings: 6
Cooking Time: 46 Minutes
Ingredients:
- 2 tablespoons extra-virgin olive oil
- 1 yellow onion, diced
- 1 fennel bulb, tops removed and bulb diced
- 3 garlic cloves, minced
- 1 cup dry white wine
- 2 cans fire-roasted tomatoes
- 2 cups chicken stock
- 1 pound medium shrimp, peeled and deveined
- 1 pound raw white fish (cod or haddock), cubed

- Salt
- Freshly ground black pepper
- Fresh basil, torn, for garnish

Directions:
1. Select SEAR/SAUTÉ and set to MED. Select START/STOP to begin. Let preheat for 3 minutes.
2. Add the olive oil, onions, fennel, and garlic. Cook for about 3 minutes, until translucent.
3. Add the white wine and deglaze, scraping any stuck bits from the bottom of the pot using a silicone spatula. Add the roasted tomatoes and chicken stock. Simmer for 25 to 30 minutes. Add the shrimp and white fish.
4. Select SEAR/SAUTÉ and set to MD:LO. Select START/STOP to begin.
5. Simmer for 10 minutes, stirring frequently, until the shrimp and fish are cooked through. Season with salt and pepper.
6. Ladle into bowl and serve topped with torn basil.

Nutrition:
- InfoCalories: 301,Total Fat: 8g,Sodium: 808mg,Carbohydrates: 21g,Protein: 26g.

Lasagna Soup

Servings:8
Cooking Time: 16 Minutes
Ingredients:
- 1 tablespoon extra-virgin olive oil
- 16 ounces Italian sausage
- 1 small onion, diced
- 4 garlic cloves, minced
- 1 jar marinara sauce
- 2 cups water
- 1 cup vegetable broth
- 1 teaspoon dried basil
- 1 teaspoon dried oregano
- ½ teaspoon dried thyme
- Freshly ground black pepper
- 8 ounces lasagna noodles, broken up
- 1 cup ricotta cheese
- ½ cup grated Parmesan cheese
- 1 teaspoon dried parsley
- ½ cup heavy (whipping) cream
- 1 cup shredded mozzarella cheese

Directions:
1. Select SEAR/SAUTÉ and set to HI. Select START/STOP to begin. Let preheat for 5 minutes.
2. Add the oil and sausage and cook for about 5 minutes. Using a wooden spoon, break apart the sausage and stir.
3. Add the onions and cook, stirring occasionally, for 3 minutes. Add the garlic and cook for 2 minutes, or until the meat is no longer pink.
4. Add the marinara sauce, water, vegetable broth, basil, oregano, thyme, pepper, and lasagna noodles. Assemble pressure lid, making sure the pressure release valve is in the SEAL position.
5. Select PRESSURE and set to HI. Set time to 6 minutes. Select START/STOP to begin.
6. In a medium bowl, combine the ricotta cheese, Parmesan cheese, and parsley. Cover and refrigerate.
7. When pressure cooking is complete, quick release the pressure by turning the pressure release valve to the VENT position. Carefully remove lid when unit has finished releasing pressure.
8. Stir in the heavy cream. Add the cheese mixture and stir. Top the soup with the mozzarella. Close crisping lid.
9. Select BROIL and set time to 5 minutes. Select START/STOP to begin.
10. When cooking is complete, serve immediately.

Nutrition:
- InfoCalories: 398,Total Fat: 22g,Sodium: 892mg,Carbohydrates: 29g,Protein: 23g.

Chicken Enchilada Soup

Servings:8
Cooking Time: 30 Minutes
Ingredients:
- 1 tablespoon extra-virgin olive oil
- 1 small red onion, diced
- 2 cans fire-roasted tomatoes with chiles
- 1 can corn
- 1 can black beans, rinsed and drained
- 1 can red enchilada sauce
- 1 can tomato paste
- 3 tablespoons taco seasoning
- 2 tablespoons freshly squeezed lime juice
- 2 boneless, skinless chicken breasts
- Salt
- Freshly ground black pepper

Directions:
1. Select SEAR/SAUTÉ and set temperature to MD:HI. Select START/STOP to begin. Let preheat for 5 minutes.
2. Place the olive oil and onion in the pot. Cook until the onions are translucent, about 2 minutes.
3. Add the tomatoes, corn, beans, enchilada sauce, tomato paste, taco seasoning, lime juice, and chicken. Season with salt and pepper and stir. Assemble pressure lid, making sure the pressure release valve is in the SEAL position.
4. Select PRESSURE and set to HI. Set time to 9 minutes. Select START/STOP to begin.
5. When pressure cooking is complete, allow pressure to naturally release for 10 minutes. After 10 minutes, quick release remaining pressure by moving the pressure release valve to the VENT position. Carefully remove lid when unit has finished releasing pressure.
6. Transfer the chicken breasts to a cutting board. Using two forks, shred the chicken. Return the chicken back to the pot and stir. Serve in a bowl with toppings of choice, such as shredded cheese, crushed tortilla chips, sliced avocado, sour cream, cilantro, and lime wedges, if desired.

Nutrition:
- InfoCalories: 257,Total Fat: 4g,Sodium: 819mg,Carbohydrates: 37g,Protein: 20g.

Mushroom And Wild Rice Soup

Servings:6
Cooking Time: 30 Minutes
Ingredients:
- 5 medium carrots, chopped
- 5 celery stalks, chopped
- 1 onion, chopped
- 3 garlic cloves, minced
- 1 cup wild rice
- 8 ounces fresh mushrooms, sliced
- 6 cups vegetable broth
- 1 teaspoon kosher salt
- 1 teaspoon poultry seasoning
- ½ teaspoon dried thyme

Directions:

1. Place all the ingredients in the pot. Assemble pressure lid, making sure the pressure release valve is in the SEAL position.
2. Select PRESSURE and set to HI. Set time to 30 minutes. Select START/STOP to begin.
3. When pressure cooking is complete, quick release the pressure by turning the pressure release valve to the VENT position. Carefully remove lid when unit has finished releasing pressure.
4. Serve.

Nutrition:
- InfoCalories: 175,Total Fat: 2g,Sodium: 723mg,Carbohydrates: 30g,Protein: 11g.

Butternut Squash, Apple, Bacon And Orzo Soup

Servings:8
Cooking Time: 28 Minutes

Ingredients:
- 4 slices uncooked bacon, cut into ½-inch pieces
- 12 ounces butternut squash, peeled and cubed
- 1 green apple, cut into small cubes
- Kosher salt
- Freshly ground black pepper
- 1 tablespoon minced fresh oregano
- 2 quarts chicken stock
- 1 cup orzo

Directions:
1. Select SEAR/SAUTÉ and set temperature to HI. Select START/STOP to begin. Let preheat for 5 minutes.
2. Place the bacon in the pot and cook, stirring frequently, about 5 minutes, or until fat is rendered and the bacon starts to brown. Using a slotted spoon, transfer the bacon to a paper towel-lined plate to drain, leaving the rendered bacon fat in the pot.
3. Add the butternut squash, apple, salt, and pepper and sauté until partially soft, about 5 minutes. Stir in the oregano.
4. Add the bacon back into the pot along with the chicken stock. Bring to a boil for about 10 minutes, then add the orzo. Cook for about 8 minutes, until the orzo is tender. Serve.

Nutrition:
- InfoCalories: 247,Total Fat: 7g,Sodium: 563mg,Carbohydrates: 33g,Protein: 12g.

Chicken Chili

Servings:8
Cooking Time: 30 Minutes

Ingredients:
- 1 tablespoon extra-virgin olive oil
- 1 yellow onion, chopped
- 4 garlic cloves, minced
- 2 pounds boneless chicken breast, cut in half crosswise
- 4 cups chicken broth
- 1 green bell pepper, seeded and chopped
- 2 jalapeños, seeded and chopped
- 1½ tablespoons ground cumin
- 1 tablespoon coriander
- 1 teaspoon dried oregano
- 1 teaspoon sea salt
- 1 teaspoon freshly ground black pepper
- 2 cans cannellini beans, rinsed and drained
- Shredded Monterey Jack cheese, for garnish
- Chopped cilantro, for garnish
- Lime wedge, for garnish

Directions:
1. Select SEAR/SAUTÉ and set to HI. Select START/STOP to begin. Let preheat for 5 minutes.
2. Add the oil and onions and cook, stirring occasionally, for 3 minutes. Add the garlic and cook for 2 minutes.
3. Add the chicken breast, chicken broth, green bell pepper, jalapeño, cumin, coriander, oregano, salt, and black pepper. Assemble pressure lid, making sure the pressure release valve is in the SEAL position.
4. Select PRESSURE and set to HI. Set time to 15 minutes. Select START/STOP to begin.
5. When pressure cooking is complete, quick release the pressure by turning the pressure release valve to the VENT position. Carefully remove lid when unit has finished releasing pressure.
6. Remove the chicken from the soup and shred it using two forks. Set aside.
7. Add the cannellini beans. Select SEAR/SAUTÉ and set to MED. Select START/STOP to begin. Cook until heated through, about 5 minutes.
8. Add shredded chicken back to the pot. Serve, garnished with the cheese, cilantro, and lime wedge (if using).

Nutrition:
- InfoCalories: 279,Total Fat: 9g,Sodium: 523mg,Carbohydrates: 18g,Protein: 32g.

Chicken Noodle Soup

Servings:8
Cooking Time: 19 Minutes

Ingredients:
- 2 tablespoons unsalted butter
- 1 large onion, chopped
- 2 carrots, chopped
- 2 celery stalks, chopped
- 2 pounds boneless chicken breast
- 4 cups chicken broth
- 4 cups water
- 1 tablespoon chopped fresh parsley
- 1 teaspoon dried thyme
- 1 teaspoon dried oregano
- ½ teaspoon sea salt
- ½ teaspoon freshly ground black pepper
- 5 ounces egg noodles

Directions:
1. Select SEAR/SAUTÉ and set to HI. Select START/STOP to begin. Let preheat for 5 minutes.
2. Add the butter. Once melted, add the onion, carrots, and celery. Cook, stirring occasionally, for 5 minutes.
3. Add the chicken, chicken broth, water, parsley, thyme, oregano, salt, and pepper. Assemble pressure lid, making sure the pressure release valve is in the SEAL position.
4. Select PRESSURE and set to HI. Set time to 8 minutes. Select START/STOP to begin.
5. When pressure cooking is complete, quick release the pressure by moving the pressure release valve to the VENT position. Carefully remove lid when unit has finished releasing pressure.
6. Remove the chicken from the soup and shred it with two forks. Set aside.
7. Add the egg noodles. Select SEAR/SAUTÉ and set to MED. Select START/STOP to begin.
8. Cook for 6 minutes, uncovered, or until the noodles are tender. Stir the shredded chicken back into the pot. Serve.

Nutrition:
- InfoCalories: 237,Total Fat: 5g,Sodium: 413mg,Carbohydrates: 17g,Protein: 30g.

Pho Tom

Servings: 6
Cooking Time: 36 Minutes
Ingredients:
- 2 tablespoons canola oil
- 1 onion, peeled and halved
- 1 piece fresh ginger, peeled
- 2 tablespoons brown sugar
- 2 tablespoons kosher salt
- 1½ tablespoons Chinese five-spice powder
- ¼ cup fish sauce
- 4 cups beef bone broth
- 8 cups water
- 1 package rice noodles, cooked according to the package directions
- 1 pound peeled cooked shrimp
- Bean sprouts, for topping (optional)
- Lime wedges, for serving (optional)
- Fresh basil, for topping (optional)
- Sriracha, for topping (optional)

Directions:
1. Select SEAR/SAUTÉ and set temperature to HI. Select START/STOP to begin. Allow to preheat for 5 minutes.
2. Add oil to the pot and allow to heat for 1 minute. Add the onion and ginger and sear on all sides, about 6 minutes. Select START/STOP to end the function.
3. Add the sugar, salt, five-spice powder, fish sauce, bone broth, and water. Stir for 1 minute to combine.
4. Assemble the pressure lid, making sure the pressure release valve is in the SEAL position.
5. Select PRESSURE and set to HI. Set the time to 30 minutes. Select START/STOP to begin.
6. When pressure cooking is complete, quick release the pressure by turning the pressure release valve to the VENT position. Carefully remove the lid when the unit has finished releasing pressure.
7. Add the desired amount of noodles to a bowl and top with 5 or 6 shrimp and some sliced onion. Ladle the pho broth to cover the noodles, shrimp, and onion. Top as desired.

Nutrition:
- InfoCalories: 242, Total Fat: 7g, Sodium: 2419mg, Carbohydrates: 25g, Protein: 22g.

Loaded Potato Soup

Servings: 6
Cooking Time: 30 Minutes
Ingredients:
- 5 slices bacon, chopped
- 1 onion, chopped
- 3 garlic cloves, minced
- 4 pounds Russet potatoes, peeled and chopped
- 4 cups chicken broth
- 1 cup whole milk
- ½ teaspoon sea salt
- ½ teaspoon freshly ground black pepper
- 1½ cups shredded Cheddar cheese
- Sour cream, for serving (optional)
- Chopped fresh chives, for serving (optional)

Directions:
1. Select SEAR/SAUTÉ and set to HI. Select START/STOP to begin. Let preheat for 5 minutes.
2. Add the bacon, onion, and garlic. Cook, stirring occasionally, for 5 minutes. Set aside some of the bacon for garnish.
3. Add the potatoes and chicken broth. Assemble pressure lid, making sure the pressure release valve is in the SEAL position.
4. Select PRESSURE and set to HI. Set time to 10 minutes, then select START/STOP to begin.
5. When pressure cooking is complete, quick release the pressure by moving the pressure release valve to the VENT position. Carefully remove lid when unit has finished releasing pressure.
6. Add the milk and mash the ingredients until the soup reaches your desired consistency. Season with the salt and black pepper. Sprinkle the cheese evenly over the top of the soup. Close crisping lid.
7. Select BROIL and set time to 5 minutes. Select START/STOP to begin.
8. When cooking is complete, top with the reserved crispy bacon and serve with sour cream and chives (if using).

Nutrition:
- InfoCalories: 468, Total Fat: 19g, Sodium: 1041mg, Carbohydrates: 53g, Protein: 23g.

Chicken Potpie Soup

Servings: 6
Cooking Time: 1 Hour
Ingredients:
- 4 chicken breasts
- 2 cups chicken stock
- 2 tablespoons unsalted butter
- 1 yellow onion, diced
- 16 ounces frozen mixed vegetables
- 1 cup heavy (whipping) cream
- 1 can condensed cream of chicken soup
- 2 tablespoons cornstarch
- 2 tablespoons water
- Salt
- Freshly ground black pepper
- 1 tube refrigerated biscuit dough

Directions:
1. Place the chicken and stock in the pot. Assemble pressure lid, making sure the pressure release valve is in the SEAL position.
2. Select PRESSURE and set to HI. Set time to 15 minutes. Select START/STOP to begin.
3. Once pressure cooking is complete, quick release the pressure by turning the pressure release valve to the VENT position. Carefully remove lid when the unit has finished releasing pressure.
4. Using a silicone-tipped utensil, shred the chicken.
5. Select SEAR/SAUTÉ and set to MED. Add the butter, onion, mixed vegetables, cream, and condensed soup and stir. Select START/STOP to begin. Simmer for 10 minutes.
6. In a small bowl, whisk together the cornstarch and water. Slowly whisk the cornstarch mixture into the soup. Set temperature to LO and simmer for 10 minutes more. Season with salt and pepper.
7. Carefully arrange the biscuits on top of the simmering soup. Close crisping lid.
8. Select BAKE/ROAST, set temperature to 325°F (160°C), and set time to 15 minutes. Select START/STOP to begin.
9. When cooking is complete, remove the biscuits. To serve, place a biscuit in a bowl and ladle soup over it.

Nutrition:
- InfoCalories: 731, Total Fat: 26g, Sodium: 1167mg, Carbohydrates: 56g, Protein: 45g.

Jamaican Jerk Chicken Stew

Servings: 6
Cooking Time: 28 Minutes
Ingredients:
- 2 tablespoons canola oil
- 6 boneless, skinless chicken thighs, cut in 2-inch pieces
- 2 tablespoons Jamaican jerk spice
- 1 white onion, peeled and chopped
- 2 red bell peppers, chopped
- ½ head green cabbage, core removed and cut into 2-inch pieces
- 1½ cups wild rice blend, rinsed
- 4 cups chicken stock
- ½ cup prepared Jamaican jerk sauce
- Kosher salt

Directions:
1. Select SEAR/SAUTÉ and set to HI. Select START/STOP to begin. Let preheat for 5 minutes.
2. Add the oil, chicken, and jerk spice and stir. Cook for 5 minutes, stirring occasionally.
3. Add the onions, bell pepper, and cabbage and stir. Cook for 5 minutes, stirring occasionally.
4. Add the wild rice and stock, stirring well to combine. Assemble pressure lid, making sure the pressure release valve is in the SEAL position.
5. Select PRESSURE and set to HI. Set time to 18 minutes. Select START/STOP to begin.
6. When pressure cooking is complete, allow pressure to naturally release for 10 minutes. After 10 minutes, quick release any remaining pressure by moving the pressure release valve to the VENT position. Carefully remove lid when unit has finished releasing pressure.
7. Add the jerk sauce to pot, stirring well to combine. Let the stew sit for 5 minutes, allowing it to thicken. Season with salt and serve.

Nutrition:
- InfoCalories: 404, Total Fat: 10g, Sodium: 373mg, Carbohydrates: 53g, Protein: 29g.

Braised Pork And Black Bean Stew

Servings: 8
Cooking Time: 30 Minutes
Ingredients:
- 2 pounds boneless pork shoulder, cut into 1-inch pieces
- ¼ cup all-purpose flour
- ¼ cup unsalted butter
- ½ small onion, diced
- 1 carrot, diced
- 1 celery stalk, diced
- 2 garlic cloves, minced
- 1 tablespoon tomato paste
- 1 tablespoon cumin
- 1 tablespoon smoked paprika
- 4 cups chicken stock
- 1 can diced tomatoes with chiles
- 1 can black beans, rinsed and drained
- 1 can hominy, rinsed and drained
- Sea salt
- Freshly ground black pepper

Directions:
1. In a large bowl, coat the pork pieces with the flour.
2. Select SEAR/SAUTÉ and set to HI. Select START/STOP to begin. Let preheat for 5 minutes.
3. Add the butter. Once melted, add the pork and sear for 5 minutes, turning the pieces so they begin to brown on all sides.
4. Add the onion, carrot, celery, garlic, tomato paste, cumin, and paprika and cook, stirring occasionally, for 3 minutes.
5. Add the chicken stock and tomatoes. Assemble pressure lid, making sure the pressure release valve is in the SEAL position.
6. Select PRESSURE and set to HI. Set time to 15 minutes. Select START/STOP to begin.
7. When pressure cooking is complete, quick release the pressure by turning the pressure release valve to the VENT position. Carefully remove lid when the unit has finished releasing pressure.
8. Select SEAR/SAUTÉ and set to HI. Select START/STOP to begin.
9. Whisk in the beans and hominy. Season with salt and pepper and cook for 2 minutes. Serve.

Nutrition:
- InfoCalories: 342, Total Fat: 12g, Sodium: 638mg, Carbohydrates: 27g, Protein: 29g.

Italian Sausage, Potato, And Kale Soup

Servings: 8
Cooking Time: 18 Minutes
Ingredients:
- 1 tablespoon extra-virgin olive oil
- 1½ pounds hot Italian sausage, ground
- 1 pound sweet Italian sausage, ground
- 1 large yellow onion, diced
- 2 tablespoons minced garlic
- 4 large Russet potatoes, cut in ½-inch thick quarters
- 5 cups chicken stock
- 2 tablespoons Italian seasoning
- 2 teaspoons crushed red pepper flakes
- Salt
- Freshly ground black pepper
- 6 cups kale, chopped
- ½ cup heavy (whipping) cream

Directions:
1. Select SEAR/SAUTÉ. Set temperature to MD:HI. Select START/STOP to begin. Let preheat for 5 minutes.
2. Add the olive oil and hot and sweet Italian sausage. Cook, breaking up the sausage with a spatula, until the meat is cooked all the way through, about 5 minutes.
3. Add the onion, garlic, potatoes, chicken stock, Italian seasoning, and crushed red pepper flakes. Season with salt and pepper. Stir to combine. Assemble pressure lid, making sure the pressure release valve is in the SEAL position.
4. Select PRESSURE and set to HI. Set time to 10 minutes. Select START/STOP to begin.
5. When pressure cooking is complete, quick release the pressure by turning the pressure release valve to the VENT position. Carefully remove lid when the unit has finished releasing pressure.
6. Stir in the kale and heavy cream. Serve.

Nutrition:
- InfoCalories: 689, Total Fat: 45g, Sodium: 1185mg, Carbohydrates: 38g, Protein: 33g.

Ninja Foodi Cookbook Guide

Desserts

Peanut Butter Pie

Servings: 8
Cooking Time: 30 Minutes
Ingredients:
- 10 peanut butter cookies, crushed
- 3 tablespoons unsalted butter, melted
- 2 packages cream cheese, at room temperature
- ¾ cup granulated sugar
- 2 eggs
- ⅓ cup creamy peanut butter
- 10 chocolate peanut butter cups, chopped
- 2 cups water
- 1 tub whipped cream topping

Directions:
1. In a small bowl, mix together peanut butter cookie crumbs and melted butter. Press the mixture into the bottom of the Ninja Multi-Purpose Pan or 8-inch baking dish.
2. In a medium bowl, use an electric hand mixer to combine the cream cheese, sugar, eggs, and peanut butter. Mix on medium speed for 5 minutes.
3. Place the chopped chocolate peanut butter cups evenly on top of crust in the pan. Pour the batter on top. Cover tightly with aluminum foil.
4. Place the water in the pot. Insert Reversible Rack into pot, making sure it is on the lower position. Place covered multipurpose pan onto rack. Assemble pressure lid, making sure the pressure release valve is in the SEAL position.
5. Select PRESSURE and set to HI. Set time to 25 minutes. Press START/STOP to begin.
6. When pressure cooking is complete, allow pressure to naturally release for 15 minutes. After 15 minutes, quick release remaining pressure by moving the pressure release valve to the VENT position. Carefully remove lid when unit has finished releasing pressure.
7. Remove the pan and chill in the refrigerator for at least 3 hours or overnight before serving topped with whipped cream.

Nutrition:
- InfoCalories: 645, Total Fat: 47g, Sodium: 383mg, Carbohydrates: 48g, Protein: 13g.

Apricots With Honey Sauce

Servings: 4
Cooking Time: 15 Min
Ingredients:
- 8 Apricots, pitted and halved
- ¼ cup Honey /62.5ml
- 2 cups Blueberries /260g
- ½ Cinnamon stick
- 1 ¼ cups Water /312.5ml
- ½ Vanilla Bean; sliced lengthwise
- 1 ½ tbsp Cornstarch /22.5g
- ¼ tsp ground Cardamom /1.25g

Directions:
1. Add all ingredients, except for the honey and the cornstarch, to your Foodi. Seal the pressure lid, choose Pressure, set to High, and set the time to s 8 minutes. Press Start. Do a quick pressure release and open the pressure lid.
2. Remove the apricots with a slotted spoon. Choose Sear/Sauté, add the honey and cornstarch, then let simmer until the sauce thickens, for about 5 minutes. Split up the apricots among serving plates and top with the blueberry sauce, to serve.

Date Orange Cheesecake

Servings: 8
Cooking Time: 20 Minutes
Ingredients:
- Butter flavored cooking spray
- 2 cups water
- 2 lbs. ricotta cheese
- 4 eggs
- ¼ cup sugar
- ¼ cup honey
- Juice & zest of ½ orange
- ¼ tsp vanilla
- 1 cup dates, soak in warm water 20 minutes, chop fine

Directions:
1. Place the trivet in the cooking pot and add 2 cups water. Spray a deep, 8-inch springform pan with cooking spray.
2. In a large bowl, beat ricotta cheese until smooth.
3. In a medium bowl, beat eggs and sugar 3 minutes. Fold into ricotta cheese.
4. In a small saucepan, heat honey over low heat, do not let it get hot, just warm.
5. Whisk in orange juice, zest, and vanilla until combined. Whisk into cheese mixture until combined.
6. Fold in dates and pour into prepared pan. Cover with foil.
7. Place the cheesecake in the cooking pot and secure the lid. Set to pressure cooking on high. Set the timer for 20 minutes.
8. When timer goes off use natural release to remove the lid. Transfer cheesecake to wire rack to cool completely. Cover and refrigerate at least 4 hours before serving.

Nutrition:
- InfoCalories 343, Total Fat 17g, Total Carbs 32g, Protein 16g, Sodium 132mg.

Fried Snickerdoodle Poppers

Servings: 6
Cooking Time: 30 Min
Ingredients:
- 1 box instant vanilla Jell-O
- 1 ½ cups cinnamon sugar /195g
- 1 can of Pillsbury Grands Flaky Layers Biscuits
- Melted butter, for brushing

Directions:
1. Unroll the flaky biscuits and cut them into fourths. Roll each ¼ into a ball. Arrange the balls on a lined baking sheet, and cook in the Foodi for 7 minutes, or until golden, on Air Crisp mode at 350 °F or 175°C.
2. Prepare the Jell-O following the package's instructions. Using an injector, inject some of the vanilla pudding into each ball. Brush the balls with melted butter and then coat them with cinnamon sugar.

Steamed Lemon Pudding

Servings: 6
Cooking Time: 90 Minutes
Ingredients:
- Nonstick cooking spray
- ¾ cup butter, unsalted, soft
- 1 cup caster sugar
- 2 eggs
- 2 cups flour
- 1 tsp baking powder
- Zest & juice from 2 lemons

Directions:
1. Lightly spray a 1 liter oven-safe bowl with cooking spray.
2. Add the butter and sugar to the bowl and beat until light and fluffy.
3. Add the eggs, one at a time, beating well after each addition.
4. Stir in the flour and baking powder until combined.
5. Fold in the lemon zest and juice and mix until smooth. Cover lightly with foil.
6. Pour 1 ½ cups water into the cooking pot and add steamer rack.
7. Place the bowl on the rack, secure the lid. Set to steam on 212°F (100°C). Cook 90 minutes, or until pudding is cooked through.
8. Remove the pudding from the cooker and let sit 5 minutes before inverting onto serving plate.

Nutrition:
- InfoCalories 446,Total Fat 17g,Total Carbs 66g,Protein 7g,Sodium 33mg.

Blueberry Peach Crisp

Servings: 8
Cooking Time: 40 Minutes
Ingredients:
- 1 cup blueberries
- 6 peaches, peeled, cored & cut in ½-inch pieces
- ½ cup + 3 tbsp. flour
- ¾ cups Stevia, divided
- ½ tsp cinnamon
- ¼ tsp salt, divided
- Zest & juice of 1 lemon
- 1 cup oats
- 1/3 cup coconut oil, melted

Directions:
1. Place the rack in the cooking pot.
2. In a large bowl, combine blueberries, peaches, 3 tablespoons flour, ¼ cup Stevia, cinnamon, and 1/8 teaspoon salt, toss to coat fruit. Stir in lemon zest and juice just until combined. Pour into an 8-inch baking dish.
3. In a medium bowl, combine oats, ½ cup Stevia, coconut oil, remaining flour and salt and mix with a fork until crumbly. Sprinkle over the top of the fruit.
4. Place the dish on the rack and add the tender-crisp lid. Set to bake on 350 °F (175°C). Bake 35-40 minutes until filling is bubbly and top is golden brown. Serve warm.

Nutrition:
- InfoCalories 265,Total Fat 11g,Total Carbs 44g,Protein 6g,Sodium 74mg.

Chocolate Soufflé

Servings: 2
Cooking Time: 25 Min
Ingredients:
- 2 eggs, whites and yolks separated
- 3 oz. chocolate, melted /90ml
- ¼ cup butter, melted /32.5ml
- 2 tbsp flour /30g
- 3 tbsp sugar /45g
- ½ tsp vanilla extract /2.5ml

Directions:
1. Beat the yolks along with the sugar and vanilla extract. Stir in butter, chocolate, and flour. Whisk the whites until a stiff peak forms.
2. Working in batches, gently combine the egg whites with the chocolate mixture. Divide the batter between two greased ramekins. Close the crisping lid and cook for 14 minutes on Roast at 330 °F or 165°C.

Chocolate Cake

Servings: 16
Cooking Time: 30 Minutes
Ingredients:
- Butter flavored cooking spray
- 8 Eggs
- 1 lb. semi-sweet chocolate chips
- 1 cup butter

Directions:
1. Place the rack in the cooking pot. Line the bottom of an 8-inch springform pan with parchment paper. Spray with cooking spray and wrap foil around the outside of the pan.
2. In a large bowl, beat eggs until double in size, about 6-8 minutes.
3. Place the chocolate chips and butter in a microwave safe bowl. Microwave at 30 second intervals until melted and smooth.
4. Fold 1/3 of the eggs into chocolate, folding gently just until eggs are incorporated. Repeat two more times.
5. Pour the batter into the prepared pan. Pour 1 ½ cups water into the cooking pot. Place the cake on the rack.
6. Add the tender-crisp lid and set to air fry on 325°F (160°C). Bake 25-30 minutes or until center is set.
7. Transfer to wire rack to cool. When cool, invert onto serving plate, top with fresh berries if desired. Slice and serve.

Nutrition:
- InfoCalories 302,Total Fat 25g,Total Carbs 15g,Protein 5g,Sodium 130mg.

Mini Chocolate Cheesecakes

Servings: 4
Cooking Time: 18 Minutes
Ingredients:
- 1 egg
- 8 ounces cream cheese, softened
- ¼ cup Erythritol
- 1 tablespoon powdered peanut butter
- ¾ tablespoon cacao powder

Directions:
1. Grease the Ninja Foodi's insert.
2. In a blender, stir in the eggs and cream cheese and pulse until smooth.
3. Add the rest of the ingredients and pulse until well combined.
4. Transfer the mixture into 2 8-ounce mason jars evenly.
5. In the Ninja Foodi's insert, place 1 cup of water.

Ninja Foodi Cookbook Guide

6. Set a "Reversible Rack" in the Ninja Foodi's insert.
7. Place the mason jars over the "Reversible Rack".
8. Close the Ninja Foodi's lid with a pressure lid and place the pressure valve in the "Seal" position.
9. Select "Pressure" mode and set it to "High" for 18 minutes.
10. Press the "Start/Stop" button to initiate cooking.
11. Switch the pressure valve to "Vent" and do a "Natural" release.
12. Open the Ninja Foodi's lid and place the ramekins onto a wire rack to cool.
13. Refrigerate to chill for at least 6-8 hours before serving.

Nutrition:
- InfoCalories: 222; Fats: 28.4g; Carbohydrates: 2.9g; Proteins: 6.5g

Blueberry Lemon Pound Cake

Servings: 12
Cooking Time: 1 Hour 5 Minutes
Ingredients:
- Butter flavored cooking spray
- 1 ¾ cups + 2 tsp flour, divided
- 2 tsp baking powder
- ½ tsp salt
- 1 ½ cups blueberries
- ¾ cup butter, unsalted, soft
- 1 cup ricotta cheese, room temperature
- 1 ½ cups sugar
- 3 eggs, room temperature
- 1 tsp vanilla
- 1 tbsp. lemon zest

Directions:
1. Spray a loaf pan with cooking spray
2. In a medium bowl, combine flour, baking powder, and salt, mix well.
3. Add the blueberries to a bowl and sprinkle 2 tsp flour over them, toss to coat.
4. In a large bowl, beat together butter, ricotta, and sugar on high speed, until pale and fluffy.
5. Reduce speed to medium and beat in eggs, one at a time. Beat in zest and vanilla.
6. Stir in dry ingredients, a fourth at a time, until combined. Fold in blueberries and pour into prepared pan.
7. Add the rack to the cooking pot and place the pan on it. Add the tender-crisp lid and set to bake on 325°F (160°C). Bake 1 hour 10 minutes or until cake passes the toothpick test. After 40 minutes, cover the cake with foil.
8. Transfer to wire rack and let cool in pan 15 minutes. Then invert and let cool completely before serving.

Nutrition:
- InfoCalories 303,Total Fat 17g,Total Carbs 32g,Protein 6g,Sodium 147mg.

Hot Fudge Brownies

Servings: 16
Cooking Time: 25 Minutes
Ingredients:
- Butter flavored cooking spray
- 2/3 cup flour
- 2/3 cup sugar
- ½ cup cocoa powder, unsweetened
- ¼ cup butter, melted
- 2 tbsp. water
- 1 tbsp. vanilla
- ½ tsp baking powder
- 1/3 cup egg substitute
- ¼ cup hot fudge sauce, fat-free, warmed

Directions:
1. Place the rack in the cooking pot. Spray an 8x8-inch baking pan with cooking spray.
2. In a large bowl, combine all ingredients, except hot fudge sauce, and mix well. Spread ½ the batter evenly in prepared pan. Pour hot fudge sauce evenly over batter then spread remaining batter over the top.
3. Place the pan on the rack and add the tender-crisp lid. Set to bake on 350°F (175°C). Bake 20-25 minutes or until brownies pass the toothpick test.
4. Transfer to wire rack to cool before serving.

Nutrition:
- InfoCalories 102,Total Fat 4g,Total Carbs 17g,Protein 2g,Sodium 35mg.

Cherry Cheesecake

Servings:8
Cooking Time: 30 Minutes
Ingredients:
- 4 packages cream cheese, at room temperature
- 1 cup granulated sugar
- 3 tablespoons cornstarch
- 3 whole eggs
- 2 egg yolks
- ¼ cup heavy (whipping) cream
- 1 teaspoon kosher salt
- 1½ cups crushed graham crackers
- ½ cup unsalted butter, melted
- 1 cup water
- 1 can cherries in syrup

Directions:
1. In a large bowl, combine the cream cheese, sugar, cornstarch, eggs, egg yolks, cream, and salt. Use an electric mixer to mix until smooth and velvety.
2. In a medium bowl, combine the graham crackers and melted butter until it resembles wet sand.
3. Line the inside of the Ninja Multi-Purpose Pan or another 9-inch round baking dish with plastic wrap. Ensure the wrap is flush to the bottom of the dish and comes fully up the sides of the pan.
4. Place the graham cracker mixture in the center of the dish. Use a silicone-tipped spatula to press the mix outward. The mix should lay completely and evenly across the bottom of the dish.
5. Pour the cheesecake batter over the crust, then use the spatula to evenly smooth it out. Tightly wrap the top of the baking dish with a new piece of plastic wrap so that the cheesecake is completely covered.
6. Place the cheesecake on Reversible Rack, making sure it is in the lower steam position. Place rack with pan in pot. Pour the water into the pot. Assemble pressure lid, making sure the pressure release valve is in the SEAL position.
7. Select PRESSURE and set to HI. Set time to 30 minutes. Select START/STOP to begin.
8. When pressure cooking is complete, allow pressure to naturally release for 10 minutes. After 10 minutes, quick release remaining pressure by moving the pressure release valve to the VENT position. Carefully remove lid when unit has finished releasing pressure.

9. Remove top layer of plastic wrap from the cheesecake. Refrigerate the cheesecake to completely cool, at least 4 hours.
10. When ready to serve, remove the cheesecake from the refrigerator and place on a serving dish or cutting board. Use top edges of the remaining plastic wrap to remove cheesecake from the pan. Pull the plastic wrap out from underneath cheesecake. Top the cheesecake with the cherries in syrup as desired and serve.

Nutrition:
- InfoCalories: 789,Total Fat: 58g,Sodium: 760mg,Carbohydrates: 57g,Protein: 13g.

Double Chocolate Cake

Servings: 12
Cooking Time: 1 Hour

Ingredients:
- ½ cup coconut flour
- 1½ cups Erythritol
- 5 tablespoons cacao powder
- 1 teaspoon baking powder
- ½ teaspoon salt
- 3 eggs
- 3 egg yolks
- ½ cup butter, melted and cooled
- 1 teaspoon vanilla extract
- ½ teaspoon liquid stevia
- 4 ounces 70% dark chocolate chips
- 2 cups hot water

Directions:
1. Grease the Ninja Foodi's insert.
2. In a large bowl, stir in the flour, 1¼ cups of Erythritol, 3 tablespoons of cacao powder, baking powder and salt.
3. In a suitable bowl, add the eggs, egg yolks, butter, vanilla extract and liquid stevia and beat until well combined.
4. Stir in the egg mixture into the flour mixture and mix until just combined.
5. In a small bowl, add hot water, remaining cacao powder and Erythritol and beat until well combined.
6. In the prepared Ninja Foodi's insert, stir in the mixture evenly and top with chocolate chips, followed by the water mixture.
7. Close the Ninja Foodi's lid with a crisping lid and select "Slow Cooker".
8. Set on "Low" for 3 hours.
9. Press the "Start/Stop" button to initiate cooking.
10. Transfer the pan onto a wire rack for about 10 minutes.
11. Flip the baked and cooled cake onto the wire rack to cool completely.
12. Cut into desired-sized slices and serve.

Nutrition:
- InfoCalories: 169; Fats: 15.4g; Carbohydrates: 4.4g; Proteins: 3.9g

Churro Bites

Servings:7
Cooking Time: 12 Minutes

Ingredients:
- Cooking spray
- 1 box cinnamon swirl crumb cake and muffin mix, brown sugar mix packet removed and reserved
- 2 large eggs
- 1 cup buttermilk
- 1 teaspoon ground cinnamon, divided
- ¼ cup packed light brown sugar
- 1½ cups water
- 1 tablespoon granulated sugar
- Chocolate sauce, for serving (optional)
- Caramel sauce, for serving (optional)
- Strawberry sauce, for serving (optional)
- Whipped topping, for serving (optional)
- Peanut butter, for serving (optional)

Directions:
1. Lightly coat 2 egg bite molds with cooking spray and set aside.
2. In a large bowl, combine the cake mix, brown sugar mix packet, eggs, buttermilk, and ½ teaspoon of cinnamon. Mix until evenly combined.
3. Using a cookie scoop, transfer the batter to the prepared mold, filling each three-quarters full. Tightly cover the molds with aluminum foil, or with the silicone cover that came with the egg molds.
4. Pour the water into the cooking pot. Place the egg molds onto the Reversible Rack in the lower steam position and lower into the pot.
5. If using a foil sling (see TIP), ensure the foil cover is tight enough to support the egg mold that will sit on top. Rotate the top egg mold slightly to ensure that the molds do not press into one another.
6. Assemble the pressure lid, making sure the pressure release valve is in the SEAL position.
7. Select PRESSURE and set to HI. Set the time to 12 minutes. Select START/STOP to begin.
8. When pressure cooking is complete, allow the pressure to naturally release for 10 minutes. After 10 minutes, quick release any remaining pressure by moving the pressure release valve to the VENT position. Carefully remove the lid when the unit has finished releasing pressure.
9. In a small bowl, stir together the brown sugar, granulated sugar, and remaining ½ teaspoon of cinnamon. Set aside.
10. Using the sling, remove the egg molds from the pot and let cool for 5 minutes.
11. One at a time, place a plate over the egg mold and flip the mold over. Gently press on the mold to release the churro bites.
12. Roll the warm churro bites in the brown sugar mixture, and sprinkle any remaining brown sugar on top. Serve with your favorite dipping sauce.

Nutrition:
- Info.

Coconut Cream "custard" Bars

Servings:8
Cooking Time: 20 Minutes

Ingredients:
- 1¼ cups all-purpose flour
- 6 tablespoons unsalted butter, melted
- 2 tablespoons granulated sugar
- ½ cup unsweetened shredded coconut, divided
- ½ cup chopped almonds, divided
- Cooking spray
- 1 package instant vanilla pudding
- 1 cup milk
- 1 cup heavy (whipping) cream
- 4 tablespoons finely chopped dark chocolate, divided

Ninja Foodi Cookbook Guide

Directions:
1. Select BAKE/ROAST, set temperature to 375°F (190°C), and set time to 15 minutes. Select START/STOP to begin. Let preheat for 5 minutes.
2. To make the crust, combine the flour, butter, sugar, ¼ cup of coconut, and ¼ cup of almonds in a large bowl and stir until a crumbly dough forms.
3. Grease the Ninja Multi-Purpose Pan or an 8-inch round baking dish with cooking spray. Place the dough in the pan and press it into an even layer covering the bottom.
4. Once unit has preheated, place pan on Reversible Rack, making sure the rack is in the lower position. Open lid and place rack in pot. Close crisping lid. Reduce temperature to 325°F (160°C).
5. Place remaining ¼ cup each of almonds and coconut in a Ninja Loaf Pan or any small loaf pan and set aside.
6. When cooking is complete, remove rack with pan and let cool for 10 minutes.
7. Quickly place the loaf pan with coconut and almonds in the bottom of the pot. Close crisping lid.
8. Select AIR CRISP, set temperature to 350°F (175°C), and set time to 10 minutes. Select START/STOP to begin.
9. While the nuts and coconut toast, whisk together the instant pudding with the milk, cream, and 3 tablespoons of chocolate.
10. After 5 minutes, open lid and stir the coconut and almonds. Close lid and continue cooking for another 5 minutes.
11. When cooking is complete, open lid and remove pan from pot. Add the almonds and coconut to the pudding. Stir until fully incorporated. Pour this in a smooth, even layer on top of the crust.
12. Refrigerate for about 10 minutes. Garnish with the remaining 1 tablespoon of chocolate, cut into wedges, and serve.

Nutrition:
- InfoCalories: 476,Total Fat: 33g,Sodium: 215mg,Carbohydrates: 39g,Protein: 6g.

Chocolate Cheesecake

Servings: 10
Cooking Time: 20 Minutes
Ingredients:
- For Crust
- ¼ cup coconut flour
- ¼ cup almond flour
- 2½ tablespoons cacao powder
- 1½ tablespoons Erythritol
- 2 tablespoons butter, melted
- For Filling
- 16 ounces cream cheese, softened
- 1/3 cup cacao powder
- ½ teaspoon powdered Erythritol
- ½ teaspoon stevia powder
- 1 large egg
- 2 large egg yolks
- 6 ounces unsweetened dark chocolate, melted
- ¾ cup heavy cream
- ¼ cup sour cream
- 1 teaspoon vanilla extract

Directions:
1. For the crust: in a suitable, mix together flours, cacao powder and Erythritol.
2. Stir in the melted butter and mix until well combined.
3. Stir in the mixture into a parchment paper-lined 7-inch springform pan evenly, and with your fingers, press evenly.
4. For filling: in a food processor, add the cream cheese, cacao powder, monk fruit powder and stevia and pulse until smooth.
5. Stir in the egg and egg yolks and pulse until well combined.
6. Add the rest of the ingredients and pulse until well combined.
7. Place the prepared filling mixture on top of the crust evenly and with a rubber spatula, smooth the surface.
8. With a piece of foil, cover the springform pan loosely.
9. In the Ninja Foodi's insert, place 2 cups of water.
10. Set a "Reversible Rack" in the Ninja Foodi's insert.
11. Place the springform pan over the "Reversible Rack".
12. Close the Ninja Foodi's lid with a pressure lid and place the pressure valve in the "Seal" position.
13. Select "Pressure" mode and set it to "High" for 20 minutes.
14. Press the "Start/Stop" button to initiate cooking.
15. Switch the pressure valve to "Vent" and do a "Natural" release.
16. Place the pan onto a wire rack to cool completely.
17. Refrigerate for about 6-8 hours before serving.

Nutrition:
- InfoCalories: 385; Fats: 35.6g; Carbohydrates: 9.8g; Proteins: 8.9g

Tiramisu Cheesecake

Servings: 12
Cooking Time: 1 Hour + Chilling Time
Ingredients:
- 16 ounces Cream Cheese, softened /480g
- 8 ounces Mascarpone Cheese, softened /240g
- 2 Eggs
- ½ cup White Sugar /65g
- 1 ½ cups Ladyfingers, crushed /195g
- 1 tbsp Cocoa Powder /15g
- 2 tbsp Powdered Sugar /30g
- 1 tbsp Kahlua Liquor /15ml
- 1 tbsp Granulated Espresso /15g
- 1 tbsp Butter, melted /15ml
- 1 tsp Vanilla Extract 5ml

Directions:
1. In a bowl beat the cream cheese, mascarpone, and white sugar. Gradually beat in the eggs, the powdered sugar and vanilla. Combine the first 4 ingredients, in another bowl. Spray a springform pan with cooking spray. Press the ladyfinger crust at the bottom. Pour the filling over. Cover the pan with a paper towel and then close it with aluminum foil.
2. Pour 1 cup or 250ml of water in your Foodi and lower the reversible rack. Place the pan inside and seal the pressure lid. Select Pressure and set time to 35 minutes at High pressure. Press Start. Press Start.
3. Wait for about 10 minutes before releasing the pressure quickly. Allow to cool completely before refrigerating the cheesecake for 4 hours.

Cranberry Pie

Servings: 8
Cooking Time: 35 Minutes
Ingredients:
- Nonstick cooking spray
- ¾ cup flour
- ½ cup sugar
- ¼ tsp salt
- 2 cups cranberries
- 1/3 cup walnuts, chopped
- ½ stick butter, melted
- ½ cup liquid egg substitute
- 1 tsp almond extract

Directions:
1. Place the rack in the cooking pot. Spray an 8-inch pie plate with cooking spray.
2. In a large bowl, stir together flour, sugar, and salt.
3. Add cranberries and walnuts and toss to coat.
4. Add butter, egg substitute, and almond extract and mix well. Spread in prepared pan and place on the rack.
5. Add the tender-crisp lid and set to bake on 350°F (175°C). Bake 30-35 minutes or until pie passes the toothpick test. Transfer to wire rack to cool.

Nutrition:
- InfoCalories 145,Total Fat 9g,Total Carbs 27g,Protein 4g,Sodium 149mg.

Flourless Chocolate Cake

Servings:8
Cooking Time: 40 Minutes
Ingredients:
- Unsalted butter, at room temperature, for greasing the pan
- 9½ tablespoons unsalted butter, melted and cooled
- 4 large eggs, whites and yolks separated
- 1 cup granulated sugar, divided
- ½ cup unsweetened cocoa powder
- ¼ teaspoon vanilla extract
- ¼ teaspoon sea salt
- 1 cup plus 2 tablespoons semisweet chocolate chips, melted
- OPTIONAL TOPPINGS:
- Whipped cream
- Fruit sauce

Directions:
1. Grease a Ninja Multi-Purpose Pan or an 8-inch baking pan with butter and line the pan with a circle of parchment paper. Grease the parchment paper with butter.
2. Close crisping lid. Select BAKE/ROAST, set temperature to 350°F (175°C), and set time to 5 minutes. Select START/STOP to begin preheating.
3. In a large bowl, beat the melted butter and egg yolks. Add ½ cup of sugar, cocoa powder, vanilla extract, and salt. Slowly add the melted chocolate and stir.
4. In a medium bowl, beat the egg whites until soft peaks form. Add the remaining ½ cup of sugar and beat until stiff peaks form.
5. Gently fold the egg white mixture into the chocolate mixture. Pour the batter into the prepared pan.
6. When unit has preheated, place pan on Reversible Rack, making sure the rack is in the lower position. Open lid and place rack with pan in pot. Close crisping lid.
7. Select BAKE/ROAST, set temperature to 350°F (175°C), and set time to 40 minutes. Select START/STOP to begin.
8. After 30 minutes, check for doneness. If a toothpick inserted into the cake comes out clean, the cake is done. If not, close lid and continue baking until done.
9. When cooking is complete, carefully remove pan from pot and place it on a cooling rack for 5 minutes, then serve.

Nutrition:
- InfoCalories: 437,Total Fat: 29g,Sodium: 109mg,Carbohydrates: 49g,Protein: 7g.

Pecan Stuffed Apples

Servings: 6
Cooking Time: 20 Min
Ingredients:
- 3 ½ pounds Apples, cored /1575g
- 1 ¼ cups Red Wine /312.5ml
- ¼ cup Pecans; chopped /32.5g
- ¼ cup Graham Cracker Crumbs/32.5g
- ½ cup dried Apricots; chopped /65g
- ¼ cup Sugar /32.5g
- ½ tsp grated Nutmeg /2.5g
- ½ tsp ground Cinnamon /2.5g
- ¼ tsp Cardamom /1.25g

Directions:
1. Lay the apples at the bottom of your cooker, and pour in the red wine. Combine the other ingredients, except the crumbs.
2. Seal the pressure lid, and cook at High pressure for 15 minutes. Once ready, do a quick pressure release. Top with graham cracker crumbs and serve!

Filling Coconut And Oat Cookies

Servings: 4
Cooking Time: 30 Min
Ingredients:
- 5 ½ oz. flour /165g
- 3 oz. sugar /90g
- 1 small egg, beaten
- ¼ cup coconut flakes /32.5g
- ½ cup oats /65g
- 1 tsp vanilla extract /5ml
- Filling:
- 4 oz. powdered sugar/120g
- 1 oz. white chocolate, melted/30ml
- 2 oz. butter /60g
- 1 tsp vanilla extract /5ml

Directions:
1. Beat all cookie ingredients, with an electric mixer, except the flour. When smooth, fold in the flour. Drop spoonfuls of the batter onto a prepared cookie sheet. Close the crisping lid and cook in the Foodi at 350 °F or 175°C for about 18 minutes on Air Crisp mode; let cool.
2. Prepare the filling by beating all ingredients together. Spread the mixture on half of the cookies. Top with the other halves to make cookie sandwiches.

Ninja Foodi Cookbook Guide

Coconut Milk Crème Caramel

Servings: 4
Cooking Time: 20 Min
Ingredients:
- 7 ounces Condensed Coconut Milk /210ml
- 1 ½ cups Water /375ml
- ½ cup Coconut Milk /125ml
- 2 Eggs
- ½ tsp Vanilla /2.5ml
- 4 tbsp Caramel Syrup /60ml

Directions:
1. Divide the caramel syrup between 4 small ramekins. Pour water in the Foodi and add the reversible rack. In a bowl, beat the rest of the ingredients. Divide them between the ramekins. Cover them with aluminum foil and lower onto the reversible rack.
2. Seal the pressure lid, and choose Pressure, set to High, and set the time to 15 minutes. Press Start. Once cooking is completed, do a quick pressure release. Let cool completely. To unmold the flan, insert a spatula along the ramekin' sides and flip onto a dish.

Delicious Almond And Apple

Servings: 4
Cooking Time: 14 Min
Ingredients:
- 3 Apples, peeled and diced
- ½ cup Milk /125ml
- ½ cup Almonds; chopped or slivered /65g
- ¼ tsp Cinnamon /1.25g

Directions:
1. Place all ingredients in the Foodi. Stir well to combine and seal the pressure lid. Cook on Pressure for 4 minutes at High. Release the pressure quickly. Divide the mixture among 4 serving bowls.

Milk Dumplings In Sweet Sauce

Servings: 20
Cooking Time: 30 Min
Ingredients:
- 2 ½ cups Sugar /325g
- 6 cups Milk /1500ml
- 6 cups Water /1500ml
- 3 tbsp Lime Juice /45ml
- 1 tsp ground Cardamom /5g

Directions:
1. Bring to a boil the milk, on Sear/Sauté, and stir in the lime juice. The solids should start to separate. Pour milk through a cheesecloth-lined colander. Drain as much liquid as you can. Place the paneer on a smooth surface. Form a ball and divide into 20 equal pieces.
2. Pour water in the Foofi and bring to a boil on Sear/Sauté. Add in sugar and cardamom and cook until dissolved. Shape the dumplings into balls, and place them in the syrup.
3. Seal the pressure lid and choose Pressure, set to High, and set the time to 5 minutes. Press Start. Once done, do a quick pressure release. Let cool and refrigerate for at least 2 hours.

Coconut Rice Pudding

Servings: 6
Cooking Time: 8 Minutes
Ingredients:
- ¾ cup arborio rice
- 1 can unsweetened full-fat coconut milk
- 1 cup milk
- 1 cup water
- ¾ cup granulated sugar
- ½ teaspoon vanilla extract

Directions:
1. Rinse the rice under cold running water in a fine-mesh strainer.
2. Place the rice, coconut milk, milk, water, sugar, and vanilla in the pot and stir. Assemble pressure lid, making sure the pressure release valve is in the SEAL position.
3. Select PRESSURE and set to HI. Set time to 8 minutes. Select START/STOP to begin.
4. When pressure cooking is complete, allow pressure to naturally release for 10 minutes. After 10 minutes, quick release remaining pressure by moving the pressure release valve to the VENT position. Carefully remove lid when unit has finished releasing pressure.
5. Press a layer of plastic wrap directly on top of the rice (it should be touching) to prevent a skin from forming on top of the pudding. Let pudding cool to room temperature, then refrigerate overnight to set.

Nutrition:
- InfoCalories: 363,Total Fat: 18g,Sodium: 31mg,Carbohydrates: 50g,Protein: 5g.

Brownie Pie

Servings: 12
Cooking Time: 25 Minutes
Ingredients:
- 2 cups panko bread crumbs
- 1 ¼ cup Stevia, divided
- ¾ cup butter, melted, divided
- 2 tsp vanilla
- 2 eggs, beaten
- ½ cup cocoa powder
- ½ cup flour
- ¼ tsp salt
- 1 cup chocolate chips

Directions:
1. In a medium bowl, combine bread crumbs, ¼ cup Stevia, and ¼ cup melted butter. Press on the bottom and sides of an 8-inch pie plate.
2. In a small saucepan, over low heat, melt remaining ½ cup butter. Stir in remaining Stevia and cook, stirring frequently, until Stevia is dissolved.
3. Remove butter mixture from heat and whisk in vanilla, and eggs until combined.
4. In a small bowl, stir together, cocoa, flour, and salt. Add to butter mixture and stir just until combined. Fold in chocolate chips.
5. Pour brownie mixture into the crust. Place the rack in the cooking pot and place the pie on it. Add the tender-crisp lid and set to air fry on 350°F (175°C). Bake 20-25 minutes. Transfer to a wire rack to cool before serving.

Nutrition:
- InfoCalories 355,Total Fat 24g,Total Carbs 47g,Protein 7g,Sodium 146mg.

Lime Muffins

Servings: 6
Cooking Time: 30 Min
Ingredients:
- 2 eggs plus 1 yolk
- 1 cup yogurt /130g
- ¼ cup superfine sugar/32.5g
- Juice and zest of 2 limes
- 8 oz. cream cheese /240g
- 1 tsp vanilla extract /5ml

Directions:
1. With a spatula, gently combine the yogurt and cheese. In another bowl, beat together the rest of the ingredients.
2. Gently fold the lime with the cheese mixture. Divide the batter between 6 lined muffin tins. Close the crisping lid and cook in the Foodi for 10 minutes on Air Crisp mode at 330 °F or 165°C.

Carrot Raisin Cookie Bars

Servings: 16
Cooking Time: 15 Minutes
Ingredients:
- Butter flavored cooking spray
- ½ cup brown sugar
- ½ cup sugar
- ½ cup coconut oil, melted
- ½ cup applesauce, unsweetened
- 2 eggs
- 1 tsp vanilla
- ½ cup almond flour
- 1 tsp baking soda
- 1 tsp baking powder
- ¼ tsp salt
- 1 tsp cinnamon
- ½ tsp nutmeg
- ½ tsp ginger
- 2 cups oats
- 1 ½ cups carrots, finely grated
- 1 cup raisins

Directions:
1. Place the rack in the cooking pot. Spray an 8x8-inch pan with cooking spray.
2. In a large bowl, combine sugars, oil, applesauce, eggs, and vanilla, mix well.
3. Stir in dry ingredients until combined. Fold in carrots and raisins. Press evenly in prepared pan.
4. Place the pan on the rack and add the tender-crisp lid. Set to bake on 350°F (175°C). Bake 12-15 minutes or until golden brown and cooked through.
5. Remove to wire rack to cool before cutting and serving.

Nutrition:
- InfoCalories 115,Total Fat 7g,Total Carbs 19g,Protein 3g,Sodium 56mg.

Baked Apples With Pecan Stuffing

Servings: 4
Cooking Time: 45 Minutes
Ingredients:
- 4 Fuji apples
- ½ cup pecans, chopped
- ¼ cup Stevia
- 2 tbsp. coconut oil, melted
- 1 tbsp. molasses
- ½ tsp cinnamon
- ½ cup water

Directions:
1. Hollow out the apples by carefully removing the core and seeds. Place in the cooking pot.
2. In a medium bowl, combine nuts, Stevia, oil, molasses, and cinnamon, mix well. Spoon into the apples, stuffing them fully.
3. Pour the water around the apples. Add the tender-crisp lid and set to bake on 350 °F (175°C). Bake 40-45 minutes. Let cool slightly before serving.

Nutrition:
- InfoCalories 329,Total Fat 17g,Total Carbs 49g,Protein 2g,Sodium 11mg.

Raspberry Crumble

Servings: 6
Cooking Time: 40 Min
Ingredients:
- 1 package frozen raspberries /480g
- ½ cup rolled oats /65g
- ⅓ cup cold unsalted butter; cut into pieces /44g
- ½ cup all-purpose flour /65g
- ⅔ cup brown sugar /88g
- ½ cup water, plus 1 tbsp /265ml
- 2 tbsps arrowroot starch /30g
- 5 tbsps sugar; divided /75g
- 1 tsp freshly squeezed lemon juice /5ml
- 1 tsp cinnamon powder /5g

Directions:
1. Place the raspberries in the baking pan. In a small mixing bowl, combine the arrowroot starch, 1 tbsp or 15ml of water, lemon juice, and 3 tbsps or 45g of sugar. Pour the mixture all over the raspberries.
2. Put the reversible rack in the lower position of the pot. Cover the pan with foil and pour the remaining water into the pot. Put the pan on the rack in the pot. Put the pressure lid together, and lock in the Seal position. Choose Pressure, set to High, and set the time to 10 minutes, then Choose Start/Stop to begin.
3. In a bowl, mix the flour, brown sugar, oats, butter, cinnamon, and remaining sugar until crumble forms. When done pressure-cooking, do a quick release and carefully open the lid.
4. Remove the foil and stir the fruit mixture. After, spread the crumble evenly on the berries. Close the crisping lid; choose Air Crisp, set the temperature to 400°F (205°C), and the time to 10 minutes. Choose Start/Stop to begin crisping. Cook until the top has browned and the fruit is bubbling. When done baking, remove the rack with the pan from the pot, and serve.

Chocolate Fondue

Servings: 12
Cooking Time: 5 Min
Ingredients:
- 10 ounces Milk Chocolate; chopped into small pieces /300g
- 1 ½ cups Lukewarm Water /375ml
- 8 ounces Heavy Whipping Cream /240ml
- 2 tsp Coconut Liqueur /60ml
- ¼ tsp Cinnamon Powder /1.25g
- A pinch of Salt

Ninja Foodi Cookbook Guide

Directions:
1. Melt the chocolate in a heat-proof recipient. Add the remaining ingredients, except for the liqueur. Transfer this recipient to the metal reversible rack. Pour 1 ½ cups or 375ml of water into the cooker, and place a reversible rack inside.
2. Seal the pressure lid, choose Pressure, set to High, and set the time to 5 minutes. Press Start. Once the cooking is complete, do a quick pressure release. Pull out the container with tongs. Mix in the coconut liqueur and serve right now. Enjoy!

Berry Vanilla Pudding

Servings: 4
Cooking Time: 35 Min + 6h For Refrigeration
Ingredients:
- 4 raspberries
- 4 blueberries
- 4 egg yolks
- ½ cup sugar /65g
- ½ cup milk /125ml
- 1 cup heavy cream /250ml
- 1 tsp vanilla extract /5ml
- 4 tbsp water + 1 ½ cups water /435ml

Directions:
1. Turn on your Foodi and select Sear/Sauté mode on Medium. Add four tbsps or 60ml for water and the sugar. Stir it constantly until it dissolves. Press Stop. Add milk, heavy cream, and vanilla. Stir it with a whisk until evenly combined.
2. Crack the eggs into a bowl and add a tbsp of the cream mixture. Whisk it and then very slowly add the remaining cream mixture while whisking. Fit the reversible rack at the bottom of the pot, and pour one and a half cup of water in it. Pour the mixture into four ramekins and place them on the rack.
3. Close the lid of the pot, secure the pressure valve, and select Pressure mode on High Pressure for 4 minutes. Press Start/Stop. Once the timer has gone off, do a quick pressure release, and open the lid.
4. With a napkin in hand, carefully remove the ramekins onto a flat surface. Let cool for about 15 minutes and then refrigerate them for 6 hours.
5. After 6 hours, remove them from the refrigerator and garnish them with the raspberries and blueberries. Enjoy immediately or refrigerate further until dessert time is ready.

Maply Soufflés

Servings: 4
Cooking Time: 10 Minutes
Ingredients:
- Butter flavored cooking spray
- 1/3 cup maple syrup
- 2 eggs, separated
- ½ tsp vanilla
- 2 tbsp. flour
- 1/8 tsp salt
- Powdered sugar for dusting

Directions:
1. Spray 4 ramekins with cooking spray.
2. In a medium bowl, beat syrup, egg yolks, and vanilla until thickened, about 1 minute.
3. Add flour and beat until combined.
4. In a large bowl, beat egg whites until stiff peaks form, about 2 minutes. Gently fold ¼ of the egg whites into syrup mixture just until combined. Fold the syrup mixture into the remaining egg whites just until combined. Divide evenly among ramekins.
5. Place ramekins in the cooking pot and add the tender-crisp lid. Set to bake on 375°F (190°C). Bake 10-12 minutes, or until puffed and golden brown. Dust with powdered sugar and serve immediately.

Nutrition:
- InfoCalories 119,Total Fat 2g,Total Carbs 21g,Protein 3g,Sodium 116mg.

Raspberry Cobbler

Servings: 8
Cooking Time: 2 Hours
Ingredients:
- 1 cup almond flour
- ¼ cup coconut flour
- ¾ cup Erythritol
- 1 teaspoon baking soda
- ¼ teaspoon ground cinnamon
- 1/8 teaspoon salt
- ¼ cup unsweetened coconut milk
- 2 tablespoons coconut oil
- 1 large egg, beaten lightly
- 4 cups fresh raspberries

Directions:
1. Grease the Ninja Foodi's insert.
2. In a large bowl, mix together flours, Erythritol, baking soda, cinnamon and salt.
3. In another bowl, stir in the coconut milk, coconut oil and egg and beat until well combined.
4. Add the prepared egg mixture into the flour mixture and mix until just combined.
5. In the pot of the prepared Ninja Foodi, add the mixture evenly and top with raspberries.
6. Close the Ninja Foodi's lid with a crisping lid and select "Slow Cooker".
7. Set on "Low" for 2 hours.
8. Press the "Start/Stop" button to initiate cooking.
9. Place the pan onto a wire rack to cool slightly.
10. Serve warm.

Nutrition:
- InfoCalories: 164; Fats: 12.5g; Carbohydrates: 10.9g; Proteins: 4.7

Poached Peaches

Servings: 4
Cooking Time: 15 Min
Ingredients:
- 4 Peaches, peeled, pits removed
- 1 cup Freshly Squeezed Orange Juice /250ml
- ½ cup Black Currants /65g
- 1 Cinnamon Stick

Directions:
1. Place black currants and orange juice in a blender. Blend until the mixture becomes smooth. Pour the mixture in your Foodi, and add the cinnamon stick.
2. Add the peaches to the steamer basket and then insert the basket into the pot. Seal the pressure lid, select Pressure, and set to 5 minutes at High pressure. When done, do a quick pressure release. Serve the peaches drizzled with sauce, to enjoy!

Tres Leches Cake

Servings: 8
Cooking Time: 38 Minutes
Ingredients:
- 1 box of yellow cake mix
- Cooking spray
- 1 can evaporated milk
- 1 can sweetened condensed milk
- 1 cup heavy (whipping) cream

Directions:
1. Close crisping lid. Select BAKE/ROAST, set temperature to 400°F (205°C), and set time to 43 minutes. Select START/STOP to begin. Let preheat for 5 minutes.
2. Prepare the cake batter according to the box instructions.
3. Grease a Ninja Multi-Purpose Pan or a 1½-quart round baking dish with cooking spray. Pour the batter into the pan. Place the pan on Reversible Rack, making sure rack is in the lower position.
4. Once unit has preheated, open lid and place rack with pan in pot. Close lid, and reduce temperature to 315°F (155°C). Cook for 38 minutes.
5. In a medium bowl whisk together the evaporated milk, condensed milk, and heavy cream.
6. When cooking is complete, remove rack with pan from pot and let cool for 10 minutes.
7. Remove pan from the rack. Using a long-pronged fork, poke holes every inch or so across the surface of the cake. Slowly pour the milk mixture over the cake. Refrigerate for 1 hour.
8. Once the cake has cooled and absorbed the milk mixture, slice and serve. If desired, top with whipped cream and strawberries.

Nutrition:
- InfoCalories: 644, Total Fat: 28g, Sodium: 574mg, Carbohydrates: 89g, Protein: 12g.

Strawberry Crumble

Servings: 5
Cooking Time: 2 Hours
Ingredients:
- 1 cup almond flour
- 2 tablespoons butter, melted
- 10 drops liquid stevia
- 4 cups fresh strawberries, hulled and sliced
- 1 tablespoon butter, chopped

Directions:
1. Lightly, grease the Ninja Foodi's insert.
2. In a suitable, stir in the flour, melted butter and stevia and mix until a crumbly mixture form.
3. In the pot of the prepared Ninja Foodi, place the strawberry slices and dot with chopped butter.
4. Spread the flour mixture on top evenly
5. Close the Ninja Foodi's lid with a crisping lid and select "Slow Cooker".
6. Set on "Low" for 2 hours.
7. Press the "Start/Stop" button to initiate cooking.
8. Place the pan onto a wire rack to cool slightly.
9. Serve warm.

Nutrition:
- InfoCalories: 233; Fats: 19.2g; Carbohydrates: 10.7g; Proteins: 0.7g

Cinnamon Mulled Red Wine

Servings: 6
Cooking Time: 30 Min
Ingredients:
- 2 cardamom pods
- 8 cinnamon sticks
- 3 cups red wine /750ml
- 1/4 cup honey /62.5ml
- 6 whole cloves
- 6 whole black peppercorns
- 6 tangerine wedges
- 2 tangerines; sliced
- 1 tsp fresh ginger; sliced /5g
- 1 tsp ground cinnamon /5g

Directions:
1. In the Foodi, combine red wine, honey, cardamom pods, 2 cinnamon sticks, cloves, tangerines slices, ginger, and peppercorns. Seal the pressure lid, choose Pressure, set to High, and set the timer to 5 minutes. Press Start.
2. Release pressure naturally for 20 minutes. Press Start. Using a fine mesh strainer, strain your wine. Discard spices.
3. Divide the warm wine into glasses and add tangerine wedges and a cinnamon stick for garnishing before serving.

Raspberry Cream Tart

Servings: 4
Cooking Time: 55 Min+ Chilling Time
Ingredients:
- 1 refrigerated piecrust, for the raspberries
- 2½ cups fresh raspberries; divided /325g
- ¼ cup sugar /32.5g
- 2 tbsps water /30ml
- 1 tbsp arrowroot starch /15g
- 1 tsp lemon juice /5ml
- ¼ tsp grated lemon zest /1.25g
- Pinch salt
- For The Filling
- 8 ounces cream cheese, at room temperature /240g
- ¼ cup heavy cream /62.5ml
- ½ cup confectioners' sugar /65g
- 1 tsp vanilla extract /5ml

Directions:
1. Roll out the pie crust and fit into a tart pan. Do not stretch the dough to prevent shrinking when cooking. Use a fork to prick all over the bottom of the dough. Place the reversible rack in the pot in the lower position of the pot and put the tart pan on top.
2. Close the crisping lid, choose Bake/Roast; adjust the temperature to 250°F or 120°C, and the cook time to 15 minutes. Press Start. When done baking, open the lid and check the crust. It should be set and lightly brown around the edges.
3. Close the crisping lid again. Adjust the temperature to 375°F or 190°C and the cook time to 4 minutes. Press Start to begin baking.
4. After 3 minutes, check the crust, which should be a deep golden brown color by now. If not, cook for the remaining 1 minute. Remove the rack and set the crust aside to cool.
5. Fetch out 1 cup of berries into the inner pot. In a small bowl, whisk the arrowroot starch and water until smoothly mixed. Pour the slurry on the raspberries along with the sugar, lemon zest, lemon juice, and salt. Mix to distribute the slurry among the raspberries.
6. Seal the pressure lid, choose Pressure; adjust the pressure to High and the cook time to 2 minutes. Press Start.

Ninja Foodi Cookbook Guide

7. Once done cooking, perform a quick pressure release and carefully open the lid. The raspberries will have softened. Add the remaining 1½ cups of raspberries, stirring to coat with the cooked mixture. Then, allow cooling.
8. To make the cream filling, in a bowl and with a hand mixer, whisk the vanilla extract and cream cheese until evenly combined and smooth. Mix in the confectioners' sugar and whisk again until the sugar has fully incorporated and the mixture is light and smooth.
9. With clean whisks and in another bowl, beat the heavy cream until soft peaks form. Fold the heavy cream into the vanilla mixture until both are evenly combined. To assemble, spoon the cream filling into the piecrust and scatter the remaining raspberries on the cream. Chill for 30 minutes before cutting and serving.

Pumpkin Latte Cake

Servings: 16
Cooking Time: 3 Hours
Ingredients:
- Butter flavored cooking spray
- 28 oz. pumpkin puree
- 2 cups whole wheat pastry flour
- 3 eggs
- 1 2/3 cups Stevia
- 2/3 cup almond milk, unsweetened
- ¼ cup coconut oil, melted
- 2 tbsp. pumpkin pie spice, divided
- 2 tsp baking powder
- 2 tsp vanilla
- 2 tbsp. espresso powder
- ½ cup honey

Directions:
1. Line the bottom only of the cooking pot with parchment paper. Spray with cooking spray.
2. In a large bowl, beat ½ the pumpkin, flour, 2 eggs, Stevia, milk, oil, 1 ½ tablespoons pie spice, baking powder, vanilla, and espresso together until smooth.
3. In a separate bowl, whisk together remaining pumpkin, egg, pie spice, and honey until smooth.
4. Pour half the cake batter into the cooking pot. Spread the pumpkin mixture on top. Then pour in remaining cake batter.
5. Add the lid and set to slow cooking on low. Cook 2-3 hours until cake passes the toothpick test.
6. Let cool in the pot for 10 minutes, then invert onto serving plate and let cool completely before serving.

Nutrition:
- InfoCalories 150,Total Fat 6g,Total Carbs 47g,Protein 4g,Sodium 22mg.

Red Velvet Cheesecake

Servings:8
Cooking Time: 25 Minutes
Ingredients:
- 2 cups Oreo cookie crumbs
- 3 tablespoons unsalted butter, melted
- 2 packages cream cheese, at room temperature
- ½ cup granulated sugar
- ½ cup buttermilk
- 2 tablespoons unsweetened cocoa powder
- 1 teaspoon vanilla extract
- 2 tablespoons red food coloring
- ½ teaspoon white vinegar
- 1 cup water

Directions:
1. In a small bowl, combine the cookie crumbs and butter. Press this mixture into the bottom of the Ninja Multi-Purpose Pan or 8-inch baking pan.
2. In a large bowl, use an electric hand mixer to combine the cream cheese, sugar, buttermilk, cocoa powder, vanilla, food coloring, and vinegar for 3 minutes. Pour this over the cookie crust. Cover the pan tightly with aluminum foil.
3. Place the water in the pot. Insert Reversible Rack into pot, making sure it is in the lower position. Place the covered multi-purpose pan onto the rack. Assemble pressure lid, making sure the pressure release valve is in the SEAL position.
4. Select PRESSURE on HI. Set time to 25 minutes. Press START/STOP to begin.
5. When pressure cooking is complete, allow pressure to naturally release for 15 minutes. After 15 minutes, quick release remaining pressure by moving the pressure release valve to the VENT position. Carefully remove lid when unit has finished releasing pressure.
6. Remove cheesecake from the pot. Refrigerate for 3 hours, or overnight if possible before serving.

Nutrition:
- InfoCalories: 437,Total Fat: 31g,Sodium: 338mg,Carbohydrates: 36g,Protein: 7g.

Mocha Cake

Servings: 6
Cooking Time: 3 Hours 37 Minutes
Ingredients:
- 2 ounces 70% dark chocolate, chopped
- ¾ cup butter, chopped
- ½ cup heavy cream
- 2 tablespoons instant coffee crystals
- 1 teaspoon vanilla extract
- 1/3 cup almond flour
- ¼ cup unsweetened cacao powder
- 1/8 teaspoon salt
- 5 large eggs
- 2/3 cup Erythritol

Directions:
1. Grease the Ninja Foodi's insert.
2. In a microwave-safe bowl, stir in the chocolate and butter and microwave on High for about 2 minutes or until melted completely, stirring after every 30 seconds.
3. Remove from the microwave and stir well.
4. Set aside to cool.
5. In a small bowl, stir in the heavy cream, coffee crystals, and vanilla extract and beat until well combined.
6. In a suitable bowl, mix the flour, cacao powder and salt.
7. In a large bowl, stir in the eggs and with an electric mixer, beat on high speed until slightly thickened.
8. Slowly, stir in the Erythritol and beat on high speed until thick and pale yellow.
9. Stir in the chocolate mixture and beat on low speed until well combined.
10. Stir in the dry flour mixture and mix until just combined.
11. Slowly stir in the cream mixture and beat on medium speed until well combined.
12. In the prepared Ninja Foodi's insert, add the mixture.
13. Close the Ninja Foodi's lid with a crisping lid and select "Slow Cooker".

14. Set on "Low" for 2½-3½ hours.
15. Press the "Start/Stop" button to initiate cooking.
16. Transfer the pan onto a wire rack for about 10 minutes.
17. Flip the baked and cooled cake onto the wire rack to cool completely.
18. Cut into desired-sized slices and serve.

Nutrition:
- InfoCalories: 407; Fats: 39.7g; Carbohydrates: 6.2g; Proteins: 9g

Dark Chocolate Brownies

Servings: 6
Cooking Time: 40 Min
Ingredients:
- 1 cup water /250ml
- 2 eggs
- ¼ cup olive oil /62.5ml
- ⅓ cup flour /44g
- ⅓ cup cocoa powder /44g
- ⅓ cup dark chocolate chips /44g
- ⅓ cup chopped Walnuts /44g
- ⅓ cup granulated sugar /44g
- 1 tbsp vanilla extract /15ml
- 1 tbsp milk/15ml
- ½ tsp baking powder /2.5g
- A pinch salt

Directions:
1. In the Foodi, add water and set in the reversible rack. Line a parchment paper on a springform pan. In a bowl, beat eggs and sugar to mix until smooth; stir in olive oil, cocoa powder, milk, salt baking powder, chocolate chips, flour, walnuts, vanilla, and sea salt.
2. Transfer the batter to the prepared springform pan and place the pan in the pot on the rack. Close the crisping lid and select Bake/Roast; adjust the temperature to 250°F or 120°C and the cook time to 20 minutes. Press Start.
3. When the time is up, open the lid and. and allow the brownie to cool for 10 minutes before cutting. Use powdered sugar to dust the brownies before serving lightly.

Créme Brulee

Servings: 4
Cooking Time: 30 Min + 6 Hours Of Cooling
Ingredients:
- 3 cups heavy whipping cream /750ml
- 7 large egg yolks
- 2 cups water /500mll
- 6 tbsp sugar /90g
- 2 tbsp vanilla extract /30ml

Directions:
1. In a mixing bowl, add the yolks, vanilla, whipping cream, and half of the swerve sugar. Use a whisk to mix them until they are well combined. Pour the mixture into the ramekins and cover them with aluminium foil.
2. Open the Foodi, fit the reversible rack into the pot, and pour in the water.
3. Place 3 ramekins on the rack and place the remaining ramekins to sit on the edges of the ramekins below.
4. Close the lid, secure the pressure valve, and select Pressure mode on High for 8 minutes. Press Start/Stop.
5. Once the timer has stopped, do a natural pressure release for 10 minutes, then a quick pressure release to let out the remaining pressure.
6. With a napkin in hand, remove the ramekins onto a flat surface and then into a refrigerator to chill for at least 6 hours. After refrigeration, remove the ramekins and remove the aluminium foil.
7. Equally, sprinkle the remaining sugar on it and return to the pot. Close the crisping lid, select Bake/Roast mode, set the timer to 4 minutes on 380 °F or 195°C. Serve the crème brulee chilled with whipped cream.

Apple Strudels

Servings: 8
Cooking Time: 25 Minutes
Ingredients:
- Butter flavored cooking spray
- 2 8 oz. whole grain puff pastry sheets
- 5 apples, cored, peeled & chopped
- ¼ cup raisins
- 1/8 cup pine nuts
- 1 tbsp. Stevia
- 1 tbsp. lemon zest
- ½ tsp cinnamon
- 1 egg

Directions:
1. Lightly spray the fryer basket with cooking spray.
2. Lay the puff pastry on a work surface and cut into 4 equal parts. Repeat with the second sheet.
3. In a large bowl, combine apples, raisins, pine nuts, Stevia, zest, and cinnamon and mix well. Spoon filling into center of each pastry piece. Fold over sides and roll up.
4. In a small bowl, whisk the egg. Place the pastries in the fryer basket in a single layer. Brush tops with egg.
5. Add the tender-crisp lid and set to air fry on 350°F (175°C). Bake 20-25 minutes or until puffed and golden brown. Serve immediately.

Nutrition:
- InfoCalories 376,Total Fat 23g,Total Carbs 17g,Protein 5g,Sodium 141mg.

RECIPE INDEX

A
- Adobo Steak 78
- Air Fried Scallops 39
- Apple Pecan Cookie Bars 15
- Apple Strudels 106
- Apricots With Honey Sauce 95
- Artichoke With Mayo 55
- Asian Beef 72
- Asian Chicken Nuggets 11
- Asparagus With Feta 52
- Awesome Shrimp Roast 42

B
- Bacon And Gruyère Egg Bites 28
- Bacon And Sausage Cheesecake 32
- Baked Apples With Pecan Stuffing 102
- Baked Cod Casserole 43
- Baked Eggs In Mushrooms 25
- Baked Eggs In Spinach 30
- Balsamic Cabbage With Endives 47
- Banana Coconut Loaf 27
- Banana Custard Oatmeal 33
- Beef And Bacon Chili 76
- Beef And Cherry Tagine 88
- Beef And Garbanzo Bean Chili 73
- Beef Bourguignon(1) 86
- Beef Brisket & Carrots 88
- Beef Broccoli 81
- Beef In Basil Sauce 89
- Beef Lasagna 74
- Beef Stir Fry 73
- Beets And Carrots 54
- Bell Pepper Frittata 34
- Berry Vanilla Pudding 103
- Blackened Tilapia With Cilantro-lime Rice And Avocado Salsa 35
- Blueberry Lemon Pound Cake 97
- Blueberry Muffins 24
- Blueberry Peach Crisp 96
- Bolognese Pizza 80
- Braised Lamb Shanks 73
- Braised Pork And Black Bean Stew 94
- Braised Short Ribs With Creamy Sauce 77
- Braised Short Ribs With Mushrooms 83
- Breakfast Burritos 26
- Breakfast Souffles 33
- Broccoli Cauliflower 54
- Broccoli Egg Scramble 31
- Broccoli, Ham, And Cheddar Frittata 29
- Brownie Pie 101
- Buffalo Chicken And Navy Bean Chili 68
- Burrito Bowls 50
- Butter Chicken 69
- Buttered Fish 42
- Butter-flower Medley 18
- Buttermilk Chicken Thighs 65
- Buttermilk Fried Chicken 63
- Butternut Squash Cake Oatmeal 28
- Butternut Squash, Apple, Bacon And Orzo Soup 92
- Butternut Turkey Stew 69

C
- Cabbage With Carrots 51
- Caponata 11
- Caramelized Cauliflower With Hazelnuts 13
- Caramelized Salmon 38
- Caribbean Pork Pot 75
- Caribbean Ropa Vieja 72
- Carne Guisada 74
- Carrot Cake Muffins 30
- Carrot Cake Oats 23
- Carrot Gazpacho 56
- Carrot Raisin Cookie Bars 102
- Cashew Cream 20
- Cauliflower Cakes 48
- Cauliflower Chunks With Lemon Sauce 53
- Cauliflower Enchiladas 53
- Cauliflower Gratin 17
- Cheddar Cheeseburgers 84
- Cheese And Mushroom Tarts 49
- Cheese Crusted Carrot Casserole 50
- Cheesy Bacon Brussel Sprouts 11
- Cheesy Baked Spinach 51
- Cheesy Chicken And Broccoli Casserole 61
- Cheesy Chicken Dip 19
- Cheesy Crab Pie 45
- Cheesy Fried Risotto Balls 21
- Cheesy Green Beans With Nuts 48
- Cheesy Ham & Potato Casserole 81
- Cheesy Jalapeno Boats 12
- Cheesy Meat Omelet 31
- Cheesy Onion Dip 16
- Cheesy Stuffed Onions 21
- Cherry Cheesecake 97
- Chicken And Sweet Potato Corn Chowder 70
- Chicken Cacciatore 59
- Chicken Chickpea Chili 68
- Chicken Chili 92
- Chicken Enchilada Soup 91
- Chicken Meatballs Primavera 61
- Chicken Meatballs With Dill Dipping Sauce 13
- Chicken Noodle Soup 92
- Chicken Potpie Soup 93
- Chicken Thighs With Cabbage 69
- Chicken Tomatillo Stew 90
- Chicken With Black Beans 65
- Chicken With Mushroom Sauce 67
- Chicken With Prunes 65
- Chicken With Roasted Red Pepper Sauce 71
- Chickpea, Spinach, And Sweet Potato Stew 90
- Chili Chicken Dip 19
- Chinese Bbq Ribs 75
- Chipotle Raspberry Chicken 62
- Chocolate Cake 96
- Chocolate Cheesecake 99
- Chocolate Fondue 102
- Chocolate Hazelnut Toaster Pastries 23
- Chocolate Soufflé 96

Chunky Pork Meatloaf With Mashed Potatoes 79
Churro Bites 98
Cinnamon Crumb Donuts 31
Cinnamon Mulled Red Wine 104
Clam Fritters 46
Coconut Cilantro Shrimp 45
Coconut Cream "custard" Bars 98
Coconut Curried Mussels 36
Coconut Milk Crème Caramel 101
Coconut Rice Pudding 101
Coconut Shrimp 43
Colorful Vegetable Medley 49
Coq Au Vin 65
Corned Beef 85
Country Chicken Casserole 61
Crab Cakes With Spicy Dipping Sauce 43
Cranberry Pie 100
Creamy Carrot Soup 49
Creamy Golden Casserole 57
Creamy Polenta & Mushrooms 54
Creamy Spinach Soup 58
Creamy Turkey And Mushroom Ragu 68
Creamy Tuscan Chicken Pasta 67
Créme Brulee 106
Crispy Cheesy Straws 15
Crispy Korean-style Ribs 84
Crispy Pork Chops 78
Crispy Sesame Shrimp 15
Crispy Spiced Cauliflower Bites 13
Crunchy Cashew Lamb Rack 87
Crunchy Chicken Schnitzels 66
Crusted Pork Chops 74
Crustless Quiche 28
Cuban Pork 80
Curried Chickpea And Roasted Tomato Shakshuka 25

D

Dark Chocolate Brownies 106
Date Orange Cheesecake 95
Delicious Almond And Apple 101
Dill Butter 16
Double Berry Dutch Baby 32
Double Chocolate Cake 98
Double Chocolate Quinoa Bowl 26

E

Easy Clam Chowder 42
Egg Spinach Bites 29
Eggplant Lasagna 54
Eggplant With Kale 54

F

Farfalle Tuna Casserole With Cheese 45
Filling Coconut And Oat Cookies 100
Fish Broccoli Stew 35
Flank Steak With Bell Pepper Salsa 82
Flaxseeds Granola 33
Flounder Veggie Soup 43
Flourless Chocolate Cake 100
Fried Snickerdoodle Poppers 95

G

Garlic Bread Pizza 57

Garlic Potatoes 55
Garlicky Pork Chops 76
Garlicky Tomato 10
Glazed Lemon Muffins 30
Glazed Salmon 42
Glazed Walnuts 15
Greek Chicken 70
Ground Beef Stuffed Empanadas 79

H

Haddock With Sanfaina 40
Hainanese Chicken 68
Ham & Spinach Breakfast Bake 23
Hamburger & Macaroni Skillet 80
Hawaiian Tofu 56
Healthier Meatloaf 78
Healthy Chicken Stew 63
Hearty Veggie Soup 49
Herb Salmon With Barley Haricot Verts 37
Herbed Lamb Chops 88
Herby Fish Skewers 15
Honey Chicken & Veggies 71
Honey Short Ribs With Rosemary Potatoes 77
Honey-garlic Chicken Wings 10
Hot & Sour Soup 51
Hot Fudge Brownies 97

I

Italian Baked Zucchini 58
Italian Flounder 39
Italian Pasta Potpie 83
Italian Pot Roast 79
Italian Sausage And Cannellini Stew 82
Italian Sausage With Garlic Mash 56
Italian Sausage, Potato, And Kale Soup 94
Italian Spinach & Tomato Soup 48

J

Jalapeno Salsa 14
Jamaican Jerk Chicken Stew 94
Jamaican Pork 82
Japanese Eggs 14

K

Korean Barbecued Satay 59
Korean Cabbage Cups 89

L

Lamb Chops And Potato Mash 77
Lasagna Soup 91
Lemon Cod Goujons And Rosemary Chips 39
Lemon Turkey Risotto 59
Lemon, Barley & Turkey Soup 70
Lime Muffins 102
Loaded Potato Skins 18
Loaded Potato Soup 93
Lone Star Chili 75

M

Maply Soufflés 103
Meatballs With Spaghetti Sauce 78
Mediterranean Cod 46

Mexican Chicken Soup	62
Mexican Pork Stir Fry	76
Mexican Street Corn Queso Dip	20
Mexican Style Green Chili Chicken	60
Milk Dumplings In Sweet Sauce	101
Minestrone With Pancetta	53
Mini Chocolate Cheesecakes	96
Mini Crab Cakes	12
Mini Steak Kebabs	17
Mocha Cake	105
Moo Shu Chicken	70
Mushroom And Wild Rice Soup	91
Mushrooms Stuffed With Veggies	20
Mussel Chowder With Oyster Crackers	38

N

New England Lobster Rolls	36
Nutmeg Peanuts	20
Nutmeg Pumpkin Porridge	25

O

Okra Stew	47
Oyster Stew	43

P

Paella Señorito	40
Palak Paneer	48
Pancetta Hash With Baked Eggs	25
Paneer Cutlet	52
Panko Crusted Cod	39
Parmesan Stuffed Mushrooms	11
Peanut Butter Pie	95
Pecan Stuffed Apples	100
Penne All Arrabbiata With Seafood And Chorizo	36
Pepper And Sweet Potato Skewers	55
Pepper Smothered Cod	37
Peppercorn Meatloaf	75
Pesto Pork Chops & Asparagus	86
Pho Tom	93
Picadillo Dish	76
Pineapple Appetizer Ribs	47
Pistachio Crusted Salmon	44
Plum Breakfast Clafoutis	27
Poached Egg Heirloom Tomato	31
Poached Peaches	103
Pomegranate Radish Mix	50
Pork Chops With Gravy	89
Pork Pie	84
Pork Shank	21
Pork Tenderloin With Ginger And Garlic	84
Pork Tenderloin With Warm Balsamic And Apple Chutney	72
Pot Roast With Biscuits	80
Potato Chowder With Peppery Prawns	40
Potato Filled Bread Rolls	53
Prosciutto Egg Bake	28
Prosciutto, Mozzarella Egg In A Cup	24
Pulled Chicken And Peach Salsa	67
Pumpkin Breakfast Bread	25
Pumpkin Coconut Breakfast Bake	24
Pumpkin Latte Cake	105

Q

Quick Indian-style Curry	55
Quinoa Stuffed Butternut Squash	52

R

Radish Apples Salad	51
Raspberry And Vanilla Pancake	34
Raspberry Cobbler	103
Raspberry Cream Tart	104
Raspberry Crumble	102
Red Chili Chicken	67
Red Velvet Cheesecake	105
Refried Black Beans And Chicken Fajitas	60
Ricotta Raspberry Breakfast Cake	33
Roasted Cauliflower Salad	57
Roasted Chicken With Potato Mash	64
Roasted Squash And Rice With Crispy Tofu	58
Roasted Tomato And Seafood Stew	90
Ropa Vieja	87
Rosemary And Garlic Mushrooms	16
Rosemary Potato Fries	14

S

Salmon & Quinoa Patties	45
Salmon Croquettes	10
Salmon Kale Meal	37
Salmon With Dill Chutney	41
Sausage & Egg Stuffed Peppers	32
Sausage & Roasted Red Pepper Linguine	83
Savory Oatmeal	34
Scalloped Potatoes	19
Sesame Crusted Chicken	60
Sesame Radish	50
Shallots With Mushrooms	18
Short Ribs With Egg Noodles	73
Shredded Chicken And Wild Rice	64
Shredded Chicken With Lentils And Rice	62
Shrimp & Asparagus Risotto	36
Shrimp And Chorizo Potpie	44
Shrimp Etouffee	41
Shrimp Fried Rice	41
Simple Beef & Shallot Curry	82
Simple Chicken Parmesan	66
Skinny Chicken & Dumplings	71
Smoked Salmon Pilaf With Walnuts	44
Smoky Horseradish Spare Ribs	75
Sour Cream & Cheese Chicken	62
Southern Pineapple Casserole	48
Southwest Tofu Scramble	26
Spanish Potato And Chorizo Frittata	24
Spiced Lamb Meatballs	85
Spicy "grilled" Catfish	46
Spicy Black Bean Dip	16
Spicy Onion Crusted Chicken Tenders	71
Spicy Turkey Meatballs	17
Spinach & Sausage Casserole	27
Spinach Hummus	10
Steak And Chips	86
Steak And Minty Cheese	16
Steamed Lemon Pudding	96
Steamed Sea Bass With Turnips	37
Sticky Baby Back Ribs	81
Sticky Barbeque Baby Back Ribs	85
Sticky Drumsticks	59
Strawberry Crumble	104

Stuffed Baked Potatoes	30
Stuffed Cabbage Rolls	86
Stuffed Manicotti	57
Stuffed Summer Squash	51
Sweet & Spicy Shrimp	41
Sweet Garlicky Chicken Wings	59
Sweet Potato Gratin	22
Sweet Potato Skins	14
Sweet Sour Fish	46
Swiss Onion Dip	13
Swordfish With Caper Sauce	39

T

Taco Meatballs	85
Taco Stuffed Avocados	66
Teriyaki Chicken Wings	17
Tex Mex Beef Stew	88
Thai Roasted Beef	87
Three-layer Taco Dip	19
Thyme Chicken With Veggies	69
Tiny Tostadas	14
Tiramisu Cheesecake	99
Tres Leches Cake	104
Tuna Zoodle Bake	35
Turkey And Brown Rice Salad With Peanuts	63
Turkey Enchilada Casserole	64
Tuscan Chicken & Pasta	62

V

Veggie Potpie	47

W

Waffle Bread Pudding With Maple-jam Glaze	29
Walnut Orange Coffee Cake	32
White Bean Hummus	12
Whole Chicken With Lemon And Onion Stuffing	66

Z

Zucchini Egg Tots	12
Zucchini Pancakes	23
Zucchini Quinoa Stuffed Red Peppers	56
Zucchinis Spinach Fry	52

Printed in Great Britain
by Amazon